INSPIRE / PLAN / DISCOVER / EXPERIENCE

SRI LANKA

SRI LANKA

CONTENTS

DISCOVER 6

EXPERIENCE 60

NEED TO KNOW 218

Left: A reclining Buddha at a temple in Colombo
Previous page: A tea plantation in the Hill Country
Front cover: Stilt fishermen, off the coast of Weligama

DISCOVER

An aerial view over Weligama Bay

WELCOME TO
SRI LANKA

This teardrop-shaped island's many attractions belie its diminutive size. Get ready to discover world-class wildlife, stunning landscapes, time-warped colonial streets and some of the ancient world's most majestic monuments. Whatever your dream trip to Sri Lanka includes, this DK Eyewitness travel guide is the perfect companion.

1 A train crossing Demodara Bridge, near Ella.

2 Relaxing by the water in Colombo's Fort.

3 The turquoise waters off Unawatuna's beach.

4 Jaffna's Maviddapuram Kandaswamy Temple.

Fringed by idyllic sandy beaches, lapped by the warm waves of the Indian Ocean, Sri Lanka's interior is an ever-changing picture. Tangled lowland rainforests in the southwestern wet zone give way to the south's endless dry plains, where elephants roam and Yala's famous leopards lounge in trees. Moving further inland, the Hill Country – at the heart of the island – is corduroyed with tea plantations, backed by misty cloud forests and rugged mountains.

The island's urban environments are similarly diverse. The capital, Colombo, serves up a helter-skelter mix of chaotic bazaars, contemporary chic and colonial grandeur. Further glimpses of Ceylon can be seen in the perfectly preserved Dutch fort at Galle and whimsical Nuwara Eliya, known as "Little England". If Colombo's foodie scene encompasses crunchy hoppers, steaming samosas and comforting curries, Nuwara Eliya's is all about afternoon tea. Kandy, meanwhile, is firmly rooted in Sri Lanka's Sinhalese heritage, with its gold-roofed Temple of the Tooth and traditional dancing, complete with elaborate costumes, gyrating moves and fire stunts.

With so many different things to discover and experience, it's hard to know where to start. We've broken the island down into easily navigable chapters, with detailed itineraries, expert local knowledge and colourful, comprehensive maps to help you plan the perfect visit. Whether you're staying for a week or longer, this DK Eyewitness guide will ensure that you see the very best that Sri Lanka has to offer. Enjoy the book, and enjoy Sri Lanka.

REASONS TO LOVE
SRI LANKA

There are so many reasons that Sri Lanka is called the "Pearl of the Indian Ocean", from steaming cups of tea and heaped bowls of curry to hallowed temples and sacred mountains. Here, we pick some of our favourites.

1 KANDY

Set among beautiful green hills, the island's cultural capital is home to the famous Temple of the Tooth, one of the world's holiest Buddhist shrines (p136).

RIDING THE RAILS 2

Take advantage of Sri Lanka's British-era railway network (p48). The line that snakes and rattles through the verdant tea terraces of the Hill Country is Asia's greatest train journey.

3 WET AND WILD

Perhaps unsurprisingly, this island offers a whole host of water sports (p34). Try your hand at surfing at Arugam Bay, kitesurfing at Kalpitiya or water-skiing at Bentota.

GALLE 4

One of Asia's most picture-perfect colonial towns, Galle rewards visitors with streets upon streets of sedate Dutch villas and marvellous sea views in every direction *(p106)*.

FESTIVALS 5

With so many different religions coexisting here, there always seems to be some festivity or celebration taking place. The headliner is undoubtedly Kandy's Esala Perahera *(p139)*.

CAPTIVATING CUISINE 6

Sri Lanka boasts a rich culinary heritage – a fusion of traditional dishes and recipes brought to the island by traders and colonialists. Don't leave without trying rice and curry *(p31)*.

TEA PLANTATIONS AND HILLS 7

Explore the spectacular Hill Country, with its tumbling waterfalls, misty cloud forests and endless swathes of green plantations, before savouring a cup of amber-hued tea *(p132)*.

ANCIENT TEMPLES AND SOARING STUPAS 8

Sri Lanka's past is written on its buildings, from the cave temples at Dambulla *(p180)* to Anuradhapura's majestic stupas *(p172)*. Don't miss the rock-top citadel of Sigiriya *(p162)*.

9 WONDERFUL WILDLIFE

You'll find all creatures great and small in Sri Lanka's parks, from hard-to-spot leopards to unmissable elephants. The island's waters are just as abundant *(p36)*.

10 ADAM'S PEAK

Make the night-time ascent of Adam's Peak *(p146)*. As dawn breaks at the summit, you're rewarded with panoramic views of the Hill Country illuminated in the first light of morning.

BLISSFUL BEACHES 11

Throw a towel down on your perfect strip of sand, whether that be one of the west coast's boutique beaches, a deserted south coast strand or a remote east coast hideaway *(p38)*.

WELLNESS 12

Sri Lanka provides solace for both body and soul, with two-week holistic Ayurveda courses, beachside yoga and meditation retreats set high in the hills *(p32)*.

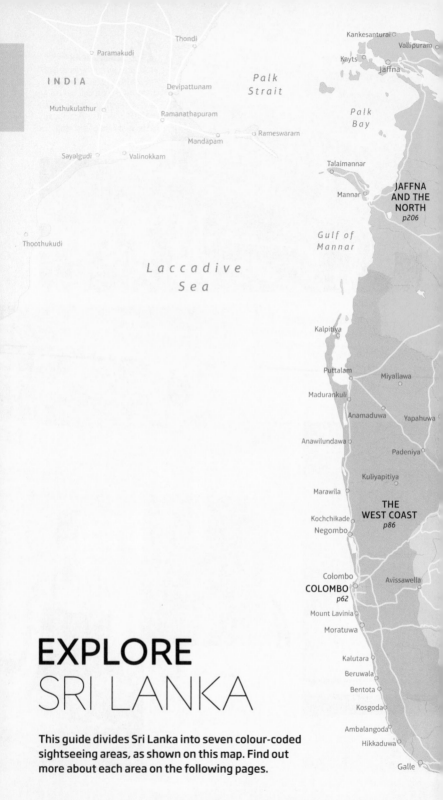

INDIA

Thondi

Paramakudi

Muthukulathur

Devipattunam

Palk
Strait

Ramanathapuram

Mandapam

Rameswaram

Sayalgudi

Valinokkam

Kankesanturai

Vallipuram

Kayts

Jaffna

Palk
Bay

Talaimannar

Mannar

JAFFNA
AND THE
NORTH
p206

Thoothukudi

Gulf of
Mannar

Laccadive
Sea

Kalpitiya

Puttalam

Miyallawa

Madurankuli

Anamaduwa

Yapahuwa

Anawilundawa

Padeniya

Kuliyapitiya

Marawila

THE
WEST COAST
p86

Kochchikade

Negombo

Colombo

Avissawella

COLOMBO
p62

Mount Lavinia

Moratuwa

Kalutara

Beruwala

Bentota

Kosgoda

Ambalangoda

Hikkaduwa

Galle

EXPLORE
SRI LANKA

This guide divides Sri Lanka into seven colour-coded
sightseeing areas, as shown on this map. Find out
more about each area on the following pages.

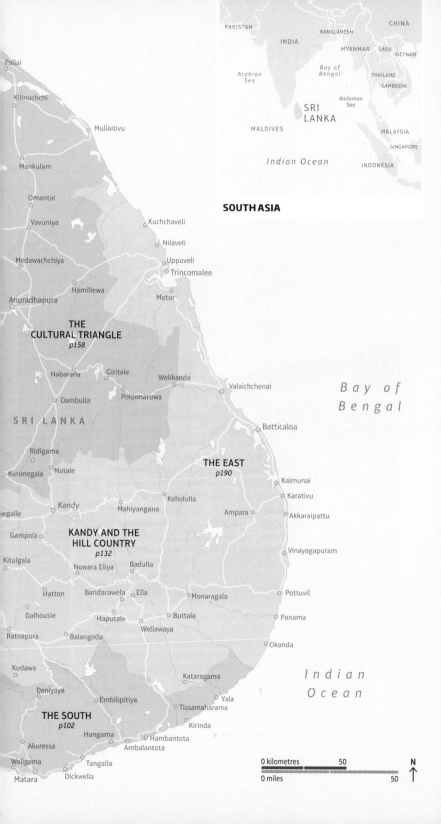

PAKISTAN
CHINA
BANGLADESH
INDIA
MYANMAR LAOS VIETNAM
Arabian
Sea
Bay of
Bengal
THAILAND
CAMBODIA
SRI
LANKA
Andaman
Sea
MALDIVES
MALAYSIA
SINGAPORE
Indian Ocean
INDONESIA

SOUTH ASIA

Pallai

Kilinochchi

Mullaitivu

Mankulam

Omantai

Vavuniya

Kuchchaveli

Nilaveli

Medawachchiya

Uppuveli
Trincomalee

Hamillewa

Mutur

Anuradhapura

**THE
CULTURAL TRIANGLE**
p158

Habarana   Giritale

Welikanda

Valaichchenai

Dambulla   Polonnaruwa

S R I   L A N K A

Bay of
Bengal

Ridigama

Batticaloa

Kurunegala   Matale

THE EAST
p190

Kehelulla

Kalmunai

egalle   Kandy   Mahiyangana

Karativu

Ampara

Akkaraipattu

Gampola

**KANDY AND THE
HILL COUNTRY**
p132

Vinayagapuram

Kitulgala

Nuwara Eliya   Badulla

Hatton   Bandarawela   Ella

Monaragala

Pottuvil

Dalhousie   Haputale   Buttala

Panama

Wellawaya

Ratnapura   Balangoda

Okanda

Kudawa

Indian
Ocean

Deniyaya

Kataragama

THE SOUTH
p102

Embilipitiya   Yala

Tissaharama

Hungama   Kirinda

Akuressa   Hambantota
Ambalantota

Weligama   Tangalla

Matara   Dickwella

0 kilometres   50
0 miles   50

N

GETTING TO KNOW
SRI LANKA

A teardrop-shaped island set in the Indian Ocean, Sri Lanka's 65,610 sq km (25,332 sq miles) are home to beautiful beaches, urban sprawls, endless swathes of tea bushes, soaring mountains and much more besides. Becoming familiar with each region will help when planning your trip.

PAGE 62

COLOMBO

Far and away the largest city in an overwhelmingly rural island, Colombo offers an absorbing exception to the Sri Lankan norm. Sprawling, disorientating and sometimes downright chaotic, the city has an energy unlike anywhere else in the country. It's a place of startling contrasts, too, from the memorably manic Pettah bazaars to serene Buddhist temples, and from graciously time-warped colonial-era streets to chic contemporary cafés, bars and boutiques.

Best for
Contemporary Sri Lankan chic and bustling bazaars

Home to
Colombo National Museum, Pettah, Fort, Gangaramaya Temple

Experience
Mingling with the crowds at sunset on Galle Face Green

PAGE 86

THE WEST COAST

Busy and brash, the west coast is the powerhouse at the heart of Sri Lanka's vibrant and booming tourism industry. Big resorts line the coast from Negombo to Bentota, interspersed with backpacker enclaves and some gorgeous boutique hotels. The west is also the island's premier activity zone, with world-class kitesurfing and dolphin-watching in Kalpitiya, superlative diving in Hikkaduwa and adrenaline-fuelled water sports in Bentota. For something more sedate, take a trip on the lagoon in Negombo or look for elephants, leopards and sloth bears in Wilpattu National Park.

Best for
Beach life

Home to
*Beautiful stretches of sand
and action-packed resorts*

Experience
*A boat ride through
Muthurajawela Wetlands*

PAGE 102

THE SOUTH

Seductively sleepy, the south is home to some of the island's best hidden beaches and boutique hideaways. It's not just a lackadaisical paradise, however, and it'd be a waste to spend all day on the sand when there are whales to watch and sea turtles to spot. And don't forget the leopards – catch sight of these camouflaged felines in Yala National Park. The towns, too, are equally enchanting: from the perfectly preserved Dutch settlement of Galle to Kataragama, the vibrant pilgrimage town. You'll experience Sri Lanka's history and raw spirituality in this corner of the island.

Best for
Wildlife-watching

Home to
*Galle, Uda Walawe National Park,
Yala West (Ruhuna) National Park*

Experience
The nightly celebrations in Kataragama

→

KANDY AND THE HILL COUNTRY

The Hill Country is Sri Lanka at its most spectacular. Here, the island abruptly contorts itself into a dramatic landscape of tangled green hills and seemingly endless tea plantations. At the heart of the region is the historic city of Kandy, proud bastion of the island's most cherished cultural traditions. Moving south, the marvellous Hill Country railway rattles past the sacred and soaring mountain known as Adam's Peak and the cloud-shrouded uplands of Horton Plains National Park – seemingly at the end of the world.

Best for
Stunning scenery

Home to
Kandy, Horton Plains National Park and World's End, Ella, Adam's Peak

Experience
A train ride on the Hill Country line

THE CULTURAL TRIANGLE

Fifteen centuries of history await in the Cultural Triangle, where the achievements of Sri Lanka's early inhabitants stand immortalized in a stunning sequence of stupas, Buddhas and temples. The majestic ruined capitals of Anuradhapura and Polonnaruwa dominate the region, but they are surrounded by a plethora of other attractions, including remote forest monasteries and the intimate cave temples of Dambulla. Topping it all is the spectacular rock citadel of Sigiriya, with its extraordinary frescoes.

Best for
Ancient monuments and stupas

Home to
Sigiriya, Polonnaruwa, Anuradhapura, Mihintale, Dambulla Cave Temples

Experience
The Gathering at Minneriya National Park – the world's largest group of wild elephants

THE EAST

Far from the madding crowds, the island's east coast offers adventurous travellers a taste of Sri Lanka off-the-beaten-track. The lagoon-fringed coastline is still largely untouched, while the war-torn towns of Trincomalee and Batticaloa are home to temples, mosques and churches, reflecting the ethnic diversity of this area. Further south, surfers flock to the world-class waves of Arugam Bay, one of Sri Lanka's most enjoyable beach retreats.

Best for
Unspoiled beaches

Home to
Trincomalee

Experience
Hiking to the top of Lover's Leap

JAFFNA AND THE NORTH

Northern Sri Lanka can often feel like a completely different country. Ravaged by decades of Civil War, the region remains little developed and even less visited. The jungle-strewn plains of the beleaguered Vanni region (between Vavuniya and the Elephant Pass) remain hauntingly empty, while remote Mannar Island lies almost within touching distance of India. The vibrant Tamil city of Jaffna is the main draw, with its towering Hindu temples and palm-fringed coastline, ringed by a beautiful arc of low-slung islands.

Best for
Hindu temples and culture

Home to
Jaffna Peninsula, Jaffna Islands

Experience
A daily puja at the great Nallur Kandaswamy Hindu temple in Jaffna

←

1 Monks exploring one of the ruins at Polonnaruwa.

2 Climbing Sigiriya rock.

3 Sri Muthumariamman temple in Matale.

4 Kandyan drummers.

Sri Lanka offers endless options for exploration, from weekends spent discovering the historic cities to longer tours taking in the entire country. Wherever you choose to go, our handpicked itineraries will help you plan the perfect trip.

2 WEEKS
in Sri Lanka

Day 1

Kick off your tour in Kandy (p136). After picking up some breakfast from Kandy Central Market, get to the Temple of the Tooth in time for the morning *puja* (temple ceremony), when exuberant drummers provide the soundtrack. After paying your respects, explore the *devales* (temples) opposite and then grab a South Indian lunch at Sri Balaji Dosa *(balaji-dosai. business.site)*. Next, jump into a tuk-tuk and spend the afternoon at the Peradeniya Botanical Gardens (p148), where you'll find everything from ferns to figs. When you're ready for dinner, head back to the city for traditional rice and curry at the Sharon Inn *(59 Saranankara Road)*.

Day 2

Hire a car and driver for the 135-km (84-mile) journey to Polonnaruwa (p166). Ask your driver to stop off en route at the Aluvihare monastery and hop between its colourful shrines (p189). After lunch at the lovely Cinnamon Lodge hotel in Habarana *(www.cinnamonhotels.com)*, take a detour to the magical forest monastery at Ritigala (p186), before continuing to Polonnaruwa.

Day 3

One of the best ways to explore this ancient city is by bike so spend the day pedalling around the remains. Don't miss the intricately carved shrines clustered in the Quadrangle or the giant rock-carved Buddhas of the Gal Vihara. After a day in the saddle, a sunset stroll around the Island Garden and Potgul Mawatha lake is the perfect way to end the day.

Day 4

Drive south to Dambulla and check into the jungle-roofed Heritance Kandalama hotel (p183). After lunch and a dip in the stunning infinity pool, set out for Sigiriya (p162) – the skyscraping citadel. Aim to arrive here at around 3pm, when the great rock begins to turn an intense shade of reddish-orange in the setting sun.

Day 5

Today, you'll explore the Dambulla Cave Temples (p180), a treasure trove of marvellous murals and imposing statues chiselled from solid rock. Afterwards, ask your driver to take you back to Kandy, pausing at the stone Nalanda Gedige temple (p189) and the Sri Muthumariamman temple in Matale (p188). Check out the latter's soaring, polychromatic *gopuram* and then check in to Helga's Folly – Sri Lanka's zaniest hotel (p137). No visit to Kandy would be complete without watching some traditional dancing and drumming. The Kandyan Arts Association gives the biggest and best performances *(72 Sangarajah Mawatha; show starts at 5pm)*.

→

Day 6

Say goodbye to your driver and catch an early ride on the island's famous Hill Country railway line *(p48)*. Cleaving through the hills south of Kandy, the landscape gradually opens up into huge, tea fields, dotted with sari-clad pickers. You'll arrive in Haputale *(p154)* in the early afternoon. Book a room at the jewel-box 'T En Zal *(p154)*, then stretch your legs with a walk around town, before heading back to the guesthouse for dinner.

Day 7

Rise early for the trip to Horton Plains National Park *(p142)*, aiming to be at the park for around 7am. Then, follow the stunning circular Loop Trail through some of Sri Lanka's highest, wildest and most dramatic scenery. It's easy to see how World's End gained its name as you take in the mist-clouded valley below. Return to Haputale and hop back on the train for the hour's ride to Ella *(p144)*. This laid-back village is beautifully situated on a Hill Country escarpment. The stylish AK Ristoro is a good choice for dinner *(p145)*.

Day 8

Lace up your walking boots to explore Ella on foot. Start with the short hike up Little Adam's Peak and then visit the nearby Newburgh Tea Factory, where you'll learn how green tea is produced. There are several cafés nearby, including Adam's Breeze *(Passara Road)*. After refuelling, continue on to the majestic Demodara Bridge. Take a picture of this graceful nine-arched bridge before looping back to Ella. This evening, dine on traditional rice and curry at Remo's *(p145)*.

Day 9

Hire a car and driver for the 90-minute drive down to Yala National Park *(p116)*, stopping off en route to take in the imposing Buddha statues at Buduruwagala *(p155)*. Cinnamon Wild Yala hotel will be your base in the park *(p116)*. Spend the afternoon taking in the surrounding jungle scenery from the hotel's observation deck before heading off to Kataragama *(p118)* in the late afternoon. Aim to arrive at the Maha Devale in time for the exuberant evening *puja*.

1 Huge Buddha at Buduruwagala.
2 Elephants in the Yala National Park.
3 A train on Demodara Bridge.
4 Cyclists in Galle's old town.
5 Jami-ul-Alfar Mosque in Pettah.

Day 10

There's a good chance of spotting leopards on a morning safari in Yala. Aim to spend around three hours driving around the park, breaking for lunch at the hotel. Once you've had your wildlife fix, drive on to the charming town of Mirissa for an Italian meal at O Mirissa Café & Bistro (p120).

Day 11

Spend the morning scouring the waves on one of Mirissa's popular whale-watching trips. Between December and April, you're very likely to see blue whales. After disembarking back at Mirissa, head for lunch at the ever-popular No. 1 Dewmini Roti Shop (p120). The rest of the afternoon is yours to enjoy some downtime on the beach – relax, you've earned it.

Day 12

Galle (p106) is your destination today. After lunch at the stylish Galle Fort Hotel (www.galleforthotel.com), walk the town's redoubtable bastions and explore the picture-perfect streets of the old town.

The Middle Eastern dishes at Chambers call at dinner time (p107).

Day 13

Take the speedy Southern Expressway to Colombo (p62). Follow our walk around the fort (p84), before lunch at the Pagoda Tea Room (p71). The Colombo National Museum offers a neat conclusion to the sights you've seen on your tour of the island (p66). If you have time, browse for souvenirs in the frenetic streets of Pettah (p68) but make sure that you're at Galle Face Green (p76) in time for sunset.

Day 14

Round off your fortnight in Sri Lanka in Negombo (p92) – a short drive away from the capital. Take a tuk-tuk tour of the city, pausing at its many churches – this is Sri Lanka's Christian heartland – and then relax on the beach. After the sun sets, chow down on traditional rice and curry at Rohan's Place (p93). It's the perfect last supper before you catch your flight home from the nearby international airport.

←

1 The Jami-ul-Alfar Mosque.

2 Exhibits in the Colombo National Museum.

3 Sambodhi Chaitya stupa.

4 Enjoying a sundowner at the Galle Face Hotel.

2 DAYS

in Colombo

Day 1

Morning Start at the beginning of the the city's history in Fort *(p70)*. Our walk *(p84)* offers a good overview of the area's main sights, including Colombo Fort Clock Tower and the colonial buildings on Janadhipathi Mawatha street. Stop for a coffee at the venerable Grand Oriental Hotel and then take a seafront stroll up breezy Chaitya Road to the bizarre Sambodhi Chaitya stupa.

Afternoon Break for lunch at the Pagoda Tea Room *(p71)*, then head into Pettah *(p68)*. The Dutch Period Museum's collection isn't that exciting but it'll give you an idea of how the colonists lived. Continuing down hectic Main Street, you'll see the unmistakable exterior of the Jami-ul-Alfar Mosque. Be sure to snap a photo of this kaleidoscopic building before picking up a snack at the similarly picturesque market outside the Old Town Hall. End up at the New Kathiresan and Old Kathiresan Kovils at 4:30pm, when these shrines come to life in a clamour of bells and clouds of smoke for the *puja*.

Evening Botanik *(p71)* is a plush place to spend the evening. Sip a cocktail on the romantic roof terrace and then chow down on some of the best Asian-style cuisine in town. If you're lucky, a live band will provide the soundtrack for your night.

Day 2

Morning Spend a couple of hours taking in the wide-ranging exhibits at the Colombo National Museum *(p66)*. Then, compare the works displayed in the National Art Gallery *(p77)* to the canvases hanging along the Green Path Art Market *(p80)*, where you can pick up an artistic memento of your trip. Ramble on through the lush Vihara Mahadevi Park *(p79)* to the turreted Devatagaha Mosque. After taking in this building, browse the chic Sri Lankan crafts for sale in Paradise Road *(p79)*, before lunch in the boutique's cosy Paradise Road The Gallery Café *(p83)*.

Afternoon A short stroll through the backstreets of Slave Island *(p76)* – so-called because this is where the Dutch kept enslaved people – brings you to Gangaramaya Temple *(p72)*. The adjacent Seema Malaka *(p78)* exemplifies architect Geoffrey Bawa's style *(p81)*. Continue north along Beira Lake *(p78)*, past several of Colombo's striking new developments, including the lopsided Altair towers, before looping west around the lake's shore. At sunset, make for Galle Face Green to watch the sun descend into the waves.

Evening Have a sundowner at the Galle Face Hotel and then head off for dinner at Monsoon *(p77)*. This stylish eatery serves up scrumptious Southeast Asian dishes.

→

1 Drummers playing in the streets outside the Temple of the Tooth.

2 Peradeniya Botanical Gardens.

3 Traders in Kandy Central Market.

4 Designing batik at the Kandyan Arts and Crafts Association.

2 DAYS

in Kandy

Day 1

Morning The obvious place to start is at the spiritual heart of Kandy – the Temple of the Tooth *(p140)*. Aim to arrive in time for the 9:30am *puja*, when drummers in Kandyan attire perform. Explore the shrine and attached museums, paying your respects to the stuffed remains of the temple's revered elephant, Raja. Immediately west of the temple are the beautiful trio of *devales (p136)*, flanked by St Paul's Church, built by the British.

Afternoon Stop for a South Indian lunch at Sri Balaji Dosa *(p21)*, then spend the afternoon exploring the tangled streets of central Kandy – a shopper's paradise. Start by walking down Dalada Vidiya, which is lined with imposing colonial buildings, to reach the ramshackle Kandy Central Market *(p138)*. Here, you'll find a colourful confusion of food and spice stalls, as well as some interesting souvenir shops. One of these – the excellent Jayamali Batiks – stocks intricate wall hangings characterized by their Sri Lankan motifs. Then, continue west down old-fashioned Colombo Street, with its pavements lined with itinerant hawkers sat behind little piles of fruit and veg. Round off the afternoon by browsing the beautiful textiles for sale at the Selyn shop *(138)* on nearby Temple Street.

Evening Start the evening by taking in some traditional Kandyan dancing and drumming. The YMBA is an intimate and low-key venue *(5 Rajapihilla Mawatha; show starts at 5:30pm)*. After the show, grab dinner at the chic little Empire Café *(empirecafekandy.com)*, right in the centre of the city.

Day 2

Morning Spend the morning at the idyllic Peradeniya Botanical Gardens *(p148)*, a short drive outside the city. One of Asia's finest arboreta, it has a marvellous array of trees from around the world. Visit the Great Lawn and then head north up Royal Palm Avenue, past the Great Circle, until you hit the river. Then, loop back clockwise around Cabbage Palm Avenue to the entrance. Catch a tuk-tuk back to central Kandy and mingle with the locals over rice and curry at the ever-popular Devon Restaurant on Dalada Vidiya.

Afternoon Immerse yourself in the region's cultural heritage at the Kandy National Museum, where you can take a closer look at *ola*-leaf manuscripts *(p137)*. The eclectic exhibits in the adjacent International Buddhist Museum *(p137)* provide an interesting contrast to these Kandyan crafts. After checking out Buddhas from around the world, stretch your legs with a leisurely circuit of beautiful Kandy Lake *(p136)*. The Kandyan Arts and Crafts Association *(p138)* is a good stopping-off point. Here, local artisans demonstrate that Kandyan craftsmanship is still alive and kicking today. Continue walking anticlockwise along the shore to reach the southern side of the lake, which is lined with a string of old monastery buildings. The view of the Temple of the Tooth across the water is bound to take your breath away.

Evening Perched on a hill, Sharon Inn *(59 Saranankara Road)* serves up some of the island's finest rice and curries. Enjoy your hearty meal while watching the city lights flickering prettily below.

←

1 An aerial view of Sigiriya.

2 A dish served at The Sanctuary at Tissawewa hotel.

3 The Sri Maha Bodhi bo tree.

4 Taking a picture of the reclining Buddha at Gal Vihara.

5 DAYS

in the Cultural Triangle

Day 1

As Sri Lanka's oldest ancient city, Anuradhapura *(p172)* is an obvious starting point for a tour of the Cultural Triangle. Make straight for the Jetavana Monastery – the section of the ruins closest to town. It's home to the biggest of the ancient city's three monumental stupas. From here, continue to the Mahavihara complex, visiting the Ruwanwelisaya stupa and the revered Sri Maha Bodhi bo tree before stopping for lunch at the nearby The Sanctuary at Tissawewa hotel *(p175)*. Spend the afternoon working your way north, past the remains of the Royal Palace to the fascinating Abhayagiri area, home to the Kuttam Pokuna bathing pool, Samadhi Buddha statue and a cluster of other memorable monuments.

Day 2

Hire a car and driver to head southeast from Anuradhapura to Polonnaruwa *(p166)*. Allow yourself an hour's break on the way to explore the magical forest hermitage at Ritigala *(p186)*. Here, the remains of old monastic buildings are hidden by jungle and connected by meditation walkways. A short drive beyond, Habarana's Cinnamon Lodge hotel *(p21)* is a good place to stop for a rice and curry lunch, before continuing to Polonnaruwa. Once you've reached your destination, take a look at the Island Garden *(p170)* – the ruins of Nissankamalla's royal palace.

Day 3

Spend the day exploring the rest of Polonnaruwa. Start at the museum *(p169)* to learn more about the city's history. Then, check out the fabulous friezes on the base of the Royal Palace Group *(p168)*. Work your way northwards via the spectacular Quadrangle *(p170)* to Gal Vihara *(p166)*. These giant Buddhas show different *mudras* (gestures; *p187*). Continue to the most northerly part of the site to take a look at the flamboyant Tivanka Patamaghara murals and the enigmatic remains of the vast Demala Maha Seya – once destined to be a huge stupa.

Day 4

It's time for a change of pace. Swap cultural sights for wildlife spotting in either the Minneriya *(p184)* or Kaudulla *(p185)* national parks. Elephants migrate freely between the two parks, so check where to go on the day. After your safari, continue south to Dambulla *(p182)* and order some lunch at the jungle-canopied Heritance Kandalama *(p183)*. Round off your animal-orientated day with a night-time visit to the idyllic Popham Arboretum *(p182)*. This forest reserve shelters myriad nocturnal animals, including slender loris, spotted deer and pangolin.

Day 5

Get ready for a blockbuster day, where you'll tick off two of the Cultural Triangle's stellar attractions. First, take in the rock-carved Buddhas and intricate murals in the Dambulla Cave Temples *(p180)*. The low-key Gimanhala Hotel *(www.gimanhala. com)* makes a pleasant lunch stop in Dambulla town. After spending the morning underground, the afternoon is all about climbing. It'll take you a couple of hours to scale the rickety stairs up Sigiriya *(p162)*. Aim to arrive at the site at around 3pm, when the heat is easing, the crowds have left and the gigantic orange-red rock glows in the late-afternoon sun.

Spice Things Up

It was cinnamon that attracted Europeans to Sri Lanka in the 17th century. Thousands of trees were cut down for their precious bark, but you'll still find cinnamon – and many other spices – in Sri Lanka's spice gardens. They may be unashamedly commercial, but these gardens are a great place to learn more about the contents of your spice rack at home and to buy some organic samples. Check out the pretty New Ranweli Spice Garden *((081) 238 7613)*, opposite the bridge to Peradeniya Botanical Gardens *(p148)*, which has informative guides and reasonably priced products.

←

Sampling spices at the restaurant at the New Ranweli Spice Garden

SRI LANKA FOR
FOODIES

Comforting curries made with creamy coconut and feisty chillis, crunchy hoppers and, of course, steaming cups of tea: local flavours and international influences meet in Sri Lanka's cuisine. Get ready to discover delicious dishes, fragrant spice gardens and cook-it-yourself courses.

TOP 3 COOKERY CLASSES

Aunty's Sri Lankan Cooking Class
Learn to cook traditional rice and curry in the heart of Colombo *(www.auntys.lk)*.

Kandy Cooking Classes
Expect intimate classes in Kandy, where you'll be taught an array of recipes *(www.kandycookingclasses.com)*.

Negombo Cooking Class
Welcoming chefs unravel the mysteries of Sri Lankan cuisine in Negombo *(www.negombocookingclass.com)*.

Cooking Up a Storm

Learn to pound spices like a local on a cookery course. Ella *(p144)* has the widest selection, but you'll find schools all over Sri Lanka. Many classes include a market tour, where you'll be introduced to some of the island's unusual fruit and veg. Look out for ash plantain, which resembles an unripe banana, and the peculiar cucumber-like snake gourd.

→

Fruit and vegetables for sale at a market in Wellawaya, near Haputale

Curry On

Forget any preconceptions you may have about what a curry is – Sri Lanka's version is completely different from its Indian neighbour's: rice and curry is a banquet of a dozen or more dishes. Fish or chicken curry is accompanied by crisp poppadoms, fiery sambals, a creamy dal and, of course, a huge mound of rice. And that's not counting the vegetable dishes, where jackfruit, ash plantain and snake gourd are often served in a classic *kiri hodhi* sauce, made from coconut milk infused with assorted spices.

→

The many dishes making up a traditional Sri Lankan rice and curry

Feeling a Little Chilli?

Sri Lankans like their curries hot. Very hot. But if you need some more fire in your food, add a spoonful of sambal (chilli sauce). The classic *pol* (coconut) sambal is made from chilli powder, chopped onions, grated coconut and dried and powdered fish, perhaps with some garlic and lime.

←

A bowl of *pol* sambal, served on the side of a potato curry

Foreign Flavours

Centuries of colonization have left their mark on the island's menu. The Dutch created *lamprais* (or "lump rice" as it's often spelt) – rice and chicken baked in a plantain leaf. Muslim settlers contributed the roti, a doughy pancake that is chopped up with other ingredients to create a *kottu*. South India is to thank for the hopper, a bowl-shaped pancake with an egg fried into the bottom. Wash down this Sri Lankan breakfast with the pervasive British import – a cup of tea.

→

A chef slicing up a roti to be used in a *kottu* roti

Namaste-ing Alive

The area to the west of Matara is the island's top yoga destination, with a number of boutique resorts like Talalla Retreat seeing you bending and balancing right on the beach *(www.talallaretreat.com)*. Serious yogis should book a two-week course at Ulpotha, an idyllic rural retreat in the Cultural Triangle *(www.ulpotha.com)*.

←

Practising yoga in a simple studio, surrounded by nature

SRI LANKA FOR
WELLNESS

Holistic healthcare and spiritual mindfulness have been a way of life in Sri Lanka for centuries. Today, the ancient principles of Ayurvedic medicine provide balm to thousands of visitors and the island offers a huge range of other wellness activities, from beachside yoga to meditation in the hills.

TOP 4 SRI LANKAN SPAS

Santani Resort
This wellness retreat near Kandy offers hydrotherapy and Ayurvedic treatments *(www.santani.lk)*.

Cape Weligama
Signature treatments use tea and cinnamon at this deluxe hotel set above Weligama Bay *(www.resplendentceylon.com)*.

Amangalla
Hot and cold plunge pools, plus a steam room and sauna *(p107)*.

Amaranthé Bay
An alluring east coast retreat offering a range of treatments *(p197)*.

Spa Day

Sri Lanka has a booming spa industry, with a huge selection of places, ranging from idyllic candle-scented retreats within luxury hotels to rustic mud-brick huts at the bottom of private gardens. Most places offer a few Ayurvedic treatments alongside other Asian specialities, including Thai and Indonesian-style massages, as well as reflexology and beauty treatments.

↑ Enjoying a deep tissue massage at the Sahana Spa in Bentota

↑ Experiencing a herbal
bath, and *(inset)* a
Ayurveda retreat

Treat Yourself

Usually lasting at least one week, Ayurvedic
courses aim to completely cleanse the body.
Bentota is home to an array of retreats *(p96)*.
If time's an issue, why not sign up for a one-off
treatment? Tackle any knots with a massage
or sit back and relax in a herbal bath. Perhaps
the most relaxing experience is a traditional
shirodhara, when a continuous stream of warm
oil is massaged into the forehead – pure bliss.

Get Your "Om" On

Perhaps unsurprisingly given
that Sri Lanka's principal
religion – Buddhism – emerged
out of the Buddha's extended
reflection while sat under an
Indian bo tree, meditation is a
popular activity. You'll find the
best selection of meditation
centres in the inspiring
environs of the Hill Country
(p148), while a number of
yoga places in the south run
meditation workshops alongside their usual beach-side
classes, offering both mental
and physical rejuvenation. To
find a beach class, it's best to
ask around locally.

→
Relaxing during a
sound bath, a type of
meditation class

Large parts of the
island's coastline are
fringed with labyrin-
thine lagoons. These
bodies of water are
diverse in their shape,
size and ecology.
Negombo (p92),
Bentota (p96), Pottuvil
(p202) and Batticaloa
(p198) are home to
some of the biggest
lagoons, complete with
mangrove swamps,
plentiful aquatic
birdlife and fishermen
pitching their nets.
Take a boat trip to
experience lagoon life.

Paddling on the Kelani
Ganga on a whitewater
rafting trip ↑

SRI LANKA FOR
WATER SPORTS

**Ringed by some 1,340 km (830 miles) of coastline, Sri Lanka serves up a
brilliant array of water-based activities. Grab a board and go surfing or
kitesurfing, don your wetsuit and mask for diving or hold on for dear life
on a whitewater rafting trip. You'll go from newbie to expert in no time.**

Let's Go Fly a Kite

Strong and steady winds offer
ideal kitesurfing conditions
along parts of the west coast.
The Kalpitiya Peninsula (p90) is
the go-to location, with dozens
of camps offering kitesurfing on
either the sea or local lakes. We
love the excellent Ruuk Village
on Kalpitiya lagoon (www.ruuk
village.com). Further north,
remote Mannar Island (p217) is a
great, and much quieter, alternative, with similarly reliable
winds and miles of unspoiled
beach. Vayu Resort is a remote
kitesurfing camp located at the
tip of the island (www.
kitesurfingmannar.com).

→

Kitesurfing on the calm
waters off a golden beach on
the Kalpitiya Peninsula

Paddle Time

Head to Kitulgala (p154) and strap in for Sri Lanka's best whitewater rafting. You'll paddle down a jungle-swathed stretch of the Kelani Ganga made famous by its starring role in the movie *Bridge on the River Kwai* (1957). The grade 2 to 3 rapids are fun, but not too challenging, and there are plenty of local operators to choose from, including Rafting Team 39 *(www.raftingteam39.com)* and Xclusive Adventures *(www.xclusive adventures.com).*

Did You Know?

Diving is best on the west coast from November to April, and out east from May to October.

Dive In

Dive schools can be found pretty much everywhere along the coast, offering a bewildering array of trips for different standards and interests. Check out the remains of the vast HMS *Hermes*, sunk near Batticaloa during World War II (p199). Sri Lanka Diving Tours offer year-round PADI courses and trips from their bases in Batticaloa, Negombo and Trincomalee, with a range of reef and wreck dives for varying abilities *(www. srilanka-divingtours.com).*

←

Learning how to scuba dive in the shallows, near Hikkaduwa

Surf's Up

With no land for a thousand miles in most directions, energetic waves crash against the island's shores. The remote east coast village of Arugam Bay (p202) has some of the best surf in Asia, but there are good waves elsewhere too, including Hikkaduwa (p100), Midigama (p123) and Weligama (p124). Breaks at different locations offer a wide range of conditions so there are surfing spots for novices, pros and everything in between. The Billabong-affiliated Dylan's Surf Company in Arugam Bay offers lessons for all standards *(www.dylan surfcompany.com).*

↑ Surfing at Narigama beach in the south coast surf town of Hikkaduwa

Whale Hello There

A major cetacean migratory route passes the south coast and – if you're lucky - you might catch sight of a majestic blue whale, the largest creature on the planet, as well as sperm, humpback and Bryde's whales *(p121)*. Mirissa Water Sports *(www.mirissa watersports.lk)* is one of the best whale-watching companies, and Blue Water Cruise *((077) 497 8306)* operates boats from both Mirissa and Trincomalee.

←

Watching a blue whale diving beneath the waves from a boat off the coast of Mirissa

SRI LANKA FOR
WILDLIFE

An almost implausible number of animals call this small island home. World-class leopard-spotting at Yala West, elephants at "The Gathering" in Minneriya and whale-watching at Mirissa are the standout wildlife encounters, but there are also excellent birding and turtle-nesting sites in-between.

INSIDER TIP
Drive On

Hundreds of drivers offer tours of Yala. Some are skilled naturalists and double as guides, or you might need to hire a guide as well. Whoever you go with, try to get an idea of their wildlife knowledge before signing up for a tour.

Spot This

You've got a greater chance of seeing a wild leopard in Sri Lanka than anywhere else on earth. Yala West *(p116)* is home to around 50 of these magnificent big cats, which have become so habituated to jeeps that they're easy to spot. Although they're rarely seen outside Yala, leopards inhabit many other parks - Wilpattu is your next best bet *(p91)*.

→

A pair of leopards in the undergrowth of Yala West National Park

Elephant-astic

Sri Lanka boasts the greatest concentration of wild elephants in Asia. They can be seen in almost every national park, but you'll have the best chance at Yala West (p116), Uda Walawe (p112), Minneriya or Kaudulla (p185). Despite the fact that the number of captive elephants has fallen steadily since the turn of the century, you're also likely to see working elephants plodding along roads and at some temples. Avoid any businesses offering elephant rides or the chance to feed or bathe elephants. The only establishment that we recommend is the Elephant Transit Home (p113).

↑ Photographing a family of elephants from a jeep in Yala West National Park

Out of Your Shell

Five species of sea turtle can be found in Sri Lanka's waters, with green turtles being the most commonly spotted (p99). Night-time nesting on Rekawa Beach (p129) is an unforgettable sight, when the turtles drag themselves out of the moonlit waves, inching slowly up the beach to lay their eggs. There are also numerous hatcheries along the west coast (p98).

← A green sea turtle gliding over the reef off Hikkaduwa beach

Feathered Friends

Sri Lanka is a twitcher's delight, with over 30 endemic species, including the Sri Lankan junglefowl and Ceylon blue magpie (p131). Lagoons and coastal flats support vivid flocks of flamingos and beaky adjutants, while rarities such as the Sri Lankan white eye and dull-blue flycatcher skulk in the rainforests. Stately birds of prey range from the majestic sea eagle through to the eccentric spot-bellied eagle owl. Sinharaja (p156) is the premier bird-watching destination, where you'll find numerous rare endemics hidden among the trees.

→ The colourful Ceylon blue magpie, endemic to the island

Twin Beaches

Separated by only 12 km (7 miles), the neighbouring beaches of Uppuveli and Nilaveli seem worlds apart (p196). Framed by towering palms, Uppuveli has a buzzing traveller's scene, with plenty of guesthouses and eateries, while Nilaveli, to the north, is still largely untouched. This expansive stretch of sand is the perfect place to take a detour from the well-worn path and catch your breath.

←

Fishermen pulling in their colourful nets onto Uppuveli Beach

SRI LANKA FOR
BEACHES

Sri Lanka offers a beach for every predilection and season – literally so, since when it's raining on the west coast, it's clear on the east. Whether you're seeking somewhere quiet to bask on icing-sugar sand or a lively party town, this island has it all.

Surf Spots

Sri Lanka's surfers' playground, Arugam Bay has epic right-hand point breaks, fast and slow rides and buzzing surf schools (p202). During the season – from July to September – this breezy seaside community comes alive with beachside brunches and yoga classes. Even if surfing is not your bag, you'll be seduced by the Bay's chilled-out vibe and soft sand. Once the surfers leave, some hotels and restaurants close up and the Bay gains off-the-beaten-track appeal.

→

Surfers climbing down Elephant Rock, near Arugam Bay

Off the Beaten Track

A horseshoe-shaped bay near Dickwella, Hiriketiya is one of the island's top boltholes for in-the-know travellers (p125). Yoga, surfing and sea-gazing are the main activities, and a small cluster of guesthouses provide good, and very chilled, lodgings. Sling a hammock at the rustic little Dot's Bay House and enjoy the waves ((077) 793 5593). With its white sand reflecting the sun, Kalkudah beach might almost seem like a mirage (p198). Apart from a few cows and dogs, it sees few visitors and lacks the tangle of resorts that usually crowd stretches of sand in Sri Lanka.

→

An aerial view of Hiriketiya Beach, showing its perfect horseshoe shape

Sporty Sands

Adrenaline junkie? Head to Bentota to get your water sports fix (p96). Take a bumpy banana boat ride, try your hand at water-skiing or learn how to windsurf. If this all sounds far too energetic, make for Mirissa and take a whale-watching trip (p120). Even if you miss out on seeing one of these gentle giants, you're bound to see scores of balletic spinner dolphins. These graceful creatures provide the ultimate aerial display as they spin in the air while leaping.

←

Wate-skiing on the calm waters of Bentota Lagoon

↑ Watching the sunset from a bar on Hikkaduwa's beach

Party Stretches

Some beaches stay hot even after the sun goes down. Dozens of bustling bars and late-night cafés ring Unawatuna's bay and regular beach parties attract travellers and locals alike (p123). Hikkaduwa (p100) – or "Hikka" as it's locally known – also sees revellers spilling out of pulsating bars and onto the sand.

SRI LANKA FOR
ARCHITECTURE

More than 2,000 years of buildings await visitors to the island, from the ancient monuments of Anuradhapura through to the iconic 20th-century creations of the architect Geoffrey Bawa. Where else can you find British colonial buildings rubbing shoulders with Buddhist stupas?

Ancient Sites

Sri Lanka's ancient buildings are monumental. The vast brick stupas of Anuradhapura *(p172)* are eclipsed in size only by the Egyptian Pyramids, while Sigiriya *(p162)* is one of the most audacious construction projects that the world has ever seen. And it's not just the size of these sites that impresses. Look out for the exquisite minutiae – Sigiriya's frescoes *(p164)* and the touches of Hindu craftsmanship added to Polonnaruwa's Buddhist buildings *(p166).*

Exploring the 200-m-
(656-ft-) high summit
of Sigiriya ↑

Bawa and Beyond

Contemporary Sri Lankan architecture has been profoundly shaped by the work of Geoffrey Bawa (p81). Bawa's distinctive style of Tropical Modernism blended elements of traditional Sinhalese and Dutch architecture with crisp, minimalist designs. His designs also blurred the division between interior and exterior spaces, as seen at Bawa's own Colombo residence, No 11, 33rd Lane (p80), where four small terrace houses have been combined into a bewildering labyrinth of ever-changing in- and outdoor perspectives. Stay at a Bawa-designed hotel, such as the jungle-clad Heritance Kandalama hotel (p183), to best appreciate the architect's unique vision.

← The exterior of the Heritance Kandalama, and (inset) a sculpture inside Jetwing Lighthouse

Colonial Cities

The three successive waves of European powers that ruled Sri Lanka left their mark on the island's landscape. Few traces of Portuguese rule survive, but reminders of the Dutch and British periods can be seen almost every-where you look. The Dutch rebuilt the island's forts – including Colombo (p70) and Galle (p108) – and bequeathed the island some distinctive verandah-fronted villas. If Galle's time-warped streets are Dutch, then Nuwara Eliya is undeniably "Little England" (p151). Check in to one of the town's whimsical half-timbered hotels, and indulge in afternoon tea on a manicured lawn to experience British Ceylon.

→ The Neo-Baroque Old Parliament Building in Colombo, funded by the British

BUDDHIST ART AND ARCHITECTURE

A range of architectural styles can be seen in Sri Lanka, but the influence of Buddhism is particularly noteworthy. The temples, *dagobas* and statues demonstrate the skills of Sri Lankan builders and sculptors, and underline the island's unique interpretation of Buddhist iconography. While the influence of Mahayana Buddhism can be seen in the size of the standing Buddhas and in the inclusion of *bodhisattvas* (enlightened beings), Hindu Tamil rulers and South Indian builders also left their mark on Buddhist architecture in the 13th century, blending Buddhist and Hindu architectural elements.

DAGOBAS

Originating from ancient Indian burial mounds, *dagobas*, or stupas, enshrine the relics of the Buddha and are thought to represent Mount Meru, the mythical mountain at the centre of the universe. Sri Lankan *dagobas* are usually simple structures, shaped as a bell, lotus or bubble, with little or no exterior decoration. Typically, *dagobas* comprise an *anda* (brick mound), which stands on a square terrace and is topped by the *harmika* (squared-off platform) from which rise the tiers of the *chattravali* (discs). The best-known examples can be seen in Anuradhapura *(p172)* and Polonnaruwa *(p166)*.

BUDDHA IMAGES

Sri Lankan artists were renowned for their ability to capture the serenity of the Buddha in their carvings, and it is said that the simplicity of the images parallels the simplicity of the *dagobas*. But don't just expect to see small, delicate statues; Sri Lanka is home to some supersized images, with many still being erected today.

↑ The bell-shaped Thuparama Dagoba in Anuradhapura

Image Features

The Ushnisha

△ The protuberance on top of the Buddha's head is symbolic of his superior mental powers. Some statues also show the *siraspata* (flame of wisdom) rising from it.

Mudras

△ The various hand gestures of the Buddha statues have symbolic significance *(p187)*. The *bhumisparsha* and *dhyana mudras* are most commonly seen in Sri Lanka.

Colossal Statues

△ Mahayana Buddhism, which required images much beyond human dimensions, had a big impact on Sri Lankan art and resulted in the construction of giant Buddha statues.

BUDDHIST TEMPLES

While *dagobas* are simple and unadorned, temples have decorative details, such as guardstones and carvings of elephants and dwarves. Semicircular stones called moonstones are placed at the foot of steps leading to many different shrines and temples. To the usual group of temple buildings, Sri Lanka added the *bodhigara* – a shrine dedicated to the sacred bo tree. The Buddha is believed to have attained enlightenment under a bo tree in India.

TEMPLE FEATURES

The image house is where the Buddha's images are kept. There are often statues of other gods or attendants, as well as paintings on the walls and ceilings, depicting events from the Buddha's life.

A *bodhigara* encloses the bo tree. Railings are erected around the sacred tree, leaving it open to the sky, with seated images of the Buddha all around. The Sri Maha Bodhi at Anuradhapura is the most significant bo tree on the island.

Moonstones are made up of a series of concentric semicircular rings. There is still debate about the symbolism of the imagery, but the rings are said to represent the spiritual journey to reach enlightenment. Elephants, horses, lions and bulls symbolize birth, old age, illness and death, respectively. Flames on the outer ring purify those who step across them.

1 The image house of the Kelaniya Raja Maha Vihara, in Colombo, houses murals depicting the Buddha's visits to the island.

2 Small Buddha statues are often found within the *bodhigara*, as seen here at a temple in Kandy.

3 Geese carrying lotus buds in their mouths, said to represent purity and wisdom, adorn this ancient moonstone at Anuradhapura.

Hills and Waterfalls

Sri Lanka's Hill Country (p132) is simply stunning, but its vast swathes of green tea bushes can make photos look a bit flat. Passing trains or strategically placed buildings add focal points to compositions or – better yet – focus on a colonial plantation sign or tea pickers dressed in brightly printed saris. Elsewhere in the Hill Country, use a tripod and try a long exposure to capture silky smooth images of cascades like Dunhinda (p150) and Bambarakanda Falls (p157).

 A picturesque tea plantation scene in the Hill country

SRI LANKA FOR
PHOTOGRAPHERS

Tumbling tea fields, paradisal beaches, vibrant cities and a wealth of wildlife make Sri Lanka a photographer's dream. Here, we show you how to snap some of the island's most iconic images, from bustling cityscapes to serene landscapes.

TOP 4 ICONIC CITY SHOTS

Temple of the Tooth
Capture the clustered shrines backdropped by the lush Udawattekele Sanctuary (p140).

Jami-ul-Alfar Mosque
The candy-striped façade of Colombo's Jami-ul-Alfar Mosque jazzes up any frame (p68).

Galle Fort
Tuk-tuks whizzing through Galle's venerable Old Gate provide a quirky contrast (p111).

Golden Buddha
Dambulla's gleaming gilded statue is the island's most irresistible big Buddha (p182).

Beaches, Boats and Fishermen

Golden sand, toppling palm trees and crashing surf make the island's beaches a pictorial dream. Perhaps the most photogenic beach scene is at Negombo, where colourful oruwas (fishing boats) are pulled right up onto the sand (p92). The fishermen hauling these boats ashore make another great subject, but ask their permission before snapping. Be aware that stilt fishermen will likely charge you for photographs (p122).

Did You Know?

The stilt fishermen you see today are usually posing rather than fishing.

Temple Life

The photographic beauty of Buddhist and Hindu temples is often in the detail rather than the whole, with their ornate friezes and statues. A white stupa against a clear blue sky is intensely photogenic, especially early or late in the day when the light brings out every detail of the mottled stone. Head to Anuradhapura for the Ruwanwelisaya Dagoba to get the shot (p172). Saffron-robed monks also make striking subjects. Ask their permission before snapping.

→

A young Buddhist monk about to open the colourful doors of a temple

Cityscapes

The island's towns and cities are full of colour and dynamism – local markets and street hawkers, elegant colonial streets and squiggly signs full of Sinhalese script. Wait for a passing rickshaw to drive into your frame to give any picture a lift or try a motion-blur effect if you have a tripod or a wall to put your camera on.

←

A bicycle whizzing past children on a street in Arugam Bay

Wild Things

A veritable ark of animals, Sri Lanka is a paradise for wildlife photographers. You'll need a lot of luck – or plenty of time – to get a good leopard image, but elephants are a lot easier to capture. Be careful that these magnificently wrinkled beasts aren't reduced to dull grey splodges on film. Perhaps the most impressive elephant shot is to be had at the annual "Gathering" at the Minneriya Wewa tank (p184).

→

A herd of wild elephants crossing a river within a national park

↑ Stilt fishermen perched above the calm waters of Koggala

Par-Tee Time

Sri Lanka isn't generally thought of as a golfing destination, but the island has a trio of excellent courses if you fancy swinging a club. Offering a pleasant respite from the bustling capital, Colombo's sylvan Royal Golf Club dates back to colonial times *(www.rcgcsl.com)* as does the picture-perfect Nuwara Eliya Golf Club, whose fairways, shaded by huge tropical trees, run picturesquely through the town centre *(www.nuwaraeliyagolfclub.com)*. The best-looking course, however, is undoubtedly the stunning Victoria Golf Club *(p148)*. Perched above the Victoria Reservoir, the rugged peaks of the Knuckles Range rise dramatically behind the greens here.

→

Teeing off on a verdant fairway at the Nuwara Eliya Golf Club

SRI LANKA FOR
OUTDOOR ACTIVITIES

Thanks to its diverse terrain, Sri Lanka offers an impressive roster of outdoor activities. Many sports and games were introduced to the island by the British, including cricket – a national obsession – but there are also some uniquely Sri Lankan pastimes to experience.

Carry On Carrom

To experience a traditional Sri Lankan pastime, join in a game of carrom. Played on a square wooden board with a pocket in each corner, the aim of the game is to flick your circular pieces into the pockets using a heavier "striker" disk. The first player to pot all of their pieces wins. Impromptu games are often set up on city streets. To watch professional players, contact the Carrom Federation of Sri Lanka who run regular tournaments ((077) 730 9234).

→

A game of carrom taking place on a board set up on a Colombo street

Take a Hike

Thanks to its undulating landscape, Sri Lanka is a trekker's delight. The Loop Trail around Horton Plains National Park is the best short-distance track (p143) but if you prefer more of a challenge, arrange a longer tour of the park with Sri Lanka Trekking Nature Holidays (www.trekkingsrilanka.com). Fancy a walk on the wild side? Head for the Knuckles Range (p148) and explore its cloud-swaddled peaks with Trekking Expeditor (www.trekking expeditor.com) or Sri Lanka Trekking Team (www.sri lankatrekking.com).

← Navigating rice paddies in a valley of the Knuckles Range

TOP 5 SRI LANKAN CRICKETERS

Muttiah Muralitharan (b 1972)
Holds the record for the most wickets in both test and one-day cricket.

Sanath Jayasuriya (b 1969)
This former captain was a great batsman.

Kumar Sangakkara (b 1977)
The second-highest one-day run-scorer.

Mahela Jayawardene (b 1977)
The first Sri Lankan player to score over 10,000 test runs.

Dhananjaya de Silva (b 1991)
The star of modern Sri Lankan cricket.

Wield the Willow

Cricket is almost another religion in Sri Lanka. The exploits of the country's test and one-day sides are watched avidly in Galle (p106), Kandy (p136) and at the venerable Sinhalese Sports Club in Colombo (p78). Catch a game or try bowling out a local team. Red Dot Tours (www. reddotsportstours.com) arranges tours with matches against school and club sides, or you can just join in a game on the beach – just don't expect the wicket to take much spin.

↑ Playing a game of cricket on a beach near Weligama, surrounded by colourful fishing boats

1864

The first service in Sri Lanka ran from Colombo to Ambepussa.

A train passing a Buddha statue on the outskirts of Galle, and *(inset)* looking out of an open window ↑

SRI LANKA FOR
RAIL JOURNEYS

Buses are often quicker and cars more convenient, but for a real taste of Sri Lanka you have to ride the rails. Grab a window seat, soak up some local know-how from your carriage companions and watch this beautiful country unfold outside your window.

Trains with a View

For enhanced views of the Hill Country line, book a seat in the "observation car". Attached to the back of certain trains, this carriage has supersized (if slightly battered) seats and larger windows. You'll need to book well in advance to get a seat in this carriage though - most tickets get snapped up the moment they're put on sale *(p224)*.

→

Enjoying the view through an open window in the observation car

Route Master

Built to transport tea from the plantations to the capital, the Hill Country line is Sri Lanka's standout railway journey. The seven-hour journey between Kandy and Badulla takes in tumbling waterfalls, mist-shrouded mountains and field upon field of tea. Roving hawkers are as much a feature of the journey as the toy-like stations and blasting horn. They go from carriage to carriage with flasks of hot drinks and freshly fried samosas. If time is precious, make the four-hour ride between Hatton and Ella – it's arguably the most scenic part of the journey. For a change of perspective, the coastal line from Colombo to Galle skims the sea as it rattles through endless palms and busy towns and villages.

> INSIDER TIP
> ## Don't Be First
>
> First class sounds great, but savvy travellers book second class tickets. The windows open in these carriages so you won't have any glare in your photos and you're more likely to be sat next to a local.

Walk the Line

Riding the rails themselves is an unbeatable experience but, for a different view of Sri Lanka's railways, take to the tracks. The best section to walk is over the Demodara Bridge (p144). If you're lucky, you'll catch the train and can wave at passengers aboard as it inches its way over the towering viaduct.

→

A blue train crossing the Demodara Bridge

A YEAR IN
SRI LANKA

JANUARY

Duruthu Poya *(Jan full moon)*. The Buddha's first visit to Sri Lanka is commemorated, with a spectacular *perahera* (parade) at Kelaniya's Raja Maha Vihara.

△ **Thai Pongol** *(14/15 Jan)*. Hindu temples celebrate the new rice harvest and honour Indra, the bringer of rains.

Galle Literary Festival *(mid-Jan)*. Readings, talks and discussions by leading authors.

FEBRUARY

Navam Poya *(Feb full moon)*. Expect a huge *perahera* at Colombo's Gangaramaya Temple.

△ **Independence Day (National Day)** *(4 Feb)*. Marks the anniversary of Sri Lankan independence in 1948.

Maha Sivarathri *(Feb/Mar)*. Devotees of the Hindu god Shiva perform a one-day fast and all-night vigil.

MAY

△ **Labour Day** *(1 May)*. Public holiday celebrating Sri Lankan workers.

Vesak Poya *(May full moon)*. The most important Buddhist *poya*, with *pandals* (decorative platforms showing scenes from the Buddha's life) erected across the country.

Eid ul-Fitr *((end of Ramadan))*. Major Muslim festival marking the end of fasting.

JUNE

△ **Poson Poya** *(May full moon)*. The introduction of Buddhism is observed with pilgrimages to Anuradhapura and Mihintale.

SEPTEMBER

△ **Dussehra** *(Sep/Oct)*. Local offshoot of the famous Indian festival, during which Hindus celebrate Rama's legendary victory over Rawana.

OCTOBER

△ **Deepavali** *(late Oct/early Nov)*. Sri Lanka's version of Diwali – the Hindu Festival of Lights – commemorating Rama's return from exile.

MARCH

△ **Good Friday** *(Mar/Apr)*. Christians congregate at Duwa, near Negombo, for the staging of a dramatic annual Easter Passion play.

APRIL

△ **Sinhalese and Tamil New Year** *(13–14 Apr)*. Buddhists and Hindus celebrate the new year with the giving of presents and casting of horoscopes.

JULY

Esala Perahera *(Jul/Aug)*. Kandy's world-famous festival features 12 days of increasingly spectacular *peraheras* celebrating the arrival of the Tooth Relic in Sri Lanka.

Kataragama Festival *(Jul/Aug)*. Exuberant religious festivities in honour of the god Kataragama, including ritual fire-walking.

△ **Vel** *(Jul/Aug)*. Dedicated to the Hindu god Skanda, a pair of *peraheras* in which the god's chariot and accompanying *vel* (spear) are pulled across Colombo.

AUGUST

△ **Nallur Festival Temple** *(Jul–Sep)*. Twenty-five-day extravaganza at Jaffna's Nallur Kandaswamy temple culminating in the spectacular procession, when the Skanda's chariot is paraded around the city.

NOVEMBER

△ **Il Poya** *(Nov full moon)*. Devout Buddhists take flowers to their local temple in honour of the Buddha's first missionary disciples. Head to Weligama to experience the procession of drummers and dancers.

DECEMBER

△ **Christmas** *(25 Dec)*. Jesus's birth is observed as a public holiday by followers of all religions, and there are traditional services in the island's churches.

A BRIEF
HISTORY

Sri Lanka's past has been shaped by trade, wars and invasions. Subjected to centuries of colonial rule, the island attained independence in 1948, only to be devastated by decades of Civil War. Since the 2002 ceasefire, visitors have flocked to the country and it's now firmly on the tourist map.

Prehistory and Anuradhapura

The island's first settlers – known as the Baladoga Man after the city where archaeologists found remains – are thought to have crossed the bridge of land that then connected the island to India in 125,000 BC. Their closest living relatives are the Veddahs (p205).

Indo-Aryans, the ancestors of the Sinhalese, arrived in Sri Lanka from around the 5th century BC. In the 4th century BC, they founded Anuradhapura (p172). Repeated invasions from India periodically convulsed this great kingdom, culminating in a devastating attack by Chola king Rajaraja in 993.

Did You Know?

Legend says that the Sinhalese are descended from Prince Vijaya, who landed here in 543 BC.

Timeline of events

c 500 BC

Indo-Aryan migrants from northern India, the ancestors of the modern Sinhalese, settle on the island.

247 BC

Mahinda converts King Devanampiya Tissa to Buddhism.

161–137 BC

Reign of Dutugemunu, who drives Tamil invaders out of Anuradhapura, seizing control of the island.

c 377 BC

The first great Sinhalese kingdom, Anuradhapura, is founded in the centre of the island's northern plains.

AD 993

Chola invaders destroy Anuradhapura and seize control of the island, reigning for 75 years.

The Kingdom of Polonnaruwa

The Cholas were driven out of the country by Sinhalese King Vijayabahu I (r 1055–1110). With Anuradhapura in ruins, the capital moved to Polonnaruwa (p166), which was further from India and easier to defend. Polonnaruwa experienced a golden age under subsequent rulers until Nissankamalla (r 1187–96) died without a successor. Tamil dynasties – the Cholas and the Pandyans – took advantage of the resulting instability to invade and pillage. In 1212, Magha (r 1215–55), a despotic Indian prince, launched a devastating attack on the island and seized power.

The Three Kingdoms

Magha's victory signalled the end of Polonnaruwa – the irrigation system fell into disrepair, disease spread and the people started migrating southwards to the safety of the Hill Country. Here, the Sinhalese rulers established a sequence of short-lived capitals, before finally settling in Kotte, near Colombo, in the 14th century. At the same time, another branch of the Sinhalese nobility built a rival centre of power in Kandy and an independent Tamil kingdom was established in Jaffna.

1 A 17th-century map of Sri Lanka.

2 Chola king Rajaraja and his guru Karuvura.

3 A statue of Parakramabhu I (r 1153–86), king of Polonnaruwa, still standing in the ancient city.

4 A mural depicting the transportation of the sacred Tooth Relic across Kandy, a Buddhist tradition that continues to this day.

1077
Vijayabahu I establishes a new capital at Polonnaruwa.

1153–86
Parakramabhu I builds lavish palaces and shrines in Polonnaruwa.

1215
Magha seizes control of the island, forcing the Sinhalese nobility to flee south.

c 1350
Rise of the Sinhalese kingdom of Kotte, close to the site of present-day Colombo.

1340
The Sinhalese diaspora continues, leading to the emergence of rival Sinhalese kingdoms at Gampola and Dedigama, as well as Kandy.

The Portuguese and Dutch

Trade became increasingly important to the Sinhalese. In 1505, a Portuguese fleet landed on the island, which they named Ceilão, and made a trading agreement with the king of Kotte. Their initial interest in Sri Lanka's cinnamon stocks rapidly grew into a desire to control the country, converting thousands of islanders to Roman Catholicism in their wake.

The Kandyans made a deal with the Dutch, promising them trade in return for military assistance against the Portuguese. The Dutch evicted the Portuguese from the island in 1658, but were in no hurry to hand over their conquests to the Kandyans, ruling the island's coastline for the next 140 years.

The British Era

The Dutch invited the British East India Company to the island in 1796 to protect it against the French, who had seized the Netherlands. In 1802, Ceylon – as it was translated in English – was handed to the British under the Treaty of Amiens. In 1815, the British deposed the Kandyan king Sri Wickrama Rajasinghe (r 1798–1815), bringing the entire island under unified rule.

↑ A painting of the last king of Kandy, Sri Wickrama Rajasinghe

Timeline of events

1505
A Portuguese fleet lands briefly in Colombo, noting its spices.

1518
The Portuguese return, constructing the Fort that will become the nucleus of Colombo.

1594
Roman Catholic missionaries begin converting islanders.

1638
King Rajasinghe II of Kandy forms an alliance with the Dutch to oust the Portuguese.

1658
Colombo, the last Portuguese stronghold, falls to the Dutch.

Under the British, a plantation economy was born. Coconut, rubber and coffee plantations were established, but it was tea that changed the physical and economic face of the island forever. Hundreds of thousands of Tamils were recruited from South India to work in the tea fields. These Tamils worked under exceptionally harsh conditions and were confined to ghettos.

The Rise of Nationalism

By the early 20th century, British Ceylon was hit by the wave of nationalism sweeping across other Asian colonies. Sparked by a revival of Buddhism and Hinduism, and driven by the Sri Lankan English-educated elite, Sri Lankans began demanding greater autonomy. This culminated in the 1915 riots. The British mistook this unrest for a conspiracy against them and reacted harshly, which resulted in further opposition. The Ceylon National Congress was formed in 1919 with the objective of self-governance. In 1931, the Donoughmore Commission (a group of four British parliamentarians) recommended a semi-responsible government and islanders were finally allowed to take part in the political process.

1 The Portuguese building a fort near Kandy.

2 The Dutch in Colombo.

3 Haputale Railway, built for the British.

4 An early 20th-century street scene.

1931

Universal suffrage was introduced to Sri Lanka, making it the first Asian colony to achieve this.

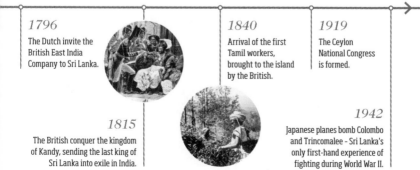

1796
The Dutch invite the British East India Company to Sri Lanka.

1815
The British conquer the kingdom of Kandy, sending the last king of Sri Lanka into exile in India.

1840
Arrival of the first Tamil workers, brought to the island by the British.

1919
The Ceylon National Congress is formed.

1942
Japanese planes bomb Colombo and Trincomalee - Sri Lanka's only first-hand experience of fighting during World War II.

1

2

Independence and Beyond

Sri Lanka peacefully gained independence in 1948, and power was handed to the conservative United National Party (UNP). After an economic decline caused by falling rubber and tea prices, the UNP lost the 1956 general election to the socialist-nationalist Sri Lanka Freedom Party (SLFP) led by S W R D Bandaranaike. This populist government passed the Sinhala Only Act, making Sinhala the country's sole official language and leading to widespread Tamil tensions. In 1971 the Janatha Vimukthi Peramuna (JVP) – a Marxist movement – staged an insurrection, which was violently suppressed by the military.

The LTTE and Civil War

Tamil feelings were further inflamed by the new constitution of 1972, which declared Buddhism the island's "foremost" religion. As tensions escalated, groups such as the Liberation Tigers of Tamil Eelam (LTTE) called for an independent Tamil state. The point of no return came during "Black July" in 1983, when the LTTE ambushed an army patrol near Jaffna. In retaliation, Sinhalese mobs swept through the cities, killing hundreds of Tamils.

↑ A poster for the LTTE, popularly known as the Tamil Tigers

Timeline of events

1948

Sri Lanka gains independence, with power being passed to the United National Party, led by D S Senanayake.

1972

Ceylon is renamed the Democratic Socialist Republic of Sri Lanka.

1983

Hundreds die during "Black July".

1959

Populist president S R W D Bandaranaike is assassinated by a Buddhist monk.

1987

Intense fighting leads to the arrival of an Indian peacekeeping force.

Fighting between the LTTE and the army escalated throughout the ensuing years. The election of UNP prime minister Ranil Wickremesinghe led to a ceasefire in 2002, but violence continued to rumble in the background. Tensions were overshadowed by the 2004 tsunami, however, when around 40,000 people died. Under the nationalist president Mahinda Rajapaksa, the army pushed north, taking the last pocket of rebel territory in 2009. Thousands of civilians died in the conflict, with widespread accusations of war crimes levelled against both sides.

Sri Lanka Today

After the fighting had ended, the island experienced a brief economic upsurge, despite Rajapaksa's increasingly nepotistic and despotic style of government. His successor, Maithripala Sirisena, made some positive reforms, but deep-seated economic problems and corruption remained.

On Easter Sunday in 2019, churches and hotels were bombed by Islamic terrorists, killing 259 people. This tragedy had a devastating effect on the country's tourist industry, although visitor numbers had nearly bounced back by the end of the year.

1 S W R D Bandaranaike. ↑

2 A Tamil Tiger guerrilla leads villagers in an exercise class.

3 A rally held in Kadawatha during the 2019 election campaign.

Did You Know?

S W R D Bandaranaike was succeeded by his widow Sirimavo – the world's first female prime minister.

2002
A ceasefire is brokered by new prime minister Ranil Wickremesinghe.

2004
A tsunami devastates much of the coast on Boxing Day, killing tens of thousands.

2005
Election of hardline Mahinda Rajapaksa leads to a collapse of the ceasefire.

2019
Gotabaya Rajapaksa wins the November election, becoming president.

2009
Final defeat of the LTTE by the Sri Lankan Army at Mullaitivu; there are accusations of war crimes on both sides.

RELIGIONS OF SRI LANKA

Religion still plays a very important role in the day-to-day life of Sri Lankans. Although the island is predominantly Buddhist (71 per cent of the population), other religions such as Hinduism (13 per cent), Islam (9 per cent) and Christianity (7 per cent) also have a marked presence here. On top of this, Animism, albeit with a Buddhist or Hindu influence, is still practised among the Veddahs, the original inhabitants of the island *(p205)*. One of the most interesting things about religion in Sri Lanka is that the same site is often sacred to the island's various religious groups, including Kataragama, which is a holy site for Buddhists, Hindus and Muslims *(p118)*.

Major Religions

Buddhism

▲ Buddhism is the belief system of the Sinhalese and has a huge influence on the country's art, architecture and literature. It was introduced to Sri Lanka by Mahinda, the son of the Indian king Asoka, in the 3rd century BC. Today, Theravada Buddhism is the most widely practised form of the religion on the island. The sect is older than the Mahayana school of Buddhism adhered to by Mahinda and preserves the orthodox teachings of the Buddha. It is based on the Pali Canon, which is believed to be the oldest record of the Buddha's teachings. All Buddhist temples in Sri Lanka follow a similar structure *(p42)*.

Hinduism

▲ Hinduism is the dominant religion of the Tamils. It was brought to the island by Tamil kings and their followers from South India. Today, Hindu communities are concentrated in the northern and eastern provinces. The Hindu belief system is based on the tenets of *samsara* (successive cycles of birth, death and rebirth), *karma* (the law of cause and effect) and *dharma* (righteousness). The three most important figures of the Hindu pantheon are Brahma, the creator of the world; Vishnu, who protects the world and preserves order; and Shiva, the god of destruction and regeneration. Try to see a temple *puja* (religious ceremony).

BUDDHIST OFFERINGS

The offering of coconut oil lamps is an important Buddhist ritual. It is followed by a wish or prayer to the Buddha, who is regarded as the "light of the three worlds" and the dispeller of darkness and ignorance. Besides oil lamps, worshippers also purchase other offerings from the stalls found near the temples. The wide variety of offerings at these kiosks ranges from lotus flowers to plastic toys.

Did You Know?

Fruits and flowers offered to a deity during Hindu *puja* ceremonies are called *prasada*.

Christianity

▲ Christians are known to have settled on the Sri Lankan coast in the early centuries AD. However, Roman Catholicism gained prominence only with the arrival of the Portuguese in the 16th century. Protestantism and other Christian denominations were introduced during the Dutch and the British eras. Since the end of colonial rule, the number of Sri Lankan Christians has declined and Roman Catholic communities are concentrated on the west coast.

Islam

▲ Islam was brought to Sri Lanka by Arab traders in the 7th century. Mostly concentrated along the coast, the Muslim community comprises less than 10 per cent of the population. All Muslims adhere to the Five Pillars of Islam: *shahadah* (professing faith), *salat* (praying five times a day), *zakat* (giving to charity), *sawm* (fasting during Ramadan) and undertaking the Hajj pilgrimage to Mecca. You'll come across many mosques on your travels around Sri Lanka, but some do not allow non-Muslims to enter. Nevertheless, they are impressive from the outside, particularly the Jami-ul-Alfar Mosque in Colombo *(p68)*.

EXPERIENCE

Swimming off a beach near Colombo

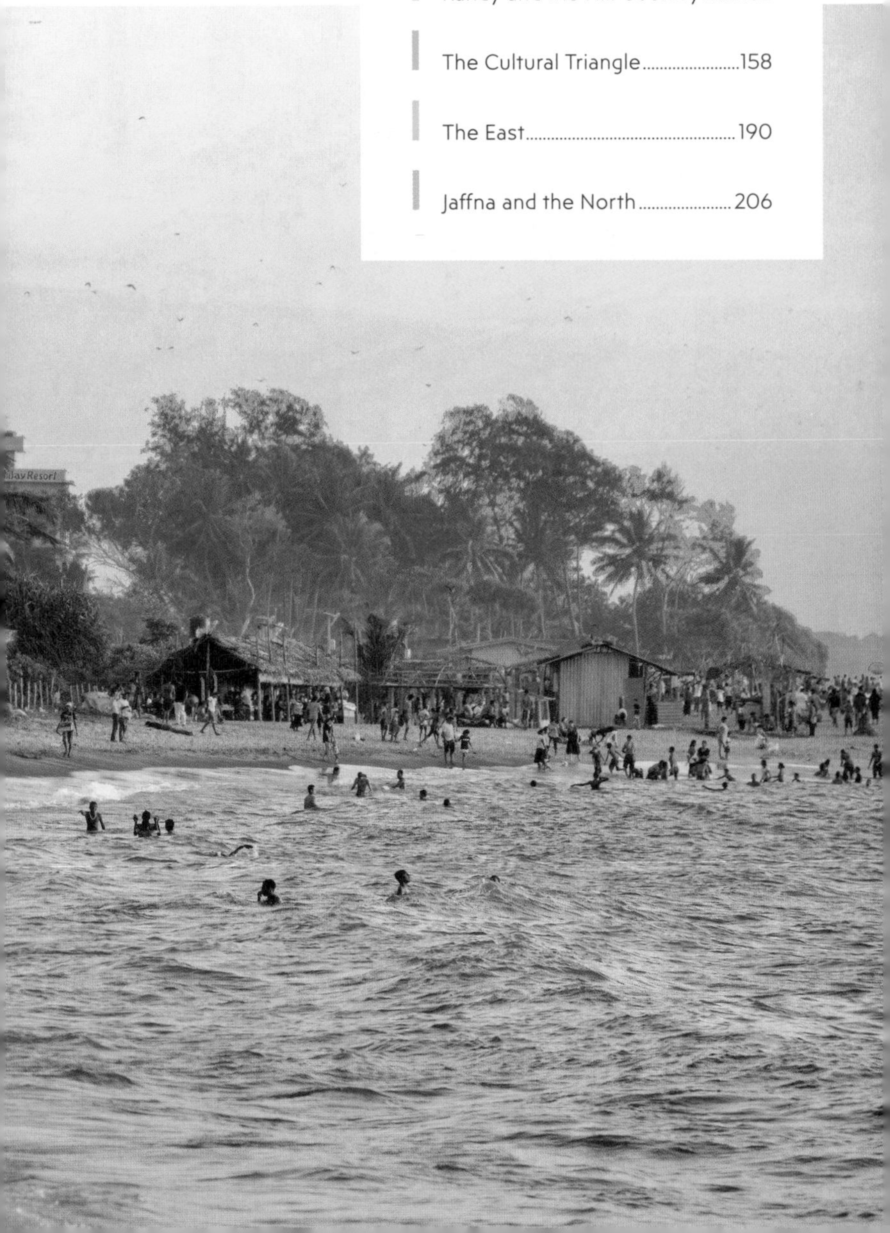

The striking Jami-ul-Alfar Mosque in Pettah

COLOMBO

Sri Lanka's dynamic capital has long been a commercial centre owing to its natural harbour. Arab traders established a trading outpost here as early as the 7th century, and Kolamba – as it was called by the Sinhalese – became a gateway between Asia and the West. Despite being a flourishing trade centre, the city only reached nationwide prominence with the arrival of the Portuguese in the 16th century. These European invaders built the fort that would become the nucleus of modern Colombo and destroyed nearby Kelaniya and Kotte. After these two major Sinhalese centres were destroyed, Colombo became the island's most important city.

The Portuguese lost control of the area in 1656 to the Dutch, who then administered Colombo for almost 150 years. The Dutch rebuilt the fort, reclaimed land from the sea using a system of canals that survives to this day and created leafy suburbs. In 1796, the city was captured by the British and was declared the capital of Ceylon in 1815. By the 1860s, it was considered one of Asia's major ports, with road and rail links to the rest of the island.

The city continued to prosper throughout the 19th century and has maintained its dominant status in post-independence Sri Lanka. However, Colombo has also had its share of tribulations. During the Civil War, the city was ravaged by suicide bombings orchestrated by the LTTE. The nation's capital took some time to recover from the war but large-scale building projects have transformed it into a thoroughly modern city, where Sinhalese, Tamil, Muslim, Burgher and expatriate communities live side by side.

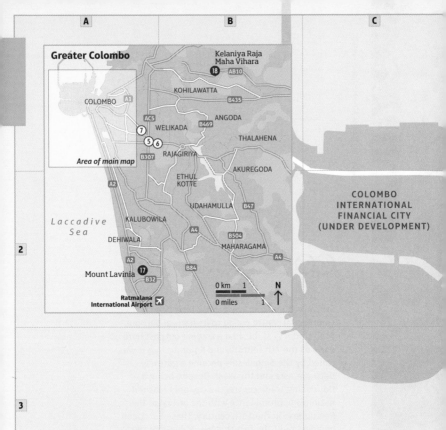

COLOMBO

Must Sees
1 Colombo National Museum
2 Pettah
3 Fort
4 Gangaramaya Temple

Experience More
5 Lotus Tower
6 Kotahena
7 Galle Face Green
8 Slave Island
9 National Museum of Natural History and National Art Gallery
10 Beira Lake
11 Seema Malaka
12 Cinnamon Gardens
13 Vihara Mahadevi Park
14 No 11, 33rd Lane
15 Green Path Art Market
16 Galle Road
17 Mount Lavinia
18 Kelaniya Raja Maha Vihara

Eat
① Café Francais
② Monsoon

Drink
③ Barefoot Café
④ Paradise Road The Gallery Café
⑤ The Verandah

Stay
⑥ Maniumpathy
⑦ Tintagel
⑧ Lake Lodge
⑨ Uga Residence

Shop
⑩ Paradise Road
⑪ Barefoot
⑫ Laksala

❶ 🎏

COLOMBO NATIONAL MUSEUM

📍F4 🏠854 Sir Marcus Fernando Mawatha, Col 7 📞(011) 269 4767 🕐9am–5pm daily 🚫Public hols 🌐museum.gov.lk

This beautiful museum houses a plethora of interesting collections, which explore what life was like in Sri Lanka from prehistoric times to the colonial era. It's a great introduction to the island's temples and ancient cities, so allow yourself a couple of hours to take it all in.

Located in a colonial-era building dating from 1877, the Colombo National Museum was founded by Sir William Henry Gregory, the British Governor of Ceylon. The museum takes up two floors of the Neo-Classical building. Artifacts on the ground floor are organized in chronological order, while the first-floor collection is arranged by theme. The most engaging galleries on the ground floor are 2 to 5, which feature exhibits from the Anuradhapura period through to the Kandyan era. The highlight here is the elaborate gold-and-red Kandyan throne which dominates room 5. A gift from the Dutch governor in 1693, it was used by generations of kings, including Sri Wickrama Rajasinghe (the last king of Kandy), until he was captured by the British in 1815 and subsequently exiled. Upstairs, there are several paintings, outlandish masks, coins, jewellery and puppets.

Artifacts on display in one of the colonnaded galleries in the museum ↑

↑ The grand exterior of the Colombo National Museum

Museum Highlights

Polonnaruwa Bronzes

In room 3, you'll find majestic dancing Shivas and voluptuous Taras. These are just some of the world-class collection of 12th-century bronze statues recovered from the ancient capital of Polonnaruwa. These artifacts demonstrate the influence of Hinduism on Sri Lankan culture.

Kandyan Throne and Regalia

▶ The brilliantly gilded throne *(right)* is accompanied by the king's golden crown and ceremonial sword. The throne was taken to England and kept at Windsor Castle between 1815 and 1934.

Urinal Stones

There are dozens of intricately carved stone slabs on one of the museum's verandas. Buddhist monks would relieve themselves on these stones in the Anuradhapura era, thereby demonstrating their contempt for worldly goods.

Kolam Masks

By turns regal, comic and grotesque, the museum's huge collection of colourful kolam masks features an entertaining medley of haughty kings, splay-toothed demons and cross-eyed yokels. Head upstairs to room 14 to check out this display. Why not pick out your favourite while you're here?

Toluvila Buddha

◀ Occupying pride of place inside the main entrance, this 5th-century granite statue of a seated Buddha *(left)*, plunged deep in meditation, is characteristic of Sri Lankan art and is considered to be a masterpiece. It was discovered in 1900 in Anuradhapura and bears a close resemblance to the Samadhi Buddha *(p176)*, although on a smaller scale.

②

PETTAH

📍E2 🚇Fort 🚌100,101

Colombo's chaotic and colourful commercial district, Pettah has hundreds of shops and open-air markets to browse. The name "Pettah" comes from the Tamil word *pettai,* meaning village, and compared with the rest of Colombo, this area has a particularly strong Muslim and Tamil influence. However, a range of different ethnicities and religions can also be found here and you'll find churches alongside Hindu temples and mosques.

① Dutch Period Museum

🏛Prince Street, Col 1
📞(011) 244 8466 ⏰9am–5pm Tue–Sat 🚫Public hols

Formerly the residence of Dutch governor Count August Carl Van Ranzow, this 17th-century colonnaded house served as a British military hospital in 1846, and as a post office in 1932. After extensive renovations, it reopened to the public in 1982 as the Dutch Period Museum, dedicated to the Dutch Colonial era in Sri Lanka.

The collection itself is only moderately interesting, with coins, military memorabilia, letters and documents, and Dutch Colonial furniture, but the mansion itself is well worth a visit. As you walk the groaning floorboards, you'll experience how colonialists lived in the 18th century.

② Jami-ul-Alfar Mosque

🏛228 2nd Cross Street, Col 11 📞(011) 245 1975
⏰5am–8pm daily

Dominating the north side of Main Street is the colourful Jami-ul-Alfar (popularly known as the "Red Mosque").

Built in 1909, the mosque's eye-catching exterior – covered in a jazzy kaleidoscope of alternating red and white stripes – is impossible to miss even among the surrounding crush of buildings and people. Designed by an untrained local architect, the mosque was inspired by Indo-Saracenic buildings, featuring an intricate confusion of Indian, Gothic and Neo-Classical elements.

③ Wolvendaal Church

🏛Wolfendahl Lane, Col 13
⏰9am–5pm Tue–Sun

The oldest Protestant church in Colombo, the Wolvendaal Dutch Reformed Church is one of the most interesting Dutch relics in Sri Lanka.

📷 PICTURE PERFECT
Picturesque Pettah

This district is a photographer's dream, particularly around the Old Town Hall and the Jami-ul-Alfar Mosque. Rise early to avoid rush hour and the hottest part of the day.

←

The unmistakable exterior of Jami-ul-Alfar Mosque on a busy street

Built in 1749, this large church, with a red-and-white Neo-Classical façade, is easy to spot. The interior is equally as elegant, with a beautiful wooden pulpit and patterned organ pipes. Look out for the Dutch names on the tombstones that pave the floor.

④
Old Town Hall

🏠 **Kayman's Gate, Col 1**

Dominating the area known as Kayman's Gate is the Moorish-style Old Town Hall, which was built in 1873. The two-storey building served as the premises of the Colombo Municipal Council for 65 years, after which it fell into disrepair and was used as a public market. Today, it is possible to climb the stairs to the second floor to see a reconstruction of a council meeting, with wax figures seated around a table.

Back downstairs, the western side of the building is lined by dozens of picturesque fruit and vegetable stalls. It's the perfect spot to take a photo or pick up a snack.

⑤
New Kathiresan and Old Kathiresan Kovils

🏠 **Sea Street**

Spied beyond an adorned *gopuram* (gateway), these two temples are dedicated to Skanda, the Hindu god of war and son of Lord Shiva, and serve the area's many Tamil residents. The temples are quiet by day but come alive at dusk during the early evening *puja* (temple ceremony) and during the annual Aadi Vel Festival, when they serve as the starting point for the colourful chariot procession.

TOP 5 PETTAH STREETS

Main Street
Assorted clothing stores line the area's main street. Check out the enticing array of colourful saris.

Front Street
Offers a huge variety of leather goods, including bags and shoes.

2nd Cross Street
The place to pick up some local textiles.

Gabo's Lane
A variety of Ayurvedic ingredients are for sale on this street.

Sea Street
Known for its gold jewellery shops.

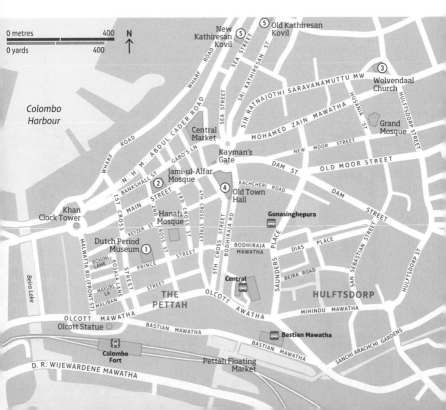

③

FORT

◉ D2 🚉 Secretariat

The heart of the city, Fort is one of the best places to stay, eat, drink and explore. Much of the area retains a largely colonial feel, particularly as you walk along Janadhipathi Mawatha, with its grand British-era buildings, but a clutch of more modern buildings line Fort's southern edge, including the World Trade Center.

① Colombo Fort Clock Tower

🏠 Junction of Chatham Street and Janadhipathi Mawatha, Col 1

Right in the centre of Fort stands this quaint clock tower. Once the tallest building in the city, it was built in 1857 by order of Lady Ward, wife of British governor Henry Ward. The tower sports a timepiece by Dent & Co – the makers of London's famous Big Ben – and is topped by a lighthouse beacon, which served as the city's maritime landmark until a new lighthouse was constructed, just to the west, in 1952.

② 🍴 Grand Oriental Hotel

🏠 2 York Street, Col 1 ⏰ Daily
🌐 grandoriental.com

Located opposite the Port of Colombo, this landmark was originally built in 1837 as an army barracks before being converted into a hotel in 1875. It soon became one of the finest hotels in the city, and Russian writer Anton Chekhov stayed here in 1890. According to some sources, his short story *Gusev* was penned during his stay. Although no longer attracting film stars or royalty, and lacking most of its former colonial elegance, the hotel still has great views of the port from its restaurant.

③ St Peter's Church

🏠 26 Church Street, Col 1
⏰ 7am–5pm daily

A Dutch governor's residence in the 17th century, this building was first used for worship in 1804 by the British as a garrison church before being officially consecrated as St Peter's Church in 1821.

THE REBIRTH OF FORT

Fort was particularly hard hit during the Civil War, when it was repeatedly targeted by LTTE suicide bombers and many of the buildings were reduced to near dereliction. Since then, the formerly war-torn shell has been transformed into one of Colombo's most vibrant districts. Redevelopment culminated in the reopening of Janadhipathi Mawatha in 2015, allowing the public access to a street which had been off limits for a generation.

EXPERIENCE Colombo

EAT

Botanik

This stylish rooftop restaurant is known for its superb Asian-influenced cuisine and great views.

🏠 7 Hospital St
🌐 botanik.lk

$$$

Ministry of Crab

A shrine to Sri Lanka's favourite crustacean, serving up plump crabs with a range of Sri Lankan and other Asian flavours.

🏠 Old Dutch Hospital
🌐 ministryofcrab.com

$$$

Pagoda Tea Room

A classic colonial-era café that famously featured in Duran Duran's *Hungry Like the Wolf* music video. Good value.

🏠 105 Chatham Street

$$$

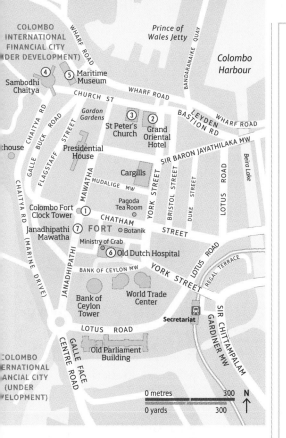

④ Sambodhi Chaitya

🏠 Chaitya Road, Col 1
🕐 Daily

This modern *dagoba* was built in 1956 to commemorate the 2,500th anniversary of the Buddha's death.

---

⑤ Maritime Museum

🏠 Chaitya Road, Col 1
🕐 10am–6pm daily

With old ships' cannons flanking the entrance, the

←

Colombo Fort Clock Tower, standing at the centre of the district

Maritime Museum is housed in a former Dutch prison. The exhibition charts the history of maritime travel in Sri Lanka, starting in the 5th century BC when Prince Vijaya from India is believed to have landed on the island with his followers.

---

⑥ 🍴 🖥 🛍 Old Dutch Hospital

🏠 Bank of Ceylon Mawatha
🕐 Daily

The low-slung, sloped-roof buildings of the Old Dutch Hospital, where officers and staff of the Dutch East India Company once convalesced, now house a cool shopping and eating complex. Relax, sample local delicacies and enjoy this lovingly restored 17th-century complex.

⑦ Janadhipathi Mawatha

Stretching north from the clock tower, the broad sweep of Janadhipathi Mawatha (formerly Queen's Street) offers a snapshot of Fort's colonial heritage. Dominating the eastern side of the street is the elegant President's House, built by the island's last Dutch ruler and now used by Sri Lankan heads of state. A statue of governor Edward Barnes stands outside, from which all road distances in the island are measured. Opposite is the flamboyant former General Post Office of 1895.

4 🔧

GANGARAMAYA TEMPLE

📍E4 🏠Sri Jinaratna Road, Col 2 🕐5am-10pm daily 🌐gangaramaya.com

Founded in the late 19th century, Gangaramaya is easily Colombo's most interesting Buddhist temple complex. It was built during Sri Lanka's Buddhist revival and comprises an unusual mix of minimalist and modern Indian architectural styles. Try to time your visit with the huge Navam Perahera festival.

The Central Courtyard

An intimate courtyard stands at the heart of the complex, centring on a small *dagoba* and a rambling bodhi tree. To one side stands the temple's principal shrine, home to a large orange-robed Buddha, flanked by elephant tusks. The wooden pavilion opposite the main shrine is the library, where piles of antique *ola*-leaf manuscripts and Buddha statues await. The upper floor can be accessed via the bodhi tree terrace, and a walk along the adjacent balcony affords a good overview of the complex.

↑ The white *dagoba* in the leafy central courtyard

Beyond the Courtyard

A cluster of more modern buildings fill the area behind the central courtyard. These structures feature an eclectic medley of religious statues and other artifacts from India, Southeast Asia and China, ranging from Hindu gods to porcelain *bodhisattvas*. Look out, in particular, for the strange collection of delicate Thai Buddhas towards the rear of the temple, stacked up high on a concrete tier like items in a Buddhist supermarket.

Back by the entrance, the grand colonial building houses the Gangaramaya's impressive museum. The collection showcases the many weird and wonderful objects that have been donated to the temple over the years, including an impressive collection of vintage cars and a stuffed elephant.

↑ The colourful Buddha in the temple's principal shrine

NAVAM PERAHERA

Dating back to 1979, Navam Perahera is a two-day event taking place in February that attracts people from all over the country and abroad. A procession of dancers, acrobats and drummers makes its way from Perahera Mawatha to the temple complex in a riot of movement, colour and music. In stark contrast are the *bhikkus* – newly ordained monks in their saffron robes who make their way sedately past the onlookers.

Did You Know?

The temple is home to the world's smallest Buddha - seen through a magnifying glass.

The shrine beneath the sprawling bodhi tree in the temple's courtyard ↑

EXPERIENCE MORE

EXPERIENCE Colombo

❺ Lotus Tower

📍E3 🏛Lotus Tower Road
🌐lotustower.lk

Soaring high above Beira Lake, and visible from across the city, the Lotus Tower is Colombo's largest and most incongruous landmark, resembling a huge concrete space rocket topped by a purple flower bud. At 35 m (115 ft) high, it is the tallest building in South Asia. One of several mega-projects financed by Chinese loans during the divisive rule of President Mahinda Rajapaksa, the tower cost 20 billion LKR to build, and work began in 2012.

Now apparently complete (at least from the outside), the Lotus Tower was originally scheduled to receive visitors in 2017, but the opening has been repeatedly delayed, with no confirmed date

← The soaring Lotus Tower overlooking Beira Lake

announced. An observation deck is among the tower's promised attractions, alongside assorted conference and recreational facilities. LED lighting is planned to illuminate the "petals" covering the summit in changing colours.

❻ Kotahena

📍F1

North of Pettah, Kotahena is Colombo's most staunchly Christian suburb – a relic of colonial times, when the city's Catholic community was granted this area of land by their Protestant Dutch rulers. There are many Catholic churches to discover here.

St Anthony's Church was built in the 19th century on the site of a small, 18th-century mud chapel. The present church is dedicated to St Anthony of Padua, the patron saint of lost and stolen articles. St Anthony is usually portrayed holding the infant Jesus in his arms. The most venerated statue of the saint can be seen on the side altar. Brought from Goa in India by a member of the church's congregation in 1822, the statue is thought to have miraculous properties.

The church is always busy on Tuesdays when people from all over the country, both Catholic and non-Catholic, come to pray to St Anthony, who was buried on a Tuesday in 1263. But this is nothing compared to the scenes on

CHRISTIANITY IN COLOMBO

Christians once lived all over the island but today the majority of Christians live along the West Coast, especially in the area around Colombo (p59). Kotahena is the spiritual centre of Catholicism on the island because Santa Lucia Cathedral is the mother church and cathedral seat of the Roman Catholic Archdiocese of Colombo, the ecclesiastical province that encompasses all of Sri Lanka, as well as the Maldives. Christians from across the archdiocese pilgrimage to Kotahena to worship at the cathedral as well as at the the suburb's many other revered churches.

↑ The impressive Neo-Classical façade of Santa Lucia Cathedral, the largest Catholic church on the island

St Anthony's Feast Day (13 June), when the church throngs with people.

Tragically, St Anthony's was one of the worst-hit targets of the April 2019 suicide bomb attacks (p57), with almost a hundred worshippers killed. The church reopened following repairs in June 2019.

Like St Anthony's, **Santa Lucia Cathedral** was once a simple mud-thatched chapel, but it's now the largest Catholic church on the island, designed to resemble St Peter's Basilica in Rome. The Neo-Classical façade is crowned by a silver dome and surmounted by a large clock, which is still wound by hand every 48 hours.

The interior, by contrast, is relatively simple. Look for the huge statue of St Lucia on the altar, who is depicted holding her eyes in the palm of her hand. Legend has it that a nobleman wanted to marry her for the beauty of her eyes. Wanting to live only to serve God, she tore them out and gave them to him.

St Anthony's Church
🏠 St Anthony's Mawatha, Col 13 📞 (011) 232 9303 🕐 6am–6pm daily

Santa Lucia Cathedral
🏠 St Lucia's Street, Col 13 📞 (011) 234 2850 🕐 6am–7pm daily 🍴 For lunch

STAY

Maniumpathy
A real taste of old Ceylon, this colonial-era villa has just eight gorgeous rooms.

📍 B1 🏠 129 Kynsey Road, Col 7
🌐 maniumpathy.com

$$$

Tintagel
Colombo's most exclusive hotel is set in the former house of Sri Lankan Prime Minister S W R D Bandaranaike (who was assassinated on the terrace here in 1959). Tintagel combines colonial style and contemporary cool, with a spa, steam room and library.

📍 A1 🏠 65 Rosmead Place, Col 7
🌐 paradiseroad hotels.com

$$$

Lake Lodge
Stylish boutique guesthouse imagined by leading Sri Lankan designer Taru. As the name suggests, it's set in a conveniently central (but very quiet) location near Lake Beira.

📍 E4 🏠 Alwis Terrace, Col 3 🌐 taruvillas.com

$$$

Uga Residence
Gorgeous boutique hotel set in the childhood home of former island president J R Jayawardene. It has only 11 rooms.

📍 E4 🏠 20 Park Street, Col 2 🌐 ugaescapes.com

$$$

❼

Galle Face Green

🅿 D3 🚌 100, 101

Stretching south along the seafront between Fort and Kollupitiya, Galle Face Green is an extensive grassy promenade. It was laid out in 1859 by Sir Henry Ward, who was the governor of British Ceylon from 1855 to 1860.

The site of horse races, cricket matches and a golf course in colonial times, Galle Face Green remains one of the city's best-loved open spaces, particularly popular towards dusk when crowds descend to fly kites, stroll along the esplanade and munch on snacks from the various food kiosks strung out along the oceanfront.

Bounding the southern end of the green is the sprawling Galle Face Hotel. Founded in 1864, this venerable colonial pile has hosted a veritable who's who of guests, from Noel Coward to Mahatma Gandhi; their photographs can be seen in the hotel's attractive Traveller's Bar. It is still one of the city's nicest places to stay.

Offering a stark contrast to the stately Galle Face Hotel, the inland side of the green is slowly being taken over by

Did You Know?

The Dutch used crocodiles to thwart any escapees from Slave Island.

huge, modern hotels. One of these, the towering Shangri-La Hotel, was significantly damaged during the April 2019 bomb attacks.

Another development changing the face of the green, indeed the city itself, is the ambitious Colombo International Financial City, which is being constructed on reclaimed land jutting into the Indian Ocean.

---

❽

Slave Island

🅿 E3

To the east of Galle Face Green is the area known as Slave Island, bounded by Beira Lake on three sides. The name is thought to date back to the Dutch occupation, when enslaved people – brought from the eastern coast of Africa – were used to rebuild Colombo's fort. The number of these enslaved people grew, and in the 18th century some staged an insurrection. However, the rebellion was quashed and from then on enslaved people were kept on the island overnight. Slavery was abolished in Sri Lanka in 1845 by the British but the name persists.

Nowhere exemplifies the massive changes sweeping through the capital better than Slave Island. Formerly a slightly shabby and run-down area, it is now being

COLOMBO INTERNATIONAL FINANCIAL CITY

From Galle Face Green, a huge swathe of reclaimed land can be clearly seen to the north. This is the site of Colombo International Financial City, a brand-new, high-rise, hi-tech mini-city, which is set to transform the face of the capital over the next 20 years. The planned development will feature a glitzy array of offices, hotels and malls. Much of the cost is being under-written by China.

transformed with a series of futuristic, high-rise developments which would look more at home in Dubai than Sri Lanka. Several of these high-rises can be found along Sir James Peiris Mawatha facing Beira Lake, including the massive Colombo City Centre, housing an upmarket hotel, large shopping mall and restaurants, and the landmark Altair building, a memorably wonky structure, already popularly known as the "Leaning Tower of Colombo".

Creeping gentrification has also seen the development of the arty Park Street Mews restaurant enclave, near the Gangaramaya temple *(p72)*, which is home to a couple of the city's top dining spots.

Away from the main roads, some of Slave Island's former character survives. The heart of the old quarter can be found around Malay Street, which is still lined with shoe-box shops and scruffy cafés, while surrounding streets are dotted with churches, mosques and temples, testifying to the multiculturalism of this part of the city.

The Island is home to **Sri Siva Subramaniya Kovil**, one of Colombo's most impressive Hindu temples. Dedicated to Skanda or Murugan, the temple was constructed for Indian troops stationed here during the British era. Its defining feature is a large *gopuram* covered in a colourful confusion of gods and goddesses, while inside shrines to various deities surround a central stone chamber. You can only visit the temple during the morning or early-evening *pujas* (temple ceremonies).

Sri Siva Subramaniya Kovil

🏠 Kew Street, Col 2 🕐 8–9am & 5–6pm daily

←

People flying kites on a Sunday on the popular Galle Face Green

↑ Sri Siva Subramaniya Kovil, one of Colombo's most impressive Hindu temples

9 🖉

National Museum of Natural History and National Art Gallery

📍 F4 🏠 Ananda Coomeraswamy Mawatha, Col 7 ☎ National Museum of Natural History: (011) 269 5366; National Art Gallery: (011) 269 3965 🕐 9am–5pm daily 🚫 Public hols

Part of the same complex as the Colombo National Museum *(p66)*, the National Museum of Natural History is dated and dusty, but those interested in the island's diverse flora and fauna will enjoy it. Check out the blue whale skeleton and pickled two-headed goat.

Next door is the National Art Gallery, which is very run-down, with no labelling or information. It comprises a large room displaying paintings by Sri Lankan artists in a range of styles.

EAT

Café Francais
Upscale restaurant offering French cuisine by the Michelin-starred Pourcel brothers.

📍 F4 🏠 48 Park Street, Col 2 🌐 cafefrancaisby pourcel.com

$$$

Monsoon
Buzzy restaurant serving up an authentic array of Southeast Asian cuisine.

📍 F4 🏠 50/2 Park Street Mews, Col 2 🌐 monsooncolombo.com

$$$

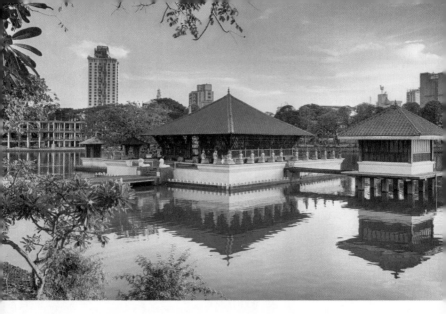

Beira Lake

📍E3

Looping around Slave Island (p76), this lake was constructed by the Portuguese to protect their fort. Today, it's a place for relaxation and recreation. The southwestern section of the lake, around the Seema Malaka temple, is particularly pretty, attracting a variety of water birds.

Behind Seema Malaka is Colombo City Centre, with a shopping mall, food court and cinema. Look out for Altair, an apartment complex made up of two leaning towers.

Seema Malaka

📍E4 🏛Beira Lake, Col 2 🕐6am-11pm daily

Set amid the placid waters of Beira Lake, Seema Malaka is a meditation temple used as an inauguration hall for monks from the nearby Gangaramaya Temple (p72). It was built in 1976 in place of a 19th-century temple that had gradually sunk into the water. The current structure was financed by a Muslim businessman who, having been ostracized by his community, decided to invest money in a Buddhist venture.

The building comprises a trio of platforms linked to the shore by a short walkway. Designed by the great Sri Lankan architect Geoffrey Bawa (p81), the temple's unusual layout was inspired by similar structures found at the island's ancient forest monasteries, such as Ritigala (p186), with open platforms for meditation linked to a small shelter (although on a far larger scale). The central covered pavilion is particularly beautiful, with its intricately constructed wooden frame roofed in handsome blue tiles.

This roof reflects the colours of the surrounding waters and the building is often reflected in Beira Lake.

Cinnamon Gardens

📍F5

Named after the spice plantations that once stood here, Cinnamon Gardens remains Colombo's leafiest and most exclusive neighbourhood. It has dozens of embassies, plus a few upmarket hotels, lining its broad, tree-shaded streets. The area is also home to several of the island's most elite private schools, surrounded by extensive cricket grounds and playing fields.

The northern part of the suburb is dominated by Vihara Mahadevi Park and the National Museum (p66). Just east of the museum is the strikingly modern Nelum Pokuna Theatre. Its flamboyant outline was inspired by the lotus-shaped *nelum pokuna* pond in Polonnaruwa (p166).

South of the museum, the old colonial **Colombo Racecourse** grandstand

> **Named after the spice plantations that once stood here, Cinnamon Gardens remains Colombo's leafiest and most exclusive neighbourhood.**

← The sun setting over Seema Malaka Temple, in the middle of tranquil Beira Lake

To the east is the **Sinhalese Sports Club**. This traditional cricket pitch, with its antiquated scoreboard, serves as one of Colombo's two Test-match cricket venues. Buy a ticket to experience the electric atmosphere.

Colombo Racecourse

🖐️ 🍴 😊 🍷 🚻 📍 Reid Avenue, Col 7

Sinhalese Sports Club

🖐️ 🍴 😊 📍 35 Maitland Place, Col 7 🌐 ssc.lk

🔟 📺

Vihara Mahadevi Park

📍 F4 📍 Ananda Coomeraswamy Mawatha (Green Path), Col 7

A large green space in the centre of Colombo, Vihara Mahadevi Park is named after the mother of King Dutugemunu (r 161–137 BC). It is a welcome shady spot with tropical trees as well as orchids and exotic plants. The park attracts a wide variety of birds, and occasionally the odd elephant may be spotted here with its *mahout* (caretaker).

The railings to the south of the park, along Green Path, display works of upcoming artists during the week

and grounds were restored and remodelled in 2011 and now serve as the island's leading rugby venue. A small, but very modern, shopping centre is attached to the pitch. To the east is the imposing Independence Commemoration Hall, an oversized and rather over-bearing re-creation in stone of the old wooden Audience Hall at the Temple of the Tooth in Kandy *(p140)*.

A short walk further south are the gleaming white buildings of the Independence Arcade, built in 1882 to house the city's asylum. They have now been repurposed as an upmarket shopping and eating complex. It's the perfect lunch spot.

SHOP

Paradise Road
Chic, contemporary Sri Lankan crafts and homeware, many featuring the brand's signature Sinhalese alphabet designs.

📍 F4 📍 213 Dharmapala Mawatha, Col 7 🌐 paradiseroad.lk

Barefoot
Sri Lanka's best-loved shop is famous for its vibrantly coloured cotton textiles, which are featured on clothes, bags and cuddly toys. Check out the café *(p83)*.

📍 E5 📍 704 Galle Rd, Col 3 🌐 barefoot ceylon.com

Laksala
The flagship branch of the government's nationwide handicrafts emporium stocks just about every kind of handicraft made on the island, from painted masks to batik.

📍 F5 📍 215 Bauddhaloka Mawatha, Col 7 🌐 laksala.gov

and students' works on Sundays *(p80)*. The white-domed Town Hall overlooks the park to the northeast. Reminiscent of the US White House, it is hard to miss. Further north is De Soysa, or Lipton Circus, one of the city's major intersections where the Devatagaha Mosque is sited.

← A seated golden Buddha in Vihara Mahadevi Park, a welcome green, shady spot

A beautiful reception room at No 11, 33rd Lane, and *(inset)* a shaded patio

No 11, 33rd Lane

⊙ E5 🏠 Off Bagatelle Road, Col 3 🕐 For tours only at 10am, 2pm & 3:30pm (book ahead) 🌐 geoffreybawa.com

In 1958, Geoffrey Bawa bought the third in a row of four bungalows on 33rd Lane and converted it into a small living unit. He persuaded the landlord to sell him the other bungalows as and when they became available, and over a period of 40 years he created this glorious townhouse, part of which can be visited today.

It was here that Bawa developed his interest in bricolage (using repurposed

materials) – incorporated into the house are articles salvaged from old buildings in Sri Lanka and South India. Stone rubbings from the ancient towns of Anuradhapura *(p172)* and Polonnaruwa *(p166)* coexist with a contemporary batik by Ena de Silva. Another feature is the set of doors painted by Donald Friend, an Australian artist. The house has a sense of infinite space, despite having been built on a small suburban plot. Light-wells and courtyards allow ample natural light and the white floors and staircase add to the tranquil air.

Visitors enter the house through what was originally the first bungalow but is now a four-storey Modernist structure with a car port where a 1950s Mercedes and a vintage Rolls Royce are displayed. Bawa's bedroom on the ground floor, with its huge stacks of books, can merely be peeked into. The first floor's main attraction are the inlaid doors by Ismeth Rahim, a well-known Sri Lankan architect. A sun-drenched stairwell leads to the rooftop terrace from the first floor.

> **INSIDER TIP**
> **Bawa Bed**
>
> What better way to experience Bawa's vision than to book a stay at No 11, 33rd Lane? A two-bed-room suite on the first floor makes for an opulent base. Book online at www.geoffrey bawa.com.

Green Path Art Market

⊙ F4 🏠 Ananda Coomeraswamy Mawatha (Green Path), Col 7

Flanking Vihara Mahadevi Park to the north and the National Art and Natural History museums to the south, the spacious, tree-lined Green Path is home to Colombo's most popular open-air art market *(kala pola)*. Weekends are particularly busy, when hundreds of colourful canvases by local art students and professional painters are hung from the railings lining the road. During bad weather, the artists display their wares in the covered display units to protect them from the rain. All works on display are for sale, usually at very reasonable prices. Why not pick up something for a wall at home?

GEOFFREY BAWA

Considered to be one of the most important Asian architects of the 20th century, Geoffrey Bawa developed the Tropical Modernist style, creating structures that blended modernity with tradition, and addressed issues of ventilation, integration and climate.

Born to wealthy Burgher parents, Bawa (1919–2003) was set to follow in his father's footsteps to become a lawyer. He soon realized that a career in law was not for him, but it was only after buying the estate at Lunuganga (p95) that he decided to become an architect. Bawa enrolled at the Architectural Association in London in 1956 and returned a year later to Colombo, where he set up a practice with other budding artists and architects. Bawa's earliest collaborator was the Danish architect Ulrik Plesner, and together they worked on projects in the Tropical Modernist style. During Bawa's 40-year career he completed more than 200 projects, of which very few survive in their original form.

↑ A portrait of Geoffrey Bawa, working on a design

BAWA BUILDINGS IN COLOMBO
The capital is home to some examples of Bawa's signature style, including No 11, 33rd Lane, Seema Malaka and the New Sri Lanka Parliament. Built to a design by Bawa between 1979 and 1982, the parliament centres around an artificial lake.

OTHER BAWA-DESIGNED BUILDINGS
Bawa's legacy of great architectural designs is not limited to Colombo. Check out Lunuganga or book a room at the Heritance Kandalama hotel (p183). A jungle hideaway with views over the Kandalama tank to Sigiriya, the hotel seems to melt into its surroundings. You can also stay at Jetwing Lighthouse - one of Bawa's last designs.

↑ Seema Malaka Temple, sitting on Beira Lake in Colombo

↑ The exterior of one of the buildings making up the New Sri Lanka Parliament

↑ The popular courtyard café of Barefoot, the famous shop on Galle Road

17 🍴 🖥

Mount Lavinia

📍 A2 🚗 12 km (7 miles) S of Colombo city centre
🚌🚍 100, 101

A beachside suburb of Colombo, Mount Lavinia is said to have been named after Sir Thomas Maitland's lover, a Portuguese-Sinhalese local dancer named Lovina. Maitland, who served as Governor General of Ceylon from 1805 to 1811, established a residence in this area in 1806. Legend has it that a tunnel connected the building to Lovina's house so the lovers could meet in secret. The building was lived in and expanded by successive governors until it was converted into the **Mount Lavinia Hotel** in the late 19th century. This imposing hotel, poised on a small promontory, towers over the beach and attracts visitors from around the world to

16

Galle Road

📍 E4 🚌🚍 100, 101

The backbone of southern Colombo, Galle Road connects the coastal suburbs to the city centre. The road splits into two one-way streets from Colombo Fort to Wellawatta, and runs for 8 km (5 miles). The further south the road advances, the less prosperous are the areas, but neighbourhoods such as Wellawatta make for an interesting wander off the tourist trail.

Immediately south of Galle Face Green (p76) is the neighbourhood of Kollupitiya, where many of the hotels as well as the Tourism Development Authority are located. Also along this stretch of road are the US and Indian embassies and the heavily guarded prime minister's official residence, Temple Trees. As the road approaches central Kollupitiya, visitors will find a number of popular cafés and shops, including the stylish Barefoot. Beware of con artists who offer to take visitors to a gem show or to an elephant festival, and persistent three-wheeler drivers looking for a fare.

Further south, Galle Road bisects the lively suburb of Bambalapitiya. This is one of the busiest areas of Colombo, with small roadside shops, large shopping malls, such

as the Majestic City Mall, and enticing restaurants.

A few kilometres south of Bambalapitiya, Wellawatta, also known as Little Jaffna, is an area with a large Tamil population. There are a number of *kovils* (temples) located here, and many family-run businesses that offer a range of goods, including saris.

The image house of Kelaniya Raja Maha Vihara, and (inset) its
↓ yellow-orange exterior

GREAT VIEW
Sandy Night

Head to Mount Lavinia beach for a night-time drink or dinner to soak up the views. From the candlelit restaurants ringing the bay you can see the twinkling lights and towers of central Colombo in the distance.

Mount Lavinia. The hotel has maintained its old-world charm despite modernization.

Mount Lavinia is a good, laid-back alternative to the bustle of Colombo. The beach is decent but can become busy at weekends and during holidays, when locals come here for the day. The sea is not great for swimming, but it is possible to watch the fishermen preparing to cast their nets. There are also a number of beachside bars and restaurants. Visitors are advised to exercise caution when walking back to their hotel after dark. The tide can become unexpectedly high, so avoid walking back along the beach at night when visibility is impaired.

Mount Lavinia Hotel
🕐 🖺 📍100 Hotel Road 📅Daily 🌐mount laviniahotel.com

18
Kelaniya Raja Maha Vihara

📍B1 🚗12 km (7 miles) NE of Colombo city centre 🚌235 🕐7am and 7pm daily (till 10:30pm on *poya* days)

Located to the northeast of Colombo is the Kelaniya Raja Maha Vihara, a venerated Sri Lankan Buddhist shrine considered second only in importance to the Temple of the Tooth (*p140*). Earlier shrines on this spot were destroyed by Indian invaders, and later by the Portuguese colonialists; the present-day structure dates from around the 18th and 19th centuries.

A fairly plain *dagoba* marks the spot where the Buddha is said to have preached during one of his three visits to Sri Lanka, although this is upstaged by the elaborate image house. Made of yellow-orange coloured stone, the eye-catching exterior boasts detailed decoration with ornate door knockers and pillars – look out for the elephants flanking the entrance. The interior is covered with paintings, the most striking of which are the 20th-century murals by Solias Mendis, a renowned artist, depicting the Buddha's visits to Sri Lanka.

The tree-shaded temple grounds are home to a large bo tree, an impressive bell tower, two large statues and a small museum. Raja Maha Vihara is also the focus of the Duruthu Perahera festival in January.

DRINK

Barefoot Café
Colombo's most chilled place for a drink, tucked away in the garden courtyard behind the famous shop (*p79*).

📍E5 📍704 Galle Road, Col 3 🌐barefoot ceylon.com

Paradise Road The Gallery Café
A super-stylish courtyard bar-restaurant set in a building designed by Geoffrey Bawa that once served as the great architect's office.

📍E5 📍2 Alfred House Road, Col 3 🌐paradiseroad.lk

The Verandah
Colonial style meets Indian Ocean views at this beautiful bar. It's the city's ultimate spot for a romantic cocktail or sundowner.

📍A1 📍Galle Face Hotel, 2 Galle Rd, Col 3 🌐gallefacehotel.com

A SHORT WALK
COLOMBO FORT

Distance 3 km (2 miles) **Nearest train station** Secretariat
Time 30 minutes

The original site of Colombo's 16th-century Portuguese fortifications, the area known as Fort is the commercial hub of the city. Although the fortifications, which lent the area its name, have long since disappeared, colonial influences are still apparent in the area's architecture. Today, parts of the area are still off limits due to the presence of the President's House, and security checkpoints and barricades are commonplace. However, navigating Fort's streets is fairly easy, and this walk is a great introduction to the city.

The low-key **Economic History Museum** *occupies the immaculately restored Centre Point Building. Constructed in 1911, the building has one of Fort's most impressive colonial interiors.*

Bang in the centre of Fort, the **Colombo Fort Clock Tower** – *a quaint clock tower-cum-lighthouse – is one of Colombo's most famous colonial landmarks.*

↑ The soaring Colombo Fort Clock Tower, now a roundabout

Colombo's most handsome colonial thoroughfare, **Janadhipathi Mawatha** *is lined with stately buildings.*

The ochre-coloured buildings of the **Old Dutch Hospital** *are now home to a fine selection of restaurants and shops.*

Maritime Museum

WHARF

CHURCH STREET

Sambodhi Chaitya

CHAITYA RD

Gordon Gardens

President's House

BUCK ROAD

GALLE BUCK

FLAGSTAFF STREET

JANADHIPATHI MW

MUDALIGE

CHAITYA ROAD (MARINE DRIVE)

FLAGSTAFF STREET

Old Colombo Clock Tower

CHATHAM

Economic History Museum

JANADHIPATHI MAWATHA

Old Dutch Hospital

BANK OF CEYLON

LOTUS RD

GALLE FACE CENTRE ROAD

0 metres 250
0 yards 250

N ↑

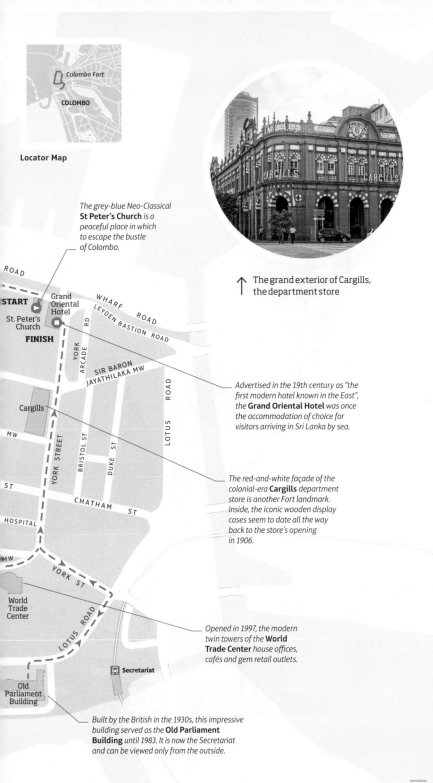

Locator Map

The grey-blue Neo-Classical **St Peter's Church** is a peaceful place in which to escape the bustle of Colombo.

↑ The grand exterior of Cargills, the department store

Advertised in the 19th century as "the first modern hotel known in the East", the **Grand Oriental Hotel** was once the accommodation of choice for visitors arriving in Sri Lanka by sea.

The red-and-white façade of the colonial-era **Cargills** department store is another Fort landmark. Inside, the iconic wooden display cases seem to date all the way back to the store's opening in 1906.

Opened in 1997, the modern twin towers of the **World Trade Center** house offices, cafés and gem retail outlets.

Built by the British in the 1930s, this impressive building served as the **Old Parliament Building** until 1983. It is now the Secretariat and can be viewed only from the outside.

START

FINISH

Colombo Fort

COLOMBO

Grand Oriental Hotel

St. Peter's Church

Cargills

World Trade Center

Old Parliament Building

Secretariat

An *oruwa*, a traditional fishing boat, on the beach at Negombo

THE WEST COAST

For centuries, this region has been Sri Lanka's
window on the world. Arab traders were
visiting (and often settling along) this coast
since time immemorial and brought Islam to the
island sometime in the 7th century. They built the
Kechimalai Mosque – Sri Lanka's first mosque –
at Beruwala, the site where they landed. Later,
European colonialists were drawn to the west
coast, too, because of its strategic position along
major trade routes. Negombo was one of the
first towns to be taken by the Portuguese, who
converted the local Karavas, Tamil and Sinhalese
fishermen to Catholicism. These European missionaries changed the face of the coast forever, leaving
swathes of florid churches in their wake, as well as
innumerable families with Portuguese surnames.
The Dutch, too, made their first settlement
here. After they helped the Kandyans push the
Portuguese out of Sri Lanka, they held Negombo
as payment. The Dutch exploited the settlement's
maritime advantages and plundered the valuable
cinnamon that grew in the surrounding jungle.

Even today, the west coast provides visitors with
their first taste of the country, as Sri Lanka's main
international airport and largest port is located
here. As a result, it is the most developed, most
populous and most cosmopolitan part of the
island, and the coastline from Negombo to
Hikkaduwa is lined with big resort hotels.

Anawilundawa

Deduru Oya

Kobeigane   Paddeniya

Hettipola

Chilaw   1   SRI MUNNESWARAM
Chilaw   TEMPLE
Lagoon

See inset map

Madampe   Kuliyapitiya   Kurunegala
Mahawewa   NORTH
Marawila   WESTERN
                                 Yakvila   Narammala
Waikkal   Pannala
         Dankotuwa   Giriulla
Kochchikade   Meerigama
                  Maha Oya
Duwa   NEGOMBO   4   Warakapola
            Bandaranaike
            International Airport   Aluthapola
Negombo   HENARATHGODA
Lagoon   BOTANICAL GARDEN
Pamunugama   5   Nittambuwa
         Ja-Ela   Gampaha
MUTHURAJAWELA   Ruwanwella
WETLANDS   6
                  Eldeniya   Kirindiwela
Hendala   A7

Colombo   Avissawella
                        Kelani Ganga
COLOMBO   Hanwella
p62
                              KANDY AND
Mount Lavinia   THE HILL
         Ratmalana   COUNTRY
         International   p132
         Airport   Makumbura
Moratuwa   WESTERN
                              Kiriella
                    Ingiriya
Panadura   Horana
Wadduwa
                  Kalu Ganga   Bulathsinhala
Laccadive
Sea
KALUTARA   7
         Katukurunda
         Airport   Baduraliya
                  Matugama
                    BRIEF GARDEN
BERUWALA   9   10
ALUTHGAMA   12
         13   BENTOTA   Pelawaththa
LUNUGANGA   11
INDURUWA AND   16
KOSGODA   Bentota Ganga
                  E1
BALAPITIYA   8   Karandeniya   THE SOUTH
                                        p102
AMBALANGODA   18   Madompe
THE WEST   Lagoon
COAST
                         HIKKADUWA
SEENIGAMA TEMPLE   15   17
                     14   GANGARAMA MAHA
         Coral Sanctuary   VIHARA

0 kilometres   20   SOUTHERN
0 miles   20   N

THE WEST COAST

Experience

① Sri Munneswaram Temple
② Kalpitiya Peninsula
③ Wilpattu National Park
④ Negombo
⑤ Henarathgoda Botanical Garden
⑥ Muthurajawela Wetlands
⑦ Kalutara
⑧ Balapitiya
⑨ Beruwala
⑩ Brief Garden
⑪ Lunuganga
⑫ Aluthgama
⑬ Bentota
⑭ Gangarama Maha Vihara
⑮ Seenigama Temple
⑯ Induruwa and Kosgoda
⑰ Hikkaduwa
⑱ Ambalangoda

EXPERIENCE

1

Sri Munneswaram Temple

🅰C4 📍57 km (35 miles) S of Puttalam ⏱5:30am–8pm daily, evening *puja* at 5pm 🔗munneswaram.com

One of the few temples dedicated to Shiva on the island, Sri Munneswaram is an important place of pilgrimage. The main shrine houses a *lingam* (a phallic symbol representing Shiva) in its inner sanctum. The complex also has a Buddhist shrine and a number of other shrines dedicated to Hindu gods.

The temple was destroyed by the Portuguese on a couple of occasions. It was later rebuilt before undergoing renovation in the 19th century, and then again in the 20th century. Hence, certain sections of the temple look newer than others.

Sri Munneswaram is also the venue for a month-long local festival that takes place in August and September. Pilgrims make offerings and chariots are paraded around the complex and through Chilaw town, about 4 km (2 miles) west of the temple.

2

Kalpitiya Peninsula

🅰B3 📍150 km (93 miles) N of Colombo 🚌

Located in the Puttalam district, between the Puttalam Lagoon and the Indian Ocean, Kalpitiya is no longer the isolated backwater it once was. The windswept peninsula and its outlying islands may be at the forefront of tourist development but the area, fringed with idyllic white-sand beaches, is largely unspoiled for the time being and makes for a superb getaway.

The peninsula has become a prime kitesurfing destination, and also offers dolphin- and whale-watching in season (*p121*) – spinner dolphins are abundant in the waters here. In addition, it is a good place to observe pelagic birds and waders, owing to the range of aquatic habitats that include mangroves and saltpans. Bird-watching enthusiasts should take a boat trip on Puttalam Lagoon. If you head out to the lagoon early in the morning – and are very lucky – you might catch sight of the Indo-Pacific Humpback dolphins, an elusive in-shore species.

Many of the boutique resorts found along the coast facilitate other exciting activities for guests, such as fishing, snorkelling and windsurfing. Among the most popular resorts are those at the alluring Alankuda Beach, on the western side of the peninsula. About 10 km (6 miles) north from Alankuda is the village of Talawila, where the 19th-century St Anne's Church attracts thousands of pilgrims for the annual Feast Day in August.

Some 20 km (12 miles) further north lies the small town of Kalpitiya. The Dutch constructed a fort here at the entrance of a lagoon on the site of an older Portuguese fortification in order to control King Rajasinghe's trade with India. The fort is currently occupied by the navy. Another reminder of the area's colonial past is the rustic St Peter's Kirk, with gravestones dating from the Dutch occupation.

The government's development plans for this beautiful and diverse area have been fraught with controversy. There have been accusations of land grabbing, as well as concerns for the local fishermen. There is also the added risk to the large coral reef

---

LEGENDS OF THE SRI MUNNESWARAM TEMPLE

Sri Munneswaram is thought to be one of the oldest Hindu temples on the island. According to folklore, the temple was established by Lord Rama after he achieved victory over Ravana, as recounted in the Hindu epic *Ramayana*. Following the battle, while returning to India in the *Puspaka* (flying chariot), Rama was suddenly seized by a sense of guilt at the blood spilled in the war. Seeing a temple on the ground below, he descended to pray. Consequently, Shiva and his consort Parvati appeared and ordered him to establish three *lingams*: at Koneswaram in Trincomalee, Thiruketheswaram in Mannar and at Munneswaram.

↑ A palm-fringed beach on the beautiful Kalpitiya Peninsula

💬 INSIDER TIP
Strings Attached

The north coast of the Kalpitiya Peninsula is home to dozens of kitesurfing camps. You can take a class at Ruuk Village (www.ruukvillage.com).

off the coast of Kalpitiya, which is under threat from fishing, pollution and human interference. If the transformation of this area of rich biodiversity into a tourist centre is sensitively managed, it will help to preserve the livelihoods of those who have lived here for generations.

---

❸ 🏷️ 🛍️

Wilpattu National Park

🅰️C3 🚗86 km (53 miles) NE of Alankuda 🚌 🕕6am–6pm daily

At 1,320 sq km (510 sq miles), Wilpattu is the largest national park in Sri Lanka. Once the most popular reserve in the country, the park was badly affected by damage and poaching during the Civil War, but has recaptured much of its old glory. Today it's one of the best wildlife-watching spots on the island, and with far fewer visitors than Yala (p116) and Uda Walawe (p112).

The park's diverse terrain covers a wide range of habitats, including thick jungle, grassy plains, a section of coastline and a series of *villus* (seasonal rainwater lakes), one of the park's unusual and characteristic features.

Leopards are the main draw – there's probably a better chance of catching sight of one in Wilpattu than anywhere else outside Yala – while elusive sloth bears are also sometimes seen. Elephants can often be spotted, along with other common island species, ranging from barking deer and water buffaloes on land through to crocodiles and water monitors lurking in the *villus*.

Birders also have rich pickings, with species including the crested serpent eagle, the brown fish owl and the brown-capped woodpecker.

You can hire a jeep and driver at the entrance to explore the park but your hotel or guesthouse may also be able to arrange this for you.

→ A leopard resting on a treetop in Wilpattu National Park

STAY

Bar Reef Resort
One of Sri Lanka's ultimate eco-retreats, set on a beautiful stretch of beach on the Kalpitiya Peninsula. There's a stunning infinity pool.

🅰️B4 🏠Alankuda Beach, Kalpitiya Peninsula 🌐barreefresort.com

$$$

Dickman Resort
Chic Negombo hideaway, with contemporary Asian styling and a picture-perfect courtyard pool.

🅰️C5 🏠Porutota Road, Negombo 🌐dickmanresort.com

$$$

The Icebear
Full of character, this Swiss-owned guesthouse occupies a prime location right on Negombo beach. Its quaint rooms are set amid lush gardens.

🅰️C5 🏠Lewis Place, Negombo 🌐icebearhotel.com

$$$

Drying fish in rows on the beach at the popular town of Negombo ↑

4

Negombo

🏴C5 🚗36 km (22 miles) N of Colombo 🚌🚐

Just north of Colombo, the sprawling town of Negombo sees plenty of tourists thanks to its location close to the international airport, making it a convenient first (or last) stop on a tour of the island.

One of the first areas to be occupied by the Portuguese, Negombo is the heartland of Sri Lankan Christianity, with colourful wayside shrines dotting the roads and dozens of large churches. One of these places of worship, St Sebastian's, was the scene of the deadliest of the 2019 bomb attacks, with over 100 people killed on Easter Sunday. Easter was always a big celebration here and a Passion play is staged on Duwa, a small island in the Negombo Lagoon, every year.

The town is divided into two halves: the beach and the old town. The beach area is where virtually all visitors stay. It's backed up by one of Sri Lanka's best selections of hotels, restaurants and bars, plus a wide (although not particularly clean) expanse of beach. Around 2 km (1 mile) south of here, the old town has a smattering of old colonial sights, including the modest gateway of the old Dutch Fort of 1672 (now the local prison). Close by, hundreds of colourful boats can be seen moored around the edge of the Negombo Lagoon, while just behind rises the imposing **St Mary's Church**, the town's principal place of worship.

St Mary's Church

🏠 Grand Street 📞 (031) 222 2128 🕐 5:30am-noon & 3-8pm daily

---

5 ⛲

Henarathgoda Botanical Garden

🏴C5 🚗29 km (18 miles) SE of Negombo 📞 (033) 222 2316 🚌 🕐7:30am-5pm daily

These historic gardens were established in 1876 under British rule. It was here that the first rubber tree, imported all the way from Brazil, is reputed to have been planted. Today, the gardens are home to an extensive range of palms, orchids and trees endemic to Sri Lanka.

> 💬 INSIDER TIP
> **In the Driving Seat**
>
> Fancy having a go at driving a tuk-tuk? Negombo has several places where you can hire your own three-wheeled vehicle. Try Alma Tours *(217 Lewis Place; (077) 762 1625).*

Although not as impressive as Peradeniya Botanical Gardens *(p148),* the gardens here are still worth a visit and make for a pleasant wander.

---

6 ⛲ 🚴

Muthurajawela Wetlands

🏴C5 🚗15 km (9 miles) S of Negombo 🚌🚐 🕐7am-6pm daily ℹ️ (011) 483 0150, call in advance to arrange a boat trip

Spread over 60 sq km (23 sq miles), this estuarine wetland, encompassing the Negombo Lagoon, as well as mangroves and marshes, makes for a rewarding half-day excursion from Negombo. The marsh's varied aquatic habitats support a diverse

coastal ecosystem. It is home to Eurasian crocodiles, macaque monkeys and water monitors, as well as one of the world's largest snakes, the Indian python. Many species of butterflies and dragonflies have also been recorded here. Various species of birds, such as kingfishers, egrets, herons, ducks and sandpipers, can also be easily spotted throughout the year. The best time for bird-watchers to visit is between September and April, when migrant birds arrive.

The visitor centre at the entrance to the marsh provides information about the wetlands. Boat trips can be arranged here or booked through hotels – a guided tour is highly recommended. It is best to arrive very early in the morning or later in the afternoon, both to spot more wildlife and to avoid the sun.

Did You Know?

Gangatilaka Vihara is one of the few hollow Buddhist stupas in the world.

7

Kalutara

C6 **42 km (26 miles) S of Colombo**

Lively Kalutara is a large town next to the estuary of the Kalu Ganga river, from which it derives its name. Formerly a spice-trading outpost, today it is a scenic resort town.

South of the bridge across the Kalu Ganga is the **Gangatilaka Vihara**, which was built in the 1960s. The temple complex houses a huge, white and entirely hollow *dagoba*, or stupa. The cavernous interior shelters a smaller *dagoba* surrounded by four golden Buddha statues. The walls of the larger *dagoba* are decorated with murals depicting scenes from the *Jataka* (the body of literature recounting the former incarnations of the Buddha). The windows below offer good views of the Kalu river and the town. On the opposite side of the road is a bo tree and other temple buildings.

Some 3 km (2 miles) to the east along the river you'll see one of the most unusual buildings in the country. **Richmond Castle** dates from 1900, when wealthy spice merchant Don Arthur de Silva Siriwardena decided to build himself a country residence. Based on the plans of a similar "castle" owned by Indian friends of Siriwardena, the graceful Italianate mansion offers an enjoyable glimpse into the lifestyles of colonial Ceylon's rich and powerful. It was built using two boatloads of teak imported from Burma, along with tiles from Italy and bathroom fittings from England. It now serves as an educational centre for deprived local kids.

Gangatilaka Vihara
Daily

Richmond Castle
Palatota-Kethhena Rd
9am–4pm daily

EAT

Lords
Lively restaurant and bar in Negombo, serving up a mainly Asian menu. The vegetarian and vegan options are particularly good.

C5 **80 Porutota Rd, Negombo** **lords restaurant.net**

$$$

Rohan's Place
A great introduction to the island's cuisine, this guesthouse restaurant serves Negombo's best home-cooked rice and curries.

C5 **59A Palangathure West, Negombo** **rohans placenegombo.com**

$$$

↑ Golden Buddha statues surrounding the stupa inside Gangatilaka Vihara

8

Balapitiya

🅰C7 🚗8 km (5 miles)
S of Kosgoda 🚌

The tiny village of Balapitiya is the starting point for boat trips up the Madu Ganga river. These river safaris offer visitors the chance to see a range of birdlife, as well as amphibians and reptiles.

There are 64 islands along this stretch of river, some of which are inhabited. One island is home to a large Buddhist temple adorned with paintings and sculptures. On another, visitors can watch a demonstration of how cinnamon oil is extracted from tree bark by island residents. For many, the highlight of the trip is passing through the dense mangrove forest or "mangrove caves", where you are surrounded on all sides by twisting trunks. Note that the boat rides are priced per boat rather than per person.

Did You Know?

Sri Lanka is the world's largest cinnamon producer, with 70 per cent of the total global output.

9

Beruwala

🅰C6 🚗15 km (9 miles)
S of Kalutara 🚉🚌

The coastal town of Beruwala is popular with those seeking a quick dose of sun and sand. The beach here is broad, and lined with resort hotels and guesthouses. After spending a restful night in your accommodation, make for the lively harbour, where a mind-boggling variety of fish are unloaded from the sizeable vessels. Bargaining begins as early as 7am, so rise early.

Historically, Beruwala is where the first Arab traders landed in Sri Lanka in the 7th century and established a Muslim settlement. To the west of the harbour, the graceful white **Kechimalai Mosque** is believed to mark the site of the landing.

Kechimalai Mosque
🕐 Daily

🏔 GREAT VIEW
To the Lighthouse

Dating from 1889, the graceful Barberyn Lighthouse dominates every vista from Beruwala beach. For the best view, take a boat to Barberyn Island to see the tower up close.

10

Brief Garden

🅰C6 🚗8 km (5 miles)
SE of Aluthgama
📞 (077) 350 9290
🕐 8am–5pm daily

Sprawling across 2 ha (5 acres), the beautiful Brief Garden is the former estate of Bevis Bawa (1909–92), the older brother of Geoffrey Bawa (p81). The estate was bought by Bevis's father in the 1920s and continued to serve as a rubber plantation until Bevis began work on the land around the house in 1929. His painstaking labour gradually transformed it into the idyllic site it is today.

The tranquil landscaped garden, with shady paths and

↑ The elegant Kechimalai Mosque, one of the oldest in Sri Lanka

↑ A water feature at the beautiful Brief Garden, created by Bevis Bawa

stone steps, is a splendid space in which to wander. A hilltop lookout, cement moonstone and the Japanese garden are just some of the many attractions. However, it is the low-slung bungalow that forms the centrepiece of the garden. Bevis Bawa was a writer and artist as well as a sculptor, and the house is filled with his artworks.

Alongside his pieces, you'll find art designed by Bawa's friends. Check out the striking mural at the top of the stairs by Australian artist Donald Friend, who stayed at Brief Garden for almost six years. You'll see photographs of Bawa's other famous house guests, who included actors Lawrence Olivier and Vivien Leigh, and British author Agatha Christie, elsewhere in the house.

After a tour of the estate, enjoy a cup of tea under the shade of the trees.

Lunuganga

🅐C7 🅐6 km (4 miles) SE of Bentota 🅞By guided tour only at 9:30am & 2pm daily 🆆lunuganga.com

The country retreat of Geoffrey Bawa *(p81)*, Lunuganga is one of the west coast's most enchanting sights. Bawa bought the estate in 1947 at the suggestion of his brother, Bevis. At the time, the property was no more than an unremarkable bungalow set amid acres of rubber trees and the architect spent 50 years moulding it into what has been called a "civilized wilderness". It was on this estate that Bawa decided to become an architect and it was here that he honed his skills. There are many buildings around the estate, such as the elegant Hen House and the serene Cinnamon Hill House, which are typical examples of Bawa's brand of architecture.

The gardens here appear so natural that it is easy to overlook the amount of work that went into transforming the land: earth has been moved, shrubs planted and tree branches weighed down to give them a certain shape. The old rubber plantations have given way to a new landscape that often unveils stunning vistas at the most unexpected moment. Look out for the view over Cinnamon Hill, which is topped by a *dagoba* and statuary of the Katakuliya temple.

For the best experience, book to have lunch here after your tour or stay overnight.

→

One of the airy rooms at Lunuganga, the former home of Geoffrey Bawa

STAY

Saman Villas
This shamelessly romantic luxury hotel clings to a small headland overlooking Bentota beach.

🅐C7 🅐Aturwella, Bentota 🆆saman villa.com

$ $ $

Club Villa
This stunning Bawa-designed villa is fringed with serene gardens and has an unbeatable beachfront location in Bentota.

🅐C7 🅐138/15 Galle Road, Bentota 🆆clubvillabentota.com

$ $ $

Lunuganga
Stay overnight at Bawa's former country retreat to soak up the architect's vision.

🅐C7 🅐Dedduwa, Bentota 🆆geoffrey bawa.com

$ $ $

Steps leading up to the Kande Vihara temple, with its white Buddha ↑

12
Aluthgama

C6 9 km (6 miles) S of Beruwala

The small coastal town of Aluthgama, to the north of Bentota Lagoon, has a hoard of photogenic markets. The town's main street is lined with shops; stretching along its west side is the vibrant fish market, where all varieties of seafood is piled on benches. The open-air produce market to the south of the road is also worth a visit. It is particularly busy on Mondays, when it is packed with vendors.

About 1 km (half a mile) inland, the serene **Kande Vihara** temple stands perched on a hilltop. It is home to a colossal white Buddha statue, sitting in the *bhumisparsha mudra* (p187).

Kande Vihara
22 Marikkar St, Dharga Town (034) 227 4453

13
Bentota

C7 9 km (6 miles) S of Aluthgama

Situated on the southern shore of the eponymous Bentota Lagoon, Bentota is Sri Lanka's classiest beach destination. A string of stylish resorts, boutique hotels and idyllic villas line the wide swathe of white sand, which is backed by dense groves of palms. This tranquil setting might explain why Bentota is the Ayurvedic capital of Sri Lanka. The resort's wellness retreats offer guests a whole host of treatments, as well as meditation and yoga.

> ### AYURVEDA
> Sri Lanka's traditional form of medicine, Ayurveda is a holistic concept. Translated as the "science of life", it works on the premise that the body is ruled by three *doshas* (humours): *vata* (air), *pitta* (bile or fire) and *kapha* (phlegm or earth). In medical terms, these refer to the nervous, digestive and immune systems, respectively. Ayurvedic treatments aim to balance the *doshas* and, thus, restore health. Popular treatments include herbal and steam baths, various forms of massage, and the classic *shirodhara*, in which a patient's forehead is doused in a continuous stream of warm oil.

TOP 5 **AYURVEDA RETREATS NEAR BENTOTA**

Amba Ayurveda
704 Welagedara, Balapitiya (077) 286 2200)
A range of packages are available at this solar-powered retreat.

Shunyata Villa
ayurveda-shunyata-villa.com
Practise yoga alongside your treatments here.

Barberyn Reef
barberynresorts.com
Relax while overlooking the ocean.

Maha Gedara
heritancehotels.com
Expect yoga, music and interesting lectures at this resort.

Sign of Life
sign-of-life-resort.com
An affordable and low-key option.

If this all sounds far too sedate, head away from the shore and into Bentota Lagoon – Sri Lanka's premier spot for water sports. Windsurfing is particularly good here, along with jet-skiing, wakeboarding and other adrenaline activities. Wildlife enthusiasts should embark on a river cruise on the lagoon. As you dip in and out of the mangrove thickets that fringe the water, you'll spot some enchantingly colourful aquatic birds, as well as the occasional monitor lizard.

Inland, Bentota village is home to a pair of interesting temples – Kande Viharaya and Galapata Raja. The village is also a major local centre for the production of coir (rope made from coconut fibres). As you walk through the village, look out for the towers of hairy coconut husks piled up alongside its roads.

WATER SPORTS IN BENTOTA

The calm waters of the broad Bentota Lagoon are perfect for a wide range of thrilling activities, making Bentota the de facto water sports capital of Sri Lanka. Come here to enjoy windsurfing, kitesurfing, jet-skiing, water-skiing and banana-boat rides on the river. In addition, angling enthusiasts can spend a rewarding day aboard a fishing boat as a variety of game fish, including marlin, barracuda and tuna, thrive in the waters. Diving and snorkelling are also popular activities along the coast and can be enjoyed from November through to April before the monsoon arrives. Equipment rental, lessons and package deals are all available at hotels, guesthouses and water sports centres in Bentota.

WATER-SKIING
One of the most popular activities on Bentota Lagoon is water-skiing, with both beginners as well as seasoned skiers guaranteed a great time.

BANANA-BOATING
A bouncy ride on the lagoon is bound to elicit screams and shrieks of delight as the inflatable boat is towed at speed, with the driver navigating some sharp turns.

DEEP-SEA FISHING BOATS
Spend around four hours out on the ocean casting for snapper and grouper fish on a deep-sea fishing trip. Anglers can take their catch back for dinner.

WINDSURFING
With strong winds creating ideal conditions, Bentota is a windsurfer's paradise. Beginners are encouraged to practise within the lagoon, whereas the more experienced surfers can take to the ocean.

DIVING
With extensive colonies of beautiful coral and schools of brightly coloured fish, Canoe Rock is one of the most notable dive sites in Bentota, accessible to divers of all levels.

↑ Water-skiing on one ski, on the calm waters of the lagoon

↑ A diver checking out a school of sweepers swimming near coral

Did You Know?

Gangarama Maha Vihara's bo tree is said to be related to the tree that the Buddha sat under.

14
Gangarama Maha Vihara

C7 **500 m (547 yards) E of Hikkaduwa**

This temple is worth visiting for its informative murals depicting the life of the Buddha. There is a bo tree and various shrines in the complex, which is often busy with locals.

15
Seenigama Temple

C7 **2 km (1 mile) N of Hikkaduwa**

The Seenigama Temple, located on a tiny island, is dedicated to Devol Deviyo, a deity invoked

by those seeking to avenge a perceived wrong. The smell of spices pervades the air during *puja*; chillies are crushed as part of the revenge ritual. The temple sustained no damage in the 2004 tsunami, which was considered very auspicious, and symbolic of the power of the deity. Local fishermen also pray at the temple for protection and a successful catch.

16
Induruwa and Kosgoda

C7 **Induruwa: 6 km (4 miles) S of Bentota; Kosgoda: 11 km (7 miles) S of Bentota**

Induruwa and its neighbour, Kosgoda, are Sri Lanka's prime turtle tourism destinations. Several endangered species of turtles nest along the coastlines of these towns. In fact, the stretch of sand near Kosgoda is the most important site for turtle nesting on the west coast and, as you might expect, there are many turtle hatcheries on the coast near the town. These are

frequented by tourists who come to watch the baby turtles being incubated. If you decide to visit the nesting sites, keep your distance and be mindful of disturbing the turtles' natural behaviours at all times.

TOP 3 TURTLE HATCHERIES

Kosgoda Sea Turtle Conservation and Research Center
htrcc.info
This is Sri Lanka's oldest turtle hatchery.

Koggala Sea Turtle Farm and Hatchery
Modarawella Wattha, Koggala (077) 783 6115
A long-running hatchery with a solid ethical reputation.

Mahamodara Sea Turtle Hatchery
417 D/1 Colombo Road, Mahamodara (075) 540 2553
A reputable organization, run by an informative mother-and-daughter team.

The Seenigama Temple, located on an island ↑

↑ Baby turtles, swimming in the Indian Ocean soon after hatching

TURTLE HATCHERIES AND CONSERVATION

Five of the world's seven species of turtles – the green turtle, the leatherback, the olive ridley, the loggerhead and the hawksbill – nest on the beaches of Sri Lanka, especially around the southwest coast. Exercise caution when approaching these nesting sites.

The Turtle Conservation Project (TCP) was set up in 1993 to conserve the dwindling population of turtles in Sri Lanka. Although the TCP no longer has field offices on the island, its mission of devising and pursuing sustainable conservation strategies through education, research and community participation is still embodied by reputable hatcheries. These organizations collect recently laid eggs from nearby rookeries or buy them from egg collectors, re-bury them in protected areas and release the hatchlings into the open sea. Many succumb to predators on their journey back to the water, but some lucky survive. Be aware of hatcheries that keep young turtles in tanks for days after they've hatched, causing them to miss out on valuable swimming time.

THREATS TO TURTLES

Turtle species remain endangered despite many programmes designed to safeguard their declining numbers. Eggs being pilfered from nesting sites for consumption or sale is perhaps the greatest threat to turtle conservation in Sri Lanka, despite heavy fines for poaching. Nesting habitats are also in peril because of coastal development that leads to pollution on beaches and the brightly lit coastline at night, which confuses hatchlings on their way to the sea. In addition, turtles are accidentally caught in fishing nets or hooked on long lines.

↑ A protected nesting site, with labels indicating when the eggs were laid

↑ Hikkaduwa's Narigama beach, and *(inset)* tropical fish at the Coral Sanctuary

⑰

Hikkaduwa

🅐C7 🅰12 km (7 miles) S of Ambalangoda 🚍🚌

This seaside town is a cautionary tale. In the 1970s Hikkaduwa was one of the first places in the island to embrace mass-market tourism, with a rash of resort hotels springing up along the once-pristine beach. The tourists came and then went in search of less developed destinations further south, leaving "Hikka" high and dry.

In the years since 2010, the town has reinvented itself yet again. Some of the resorts have been renovated or demolished and the town has established a reputation as the west coast's party capital among young travellers. It is still a bit of a mess, admittedly, but compensates for this with good surfing, diving, a few batik workshops (where intricately patterned fabrics are produced), and one of the island's best beach-party scenes.

Hikka's major visitor attraction is the Coral Sanctuary at the northern end of the beach, which was declared a national park in 2002 – it's officially called the Hikkaduwa National Marine Park. Unfortunately, the park has been a victim of the elements as well as of its own success. The coral reef was badly affected by bleaching in 1998, and was damaged further by debris from the 2004 tsunami. Over the years, it has also been ravaged by pollution, dynamite fishing, harvesting of the coral for lime and by people walking on the reef. Although most of the coral is now dead, there are certain areas where it is beginning to recover.

Visitors can observe the coral from a glass-bottomed boat; trips are offered everywhere in Hikkaduwa but these are largely unregulated and the boats can damage the coral if they bump against it. A better way to explore the reef is to go snorkelling. It is a delight to spot colourful tropical fish, but watch out for the hordes of boats on the water above.

North of Hikkaduwa, the moving **Tsunami Museum** displays photographs of the disaster and describes subsequent reconstruction efforts.

DIVING IN HIKKADUWA

One of Sri Lanka's most popular dive destinations, Hikkaduwa has a good range of sites. Some, such as those off the Coral Sanctuary, offer swim-through caves and valleys. Tropical fish abound, but the best reason to go underwater here is to admire the red and orange coral. There are also a number of shipwrecks that can be explored, such as *The Earl of Shaftesbury*, a 19th-century sailing ship, and SS *Conch*, an oil tanker that sank in 1903. Today, gleaming fish swim in and out of their portholes. Diving conditions are best from November to May and there are plenty of dive schools to choose from.

> Renowned for its colourful traditional Sri Lankan masks, the town of Ambalangoda makes for an interesting stopover on the road to Hikkaduwa.

There are a number of other tsunami museums in the area, but this is the original one. Look for the red-and-white sign opposite the 94 km post on the road to Galle.

Tsunami Museum
⊗ 🏠 Telwatta junction
📞 (077) 945 4490
🕐 9am–5pm daily

18
Ambalangoda

🅰C7 🏠 24 km (15 miles) S of Bentota 🚌🚆

Renowned for its colourful traditional Sri Lankan masks, the town of Ambalangoda makes for an interesting stopover on the road to Hikkaduwa. Hand-carved and hand-painted, these masks were originally worn by performers in low-country (southern) dances, especially Kolam, an elaborate dance-drama, and Sanni Yakku, a form of devil dance.

The **Ariyapala & Sons Mask Museum**, in the town centre, comprises two well laid-out rooms that display a superb collection of masks focusing on low-country dances. The shop upstairs has masks for sale, and it is possible to see them being made in the workshop next door.

There are many other shops scattered around town that sell the masks, but it is advisable to assess the workmanship before buying one. It is very rare to see the dance performances for which these masks were carved, but the Bandu Wijesooriya School of Dance sometimes stages shows during the tourist season. Contact the Ariyapala & Sons Mask Museum for the schedule.

Ambalangoda isn't all about masks. About 8 km (5 miles) inland from the town, in the village of Karandeniya, the Galagoda Sailatharamaya Temple houses one of the longest reclining Buddha statues in Sri Lanka. The sculpture is all the more striking for its faded orange and red paint, which contrasts starkly with the newer statues elsewhere in the complex. A donation is required to enter the temple complex.

Further south, near Meetiyagoda, there are many moonstone mines. Peer down the mine shafts to see the dirt being sieved, and observe the gemstones being cut and polished outside.

Ariyapala & Sons Mask Museum
🕐 🏠 426 Main St
🕐 8:30am–5:30pm daily 🌐 masks ariyapalasl.com

TOP 3 BATIK WORKSHOPS

Dudley Silva
Sri Lanka's leading batik artist (53 Elpitiya Road, Ambalangoda; (091) 225 9411).

Genuine Batiks (Jungle Workshop)
Only uses natural dyes (Wewala, Hikkaduwa).

Laksiri Batiks
A traditional designer (Baddegama Road, Hikkaduwa; (077) 358 7255).

DRINK

Funky de Bar
This tiny seafront venue is one of Hikka's most popular places for a drink, and possibly a dance, with weekly club nights.

🅰C7 🏠 538/1 Galle Road, Wewala, Hikkaduwa
📞 (077) 752 1003

Mambo's
A local institution, attached to Hikka's leading surf shop, with a suitably chilled vibe and weekend dance nights.

🅰C7 🏠 434/3 Galle Road, Narigama, Hikkaduwa
🌐 mambos.lk

Surf Control Rooftop Lounge
Expect great tunes and tipples – the cocktails are particularly delicious – at this relaxed rooftop lounge in Hikkaduwa. There's also a small food menu if you get peckish.

🅰C7 🏠 450 Galle Road, Wewala, Hikkaduwa
📞 (076) 980 6636

→
A traditional mask at the Ariyapala & Sons Mask Museum

THE SOUTH

Historically, the south has always been left out of power struggles thanks largely to its distance from the great northern capitals of Anuradhapura, Polonnaruwa and – later – Kandy. Spared from the recurrent Indian invasions and Hindu influences, which periodically convulsed the north, southern Sri Lanka developed into a stronghold of traditional Sinhalese Buddhism. The area became part of the ancient kingdom of Ruhunu, with Mahagama (modern-day Tissamaharama) as its capital and principal settlement. Fittingly, it was in Ruhunu that the Sinhalese hero, King Dutugemunu (r 137– 161 BC), was raised and from where he launched his conquest of the island, driving out the Indian invaders who had taken control of the north. This distant piece of semi-mythical history still strikes a chord with Sinhalese nationalists today.

Despite the brief prominence of the ports of Galle and Matara under the Dutch, Ruhunu preserved its separation from the rest of the island. When Colombo eclipsed the importance of these southern ports in the late 19th century, the south became more and more rural. The years since independence have done little to awaken the south from its centuries-long somnolence, despite disastrous attempts by former president Mahinda Rajapaksa to revive the economic fortunes of his native Hambantota. The region did at least escape the Civil War largely unscathed, but the 2004 tsunami devastated much of the coast. Little evidence of this destruction remains and the beaches, national parks and historic towns of the south are now firmly on the tourist trail.

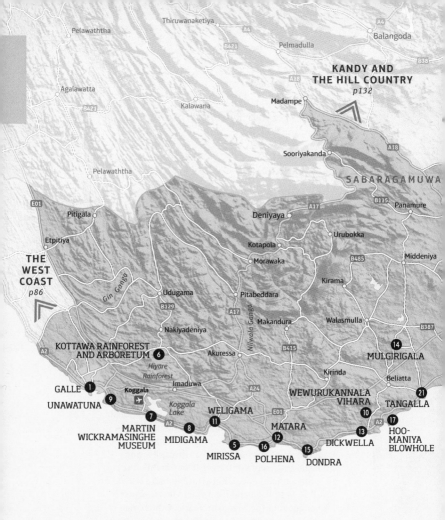

KANDY AND
THE HILL COUNTRY
p132

THE
WEST
COAST
p86

SABARAGAMUWA

Pelawaththa
Thiruwanaketiya
Balangoda
Pelmadulla
Madampe
Agalawatta
Kalawana
Sooriyakanda
Panamure
Pelawaththa
Pitigala
Deniyaya
Urubokka
Middeniya
Etpitiya
Kotapola
Morawaka
Kirama
Udugama
Pitabeddara
Nakiyadeniya
Makandura
Walasmulla
KOTTAWA RAINFOREST
AND ARBORETUM
Akuressa
MULGIRIGALA
Hiyare
Rainforest
Kirinda
Beliatta
GALLE
Imaduwa
WEWURUKANNALA
VIHARA
TANGALLA
Koggala
UNAWATUNA
Koggala
Lake
WELIGAMA
HOO-
MANIYA
BLOWHOLE
MARTIN
WICKRAMASINGHE
MUSEUM
MATARA
DICKWELLA
MIDIGAMA
MIRISSA
POLHENA
DONDRA

THE SOUTH

0 kilometres   20

0 miles   20

N

THE EAST
p190

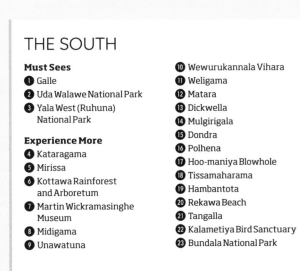

THE SOUTH

↑ A street in Galle's old Dutch quarter, lined with restaurants, at night-time

❶

GALLE

⚑C7 🚗125 km (78 miles) S of Colombo 🚉🚌 ℹ️ 12 Rampart Street; www.galleheritage.gov.lk

The most important town on the south coast, Galle has an old Dutch quarter – enclosed within a fort – and a sprawling New Town located outside the fort's walls. In both quarters, you'll find historic buildings, hip galleries, a buzzing café scene and elegant eateries.

①
Dutch Reformed Church

⚑Church Street ⏰9am-5pm daily

The Dutch Reformed Church was built in the 18th century by Commander Casparus de Jong to commemorate the birth of his daughter. The church has a high, vaulted ceiling and an imposing pulpit, topped by a large, impressive canopy. However, the most striking feature of the church is the ornate tombstones laid into the floor and adorning the walls, which were moved here from Dutch cemeteries, attesting to the high death rate of the early colonists. More tombstones can be seen in the church's grounds.

②
National Maritime Archaeology Museum

⚑Church Street ⏰9am-5pm Tue-Sat 🌐museum.gov.lk

Housed in an old Dutch warehouse, this large museum showcases marine artifacts. The visit begins with a film screening that details the history of various shipwrecks, such as the HMS *Hermes (p199)*, off the east coast of Sri Lanka. Items recovered from some of these sites are on display in the halls, and include maps, earthenware, beer mugs, smoking pipes and artillery guns. Look out for the beardman mug, excavated from the wreckage of the Dutch ship *Avondster*.

③
Galle National Museum

⚑Church Street ⏰9am-5pm Tue-Sat 🌐museum.gov.lk

Located in a 17th-century building next to the Amangalla Hotel, the Galle National Museum exhibits traditional Sri Lankan dance masks, ancient woodcarvings, ornamental objects and items dating to the Portuguese and Dutch periods. Some of the most interesting displays include weapons, furniture and porcelain, belonging to

---

OLD CRICKET GROUND

Officially called the Galle International Stadium, the Galle Cricket Ground is one of the sport's most iconic venues, with its quaint pavilions and spectator stands dramatically set against the backdrop of Galle Fort and the Indian Ocean. It's also one of the Sri Lankan team's luckiest venues, with six wins in the first 11 tests played here.

the Dutch East India Company, and some exhibits relating to crafts such as lace-making. Note, however, that the museum is rather dark and dingy and has not been renovated for many years.

④
Historical Mansion Museum

🏠 31-39 Leyn Baan Street
📞 (091) 223 4114 🕐 9am-6pm Mon-Thu & Sat, 9am-12pm & 2-6pm Fri

This restored Dutch mansion houses a private collection of antiques and bric-a-brac, belonging to Abdul Gaffar, a resident of Galle. Laid out in rooms around a small courtyard, the museum displays a number of interesting objects, such as a cabinet dedicated to vintage telephones and cameras, all of which have been accumulated by the owner during the last few decades. Lace-makers, gem-cutters and jewellery-makers can be seen at work in the building's courtyard and

their wares are for sale, as are many of the displays in the museum. It's the perfect place to pick up a souvenir.

⑤
All Saints Church

🏠 Church St 🕐 8am-5pm daily 🌐 allsaintsgalle.org

Rising above the surrounding buildings at the heart of the Fort is the imposing outline of All Saints Church – a rare British-era monument in a web of streets lined with cookie-cutter Dutch buildings, topped with red-tiled roofs. Designed in 1868 by J G Smithers, the government architect who was also responsible for the far more elegant National Museum in Colombo, the church's squat outline and Gothic Revival-style architecture provides an incongruous contrast with its neighbouring buildings. Inside, the gloomy interior, filled with heavy pews carved from Burmese teak and decorated with the Star of David, is impressively solemn.

Must See

STAY

Amangalla

This exclusive hotel is housed in the stately Dutch Governor's residence, which was built in 1684. The hotel's bar and restaurant are both open to non-residents, offering the chance to enjoy the gorgeously restored period interiors.

🏠 Church Street
🌐 aman.com

$$$

EAT

The Old Railway Café

This cosy café, overlooking the train station, serves up slick bistro fare, as well as cakes and smoothies.

🏠 42 Havelock Place
🌐 theoldrailwayshop.com

$$$

Chambers

If you've overdosed on rice and curry, enjoy something a bit different at this Middle Eastern eatery. Choose from tagines, mezze and kebabs.

🏠 40 Church Street
📞 (091) 224 4320

$$$

Bombay Brasserie

Another break from the culinary norm, with a Mumbai-street-food-inspired menu, offering parathas, pav bhaji and assorted curries.

🏠 14 Leyn Baan Cross Street 📞 (076) 242 8464

$$$

A SHORT WALK
GALLE FORT

Distance 1 km (0.5 miles) **Nearest station** Galle
Time 15 minutes

With excellent examples of colonial architecture and well-preserved fortifications, Galle Fort is an atmospheric place to wander around. Located in the heart of the town, the fort encompasses the old Dutch quarter, and is far removed from the busy town just outside its walls. Galle's harbour had been attracting traders, sailors and explorers to its shores for centuries before the Portuguese built a fort on the promontory here in 1589, but it was during the Dutch occupancy that Galle Fort had its heyday. When the Dutch seized the port in 1640, they extended the fortifications, which survive to this day, and the fort became the hive of Sri Lankan industry.

↑ The stark white exterior of the Dutch Reformed Church

*A Galle Fort landmark, the **Clock Tower** was constructed in 1882, on the spot where a Dutch belfry once stood.*

START

RAMPART STREET

LIGHTHOUSE STREET

MIDDLE STREET

*An attractive Colonial building, the **Dutch Reformed Church** was originally constructed in 1755 on the site of a Portuguese convent. It was restored in 2004.*

Post office

CHURCH STREET

Did You Know?

The fort ramparts withstood the tsunami while the surrounding modern buildings collapsed.

*Dating from the 19th century, **All Saints Church** was specifically built for the British community and remains primarily Anglican.*

PEDLAR STREET

Clan House *once accommodated the offices of English insurance company Lloyd's of London. Check out the ships arrivals board outside.*

FINISH

A striking mask on display in the Galle National Museum

GALLE

Galle Fort

Locator Map

0 metres 100
0 yards 100

N

The **Galle National Museum** has archaeological and anthropological exhibits recovered from Sri Lanka's southern region. Exhibits include traditional masks and woodcarvings.

Originally built for the Dutch governor in 1684, this building was later converted into the New Oriental Hotel. It was one of Galle's most popular hotels and many ocean-liner passengers stayed here in the 19th century. The hotel was renamed **Amangalla** in 2005.

Dutch bell tower

Opened in 2009, the **National Maritime Archaeology Museum** is housed in a former Dutch warehouse, where ships' provisions and valuable cargo such as cinnamon, cloth and cowrie shells were stored.

CHURCH STREET

QUEENS STREET

Dutch Government House

LEYN BAAN STREET

A private collection of antiques and miscellaneous objects belonging to Abdul Gaffar, a local gem merchant, is on display in the **Historical Mansion Museum**.

The veranda of the Historical Mansion Museum, furnished with period objects

A SHORT WALK
FORT RAMPARTS

Distance 3 km (2 miles) **Walking time** 45 minutes
Difficulty Easy **Nearest station** Galle

While constructing Galle Fort, the Portuguese concentrated on bolstering its landward side. When the Dutch expanded the fortifications they corralled the headland as well. The western ramparts, which are the most accessible, give the best idea of what the original Dutch fortifications would have looked like. The overall defences run for 3 km (2 miles) and the outer and inner walls are more than 1 m (3 ft) thick. The best way to appreciate these defences is to walk along the ramparts. Visitors may follow the suggested route or amend it, making forays into the fort and then clambering back up to the ramparts. Go in the morning or during the evening to avoid the harsh midday sun. Triton Bastion is a lovely spot in which to hang out at dusk.

*The **Main Gate** is part of the newer additions to the Fort, made by the British in the 19th century.*

START
Main Gate

ESPLANADE ROAD

LIGHTHOUSE STREET

MIDDLE STREET

RAMPART STREET

*The **Shri Sudharmalaya Temple** complex houses a stark white dagoba dating from 1886. A bo tree can be seen on the opposite side of the road.*

FINISH
Shri Sudharmalaya Temple

PARRAWA ST

CHADO STREET

PARRAWA STREET

PEDLAR

The Triton Bastion

↑ The striking white lighthouse crowning Point Utrecht Bastion

*Cricket games are often underway around **Triton Bastion**. It's a great spot to watch the sunset and comes to life at dusk.*

0 metres   200
0 yards   200

N ↑

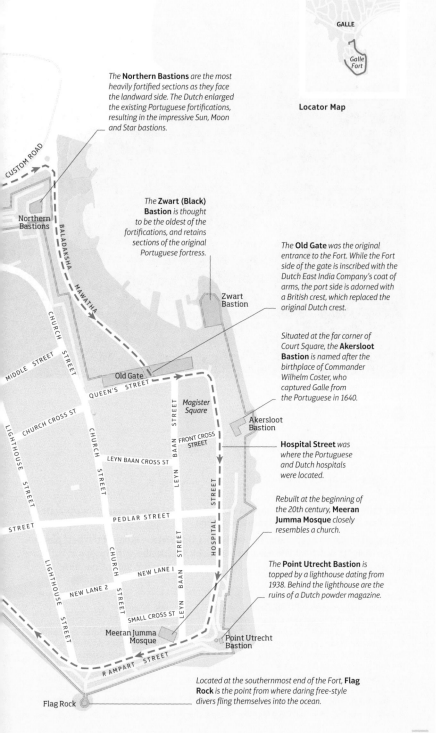

GALLE

Galle
Fort

Locator Map

The **Northern Bastions** are the most heavily fortified sections as they face the landward side. The Dutch enlarged the existing Portuguese fortifications, resulting in the impressive Sun, Moon and Star bastions.

CUSTOM ROAD

Northern Bastions

BALADAKSHA MAWATHA

The **Zwart (Black) Bastion** is thought to be the oldest of the fortifications, and retains sections of the original Portuguese fortress.

The **Old Gate** was the original entrance to the Fort. While the Fort side of the gate is inscribed with the Dutch East India Company's coat of arms, the port side is adorned with a British crest, which replaced the original Dutch crest.

Zwart Bastion

CHURCH STREET

MIDDLE STREET

CHURCH CROSS ST

Old Gate

QUEEN'S STREET

CHURCH STREET

LEYN BAAN STREET

Magister Square

Situated at the far corner of Court Square, the **Akersloot Bastion** is named after the birthplace of Commander Wilhelm Coster, who captured Galle from the Portuguese in 1640.

Akersloot Bastion

FRONT CROSS STREET

LEYN BAAN CROSS ST

LIGHTHOUSE STREET

STREET

LEYN BAAN STREET

HOSPITAL STREET

Hospital Street was where the Portuguese and Dutch hospitals were located.

Rebuilt at the beginning of the 20th century, **Meeran Jumma Mosque** closely resembles a church.

PEDLAR STREET

CHURCH STREET

The **Point Utrecht Bastion** is topped by a lighthouse dating from 1938. Behind the lighthouse are the ruins of a Dutch powder magazine.

NEW LANE 1

NEW LANE 2

LEYN BAAN STREET

LIGHTHOUSE STREET

SMALL CROSS ST

Meeran Jumma Mosque

Point Utrecht Bastion

RAMPART STREET

Flag Rock

Located at the southernmost end of the Fort, **Flag Rock** is the point from where daring free-style divers fling themselves into the ocean.

2

UDA WALAWE NATIONAL PARK

🗺 E6 🏠 80 km (50 miles) NE of Tangalla 📞 (047) 347 5892 🕐 By arranged tour/private car only, 6am–6pm daily (last tickets are sold at 5pm)

One of Sri Lanka's most popular national parks, Uda Walawe is one of the best places on the island to watch wildlife. Elegant aquatic birds glide above the reservoir, buffaloes wallow in the water and herds of graceful elephants roam this natural paradise.

Spread over an expanse of 300 sq km (116 sq miles), Uda Walawe was created in 1972 to protect the catchment area around the area's enormous reservoir. The landscape of scrub jungle, grasslands and an abandoned teak plantation harbours a variety of wildlife, ranging from sambar deer to the rarely sighted sloth bear, but the park is best known for its large resident population of elephants. Home to about 600 of these pachyderms, Uda Walawe is a great place to observe elephants in their natural habitat. The park also supports a thriving population of water birds and birds of prey.

💬 INSIDER TIP
Park Life

Hire a 4WD from outside the park gate to explore Uda Walawe. The best time to sight elephant herds is early in the morning or in the late afternoon, while November to April is the recommended season for bird-watching enthusiasts.

ELEPHANT TRANSIT HOME

Supported by the Born Free Foundation, the Elephant Transit Home lies about 5 km (3 miles) west of the park entrance. Orphaned elephants are raised at the home until they are about 4 or 5 years old, when they are released back into the wild. Visitors here are kept at a distance from the elephants. There is a viewing platform, from where you can watch young elephants being fed. Feeding times are scheduled daily at 9am, noon, 3pm and 6pm. Be sure to arrive early.

←

A herd of elephants grazing on grass in Uda Walawe National Park

1 The Elephant Transit Home takes care of around 40 orphans at any one time.

2 The Uda Walawe Reservoir was built in the 1960s to irrigate nearby agricultural areas and to power a hydroelectric plant.

3 A vehicle is required to enter and explore the park.

ELEPHANTS IN SRI LANKA

The elephant is an integral part of the history, culture and religions of Sri Lanka. Of enormous spiritual significance to the island's Buddhist and Hindu populations, elephants are commonly depicted in temple architecture and you should be aware that most Buddhist temples keep a resident elephant within their premises. Despite the presence of these captive elephants and other instances of human-elephant conflict, including deforestation and exploitative tourist attractions, there are still plenty of places where you can see elephants in the wild. Uda Walawe, Yala West and Minneriya national parks are some of the best places in Sri Lanka to see these pachyderms.

THE SRI LANKAN ELEPHANT

Distinct from the African elephant, the Asian elephant has smaller ears, a flat back and a one-fingered trunk. Additionally, only a small percentage of male elephants have tusks compared with their African counterparts. Wild elephants usually live in a close-knit group of around 15, and eat about 150 kg (331 lb) of food every day.

ELEPHANTS THROUGH TIME

During the reign of the Sinhalese kings, no elephant could be killed without the ruler's permission. However, when the British came to power, this protection was withdrawn. The British saw them as pests and paid a bounty for each elephant killed, leading to their mass slaughter.

↑ A moonstone ornamented with elephants in the ancient city of Polonnaruwa

The ears are capable of detecting sounds as low as 14 hertz. This enables elephants to communicate with each other over long distances.

Female elephants are usually smaller and lighter than the males.

SACRED ELEPHANTS

Buddhists and Hindus associate elephants with strength and courage. It is also widely believed that keeping an elephant in the temple brings good luck and prosperity. Often richly decorated, these majestic elephants are the prominent feature of annual religious processions in the country, including the Esala Perahera. The Maligawa Tusker - the elephant that carries the sacred Tooth Relic during this festival - is the most revered pachyderm in the country. In 2019, however, the world was shocked by images of an emaciated elephant that took part in this festival. Be wary of all instances of animal exploitation.

WORKING ELEPHANTS

During the time of the Sinhalese kings, elephants were used for transportation and for construction work. In the colonial era, they were trained to move heavy artillery and clear land for tea plantations. Today, they continue to work in the timber industry and, more commonly, in the tourism sector. Avoid all attractions offering rides, which damage the animals' backs, and anywhere that allows visitors to interact with the elephants, including feeding and washing. It's always best to see elephants in national parks.

HUMAN-ELEPHANT CONFLICT

A growing population, agricultural expansion and infrastructure development have led to the elephant's loss of habitat and disruption of movement. Nearly 150 elephants are killed every year when they stray in search of food into areas inhabited by humans. With their enormous bodies and huge appetites, they end up destroying property, trampling crops and occasionally taking lives. Preventive measures that have been taken include the development of national parks and elephant corridors, relocation of frequent offenders and erection of electric fences. However, the problem still persists.

The skin colour of the Sri Lankan elephant is the darkest of all subspecies of the Asian elephant. Areas of depigmentation can be seen particularly on the ears, trunk and belly.

The trunk is not just used to drink, but also to grasp things using the finger-like extension at its tip.

↑ "The Gathering" of elephants at Minneriya and Kaudulla National Parks

3 ⊗ ⊕

YALA WEST (RUHUNA) NATIONAL PARK

🅰E7 📍20 km (12 miles) NE of Tissamaharama 🕐6am–6pm daily
🗓Sep–Oct (call ahead to check) ℹBy the park entrance; (047) 348 9297

Situated in the southeastern part of Sri Lanka, the expansive Yala National Park is divided into five blocks. Covering an area of 141 sq km (54 sq miles), Block I or Yala West (Ruhuna) is the most visited part of the park, largely due to its accessibility and leopard population.

Punctuated by rocky outcrops, the park's sprawling landscape varies from thorny scrub forests and open grasslands to dense jungles and coastal lagoons. The park features a great variety of fauna, including elephants, spotted deer, crocodiles and, of course, leopards. Home to around 35 leopards, Yala West is said to be one of the best places in the world to observe and photograph these felines. The birdlife here is also very diverse, with migrants swelling the numbers of the resident population in winter. On top of this, Yala is home to a number of cultural sights, such as Situlpahuwa *dagoba* and the ruins of Magul Maha Vihara.

Exploring the Park

A 4WD vehicle is required to enter and explore the park, since walking is not permitted here. Jeeps can be easily arranged through one of the many tour operators and guesthouses in Tissa *(p128)*. All vehicles are assigned a tracker, who accompanies visitors into the park. While it's possible to explore the place on a full- or half-day safari, most people choose the latter as a whole day can be exhausting. The ideal time to visit the park is either early in the morning or late afternoon. Visitors are advised to avoid making noise as it can frighten the animals and lower the chances of a sighting. The best time to spot leopards is during the dry season, from May to September.

↑ 4WDs watching a leopard crossing a dirt road in Yala West National Park

STAY

Cinnamon Wild Yala
An attractive safari resort, located very close to the park. Elephants can often be seen from the hotel's observation deck.

📍Palatupana
🌐cinnamonhotels.com

⑤⑤⑤

—

Leopard Trails
One of several upmarket tented safari camps around the edge of the park. Leopard Trails offers a luxurious, wilderness experience.

📍Wilpattu Sanctuary Road, Pahala Maragahawewa
🌐leopardtrails.com

⑤⑤⑤

—

Chaaya Wild
Choose from the "beach" or "jungle" bungalows at Chaaya Wild. Relax on the observation deck.

📍Kirinda Palatupana
🌐chaayawild.com

⑤⑤⑤

Lush grassland in Yala West
National Park, overlooked
by Elephant Rock ↑

The colourful entrance to Maha Devale, decorated with peacocks

EXPERIENCE MORE

4

Kataragama

🅰E6 🚗19 km (12 miles) NE of Tissamaharama 🚌

Sacred to Buddhists, Hindus and Muslims alike, Kataragama is one of the most revered places of pilgrimage in Sri Lanka. Named after the god, the town is at its busiest during the Kataragama Festival.

The sacred precinct is to the north of Kataragama and is separated from the town by the Menik Ganga river. Upon entering the precinct, visitors pass a series of shrines before reaching the **Maha Devale** – the main complex. Inside are three shrines, one of which is dedicated to the god Kataragama, represented by his symbol, a *vel* (spear).

Look out for the images of the peacock that served as Kataragama's *vahana* (vehicle) on the wall surrounding the main courtyard.

The precinct comes alive during the evening *puja*, with queues of supplicants bearing fruit platters and other offerings. Pilgrims also smash coconuts against stones in front of the shrine – it is considered unlucky if the coconut fails to break. The ringing of temple bells, the sound of roving musicians and the mass of people make for a frenetic experience.

Next to the Maha Devale is the **Kataragama Museum**, which houses religious objects and copies of the rock carvings at Buduruwagala *(p155)*. An avenue behind Maha Devale leads to the **Kiri Vihara**, a *dagoba* dating from the 1st century BC. It is believed that the Buddha came here during his third visit to Sri Lanka and that the *dagoba* enshrines his hair relic.

KATARAGAMA – THE GOD

Of Sri Lanka's gods and goddesses, Kataragama is the most confusing. For the Sinhalese, Kataragama is one of the four divine protectors of the island and the Buddhist faith. Sri Lanka's Hindu Tamils, meanwhile, regard him as a form of Skanda, the son of Shiva. As such, Kataragama is the perfect example of the classic Sri Lankan fusing of Buddhist and Hindu beliefs. Additionally, local Muslims and Christians can also be found worshipping at his shrine.

Maha Devale
🏠Dewala Road 📞(047) 223 5122 🕐For *pujas* at 4:30am, 10:30am & 6:30pm Mon-Fri, 10:30am & 6:30pm Sat & Sun

Kataragama Museum
♿ 🏠Peeta Veediya
🕐8:30am-4:30pm daily

Kiri Vihara
🏠Kiri Vihera Mawatha
🕐4:30am-11pm Mon-Fri, 4:30am-midnight Sat & Sun

KATARAGAMA FESTIVAL

The famous Kataragama Festival takes place at the time of the Esala full moon in July or August. During the festival, thousands of Hindus and Buddhists descend on the town to express devotion to the deity, to ask for forgiveness for their sins, to make vows and to request favours. The festival is best known for the various forms of physical mortification and self-mutilation that pilgrims undertake as a form of penance.

MORTIFICATION AND MUTILATION

You'll see many expressions of piety during the festival. Coconuts topped with burning camphor are broken inside the temple to symbolize humility. Some devotees roll on burning hot sand near the temple to ask for forgiveness for their sins. Others go to greater lengths and pierce their skin with hooks and other sharp objects. Another unnerving spectacle is when a devotee is pierced with hooks and is then strung up on a pole, hanging face down.

THE END OF THE FESTIVAL

A couple of days before the end of the festival there is a fire-walking ceremony where worshippers, thought to be in a self-induced trance, walk barefoot across burning embers while chanting. Surprisingly, most emerge unscathed. Then, on the last night of the *perahera*, the sacred relic, or *yantra*, is taken from the Maha Devale atop an elephant and left overnight at the *kovil* dedicated to Valli. The water-cutting ceremony at the Menik Ganga river marks the end of the festival. Once the priest has "cut" the water, pilgrims rush to the spot to absolve their sins by bathing.

↑ A devotee rolling on hot sand, just one of the physical mortifications practised during the festival

↑ The water-cutting ceremony, and *(inset)* a burning coconut, symbolizing humility

⑤
Mirissa

🗺 D7 **📍 7 km (4 miles) SE of Weligama** 🚌

The village of Mirissa is one of the most popular tourist destinations in the south – and with good reason. The beach is one of the prettiest along the coast, with a fine stretch of sand ringing an intimate cove backed by dense palm trees. It's particularly pretty at night, when innumerable restaurant tables are set out on the candlelit sands. Big resort hotels are notably absent, adding to the low-key charm.

Many visitors also come to Mirissa thanks to the village's status as the whale-watching

> **The beach is one of the prettiest along the coast, with a fine stretch of sand ringing an intimate cove backed by dense palm trees.**

"capital" of Sri Lanka. Dozens of trips depart daily in season (Dec–April). Boats leave early in the morning and spend around four hours out at sea, although unfortunately the sheer number of visitors often results in overcrowding, with boats jostling noisily for position whenever a whale is sighted. In addition, beware of the cut-price trips offered by beach touts, which often use overcrowded, and possibly even unsafe, boats.

There's also some decent snorkelling and surfing, and local operators offer enjoyable sunrise and sunset cruises. Make for Giragala or Parrot Rock (at the beach's eastern end) for great views of the sun dipping down into the ocean. Further views can be had by heading out to the Buddhist Kandavahari temple, to the south of the beach and accessible via steps from the main road, which offers sweeping ocean vistas.

↓ The idyllic, palm-fringed sandy beach at unspoiled Mirissa

EAT

O Mirissa Café & Bistro
Mirissa's best Italian serves up super-fresh seafood and wood-fired pizza.

🗺 D7 **📍 271 Udupilla Junction, Mirissa** **📞 (077) 444 1452**

💲💲💲

Shady Lane Mirissa
Health-food café serving plenty of vegetarian and vegan dishes, as well as Mirissa's best breakfast.

🗺 D7 **📍 Diyagalana Road, Mirissa** **📞 (077) 082 5420**

💲💲💲

No. 1 Dewmini Roti Shop
A Mirissa institution, with *rotis* in every imaginable flavour.

🗺 D7 **📍 Udupilla Road, Mirissa** **📞 (071) 516 2604**

💲💲💲

↑ Colourful boats in Mirissa's harbour, the starting point for whale-watching trips

WHALE- AND DOLPHIN- WATCHING IN SRI LANKA

Since the end of the Civil War, whale- and dolphin-watching has really taken off in Sri Lanka. The country sits alongside one of the world's great cetacean migratory routes, and sightings are guaranteed for large parts of the year. Mirissa and Dondra Head on the south coast are perfectly placed for some excellent whale-watching, with the former being the hub for expeditions and accommodation. While the migratory season lasts from December to April, the first and the last months are the best time to spot blue and sperm whales, as well as dolphins.

WHALES

Blue whales can be seen off the Mirissa and Trincomalee *(p194)* coasts. A member of the baleen family of whales, they are thought to be the largest mammals ever to have lived and can reach up to 30 m (98 ft) in length. They pass Mirissa between December and April and can be seen off Trincomalee from February through to August as they continue their migration around the island from the south coast. As a result, Sri Lanka offers around 10 months of blue-whale-watching every year at different places along the coast. Also watch out for sperm whales, particularly around Kalpitiya *(p90)*, where they're spotted between November and March.

↑ The unmistakable sight of a blue whale's tail

DOLPHINS

Striped, spotted and bottlenose dolphins can all be seen in the waters off the island, while Risso's dolphins are less frequently spotted. They are a great tourist attraction but are increasingly being threatened by poaching. Despite this, spinner dolphins are regularly seen during whale-watching trips. One of the most commonly sighted marine mammals in Sri Lanka, these creatures enthral their audience by leaping in the air and spinning a number of times before diving back into the ocean.

↑ A small pod of striped dolphins jumping through the waves

STILT FISHERMEN

Stilt fishermen are synonymous with Sri Lanka. It's quite a recent practice however, only dating from the Second World War, when food was scarce. The stilts are carved with notches to help the fishermen climb up to their crossbar, where they carefully balance themselves as they fish. The best place to catch sight of them is the coastline between Midigama and Koggala, particularly around Ahangama. They can usually be seen during the early morning hours or at dusk. Note that those out on the poles later in the day are primarily there for the tourists, and will charge a small fee for photographs.

6

Kottawa Rainforest and Arboretum

🅰 C7 🕐 17 km (11 miles) NE of Galle 🕐 7am–5pm daily

Situated not far from Galle (p106), the Kottawa Rainforest and Arboretum makes for an interesting day excursion. This isolated area, with a 1-km- (0.5-mile-) long walking trail, offers an easily accessible introduction to the Sri Lankan rainforest. The trail is shaded by towering dipterocarps (a family of rainforest trees). Meander around the under-growth while admiring the epiphytes (parasitic plants) and keeping an eye open for reptiles, giant squirrels and purple-faced leaf monkeys. Leeches are rife here, especially in the wet season, so appropriate walking gear is a must.

If you can't make it to Sinharaja (p156), the next best option is a visit to the

> The reserve is home to an array of endemic flora and fauna, including rare lizards and 16 endemic birds (although they can be tricky to spot amid the dense vegetation).

Kanneliya Forest Reserve to the northeast of Kottawa, which has a similarly rich ecosystem. The reserve is part of Kanneliya-Dediyagala-Nakiyadeniya (KDN) forest reserve, the second-largest area of primary rainforest on the island, and also a major catchment area for the Gin and Nilwala gangas, two of the south's biggest rivers. The reserve is home to an array of endemic flora and fauna, including rare lizards and 16 endemic birds (although they can be tricky to spot amid the dense vegetation). There are also a couple of pretty little water-falls and a large natural pool in which to take a dip. Note that visits take place with a compulsory guide.

Kanneliya Forest Reserve

🈺 🅰 Udugama-Hiniduma Road, Koralegama 🕐 8am–5pm daily

7

Martin Wickramasinghe Museum

🅰 D7 🕐 12 km (7 miles) E of Unawatuna 🚌 🕐 9am–5pm daily 🌐 martinwickramasinghe.info

The Martin Wickramasinghe Museum lies in the small town

36

The number of different snake species in the Kanneliya Forest Reserve.

of Koggala. The museum does not see many tourists, but those who do go are rewarded with a glimpse of what life was like on the island in the early 20th century. The museum is inspired by, and devoted to, Martin Wickramasinghe (1890–1976), a renowned Sri Lankan writer who, although fluent in English, chose to write in Sinhalese. During his career, he penned a number of novels as well as non-fiction works, such as Gamperaliya (The Transformation of a Village, 1944), Madol Doova (Mangrove Island, 1947), Yuganthaya (The End of an Era, 1949) and Kaliyugaya (Age of Darkness, 1957).

Spread around a huge garden, the museum complex comprises two sections: the Folk Museum and the writer's

→

The sheltered semicircular bay at Unawatuna

house. The Folk Museum displays a range of exhibits from traditional village life. There are tools, cooking utensils, traditional games, a superb collection of masks and puppets, and a re-created village kitchen. Behind the museum is a display of traditional modes of transport, including carts.

The house where Martin Wickramasinghe was born and spent his early life can be found towards the rear of the garden. Wandering through its rooms, visitors can see furniture such as the writer's desk, as well as photographs, awards and books charting his life and career.

---

8 Midigama

C D7 **C** 18 km (11 miles) SE of Unawatuna 🚇🚌

Far quieter than Hikkaduwa (p100), the small village of Midigama is a surfer's paradise. It offers some of the most consistent conditions in Sri Lanka for surfers of intermediate and advanced levels. Popular spots include Lazy Left, a left break that is easily accessed from the beach, and Ram's Right, over a shallow reef in front of the famous Ram's Surfing Beach guesthouse.

9 Unawatuna

C C7 **C** 5 km (3 miles) SE of Galle 🚇🚌

The village of Unawatuna is one of Sri Lanka's most popular resorts. It has a fine stretch of beach set in an attractive bay protected by a headland that offers year-round swimming. Numerous guesthouses dot the village, and restaurants, shops and tour operators can be found on almost every corner.

Despite the construction of a high-rise hotel and increasing commercialization, Unawatuna has retained its laid-back charm. The water here is calm for most of the year and there are a number of water sports on offer, including snorkelling, jet-skiing and wreck-diving. Back on dry land, there are cookery lessons and yoga classes. Unawatuna also offers a vibrant nightlife, particularly during the high season.

At the western end of the beach is a *dagoba*, from where there are some good views over the surrounding area. Another attraction is Rumassala, a rocky outcrop behind the village. Legend states that it is a fragment of the Himalayas dropped by the Hindu monkey god Hanuman. Higher up the Rumassala

hillside is the modern, white Japanese Peace Pagoda, from where visitors can enjoy great views over the Galle Fort. The hill is also known for the number of rare plants and medicinal herbs that grow on it.

On the other side of the hill is Jungle Beach, a good spot for snorkelling. Hire a three-wheeler to reach the beach.

10

Wewurukannala Vihara

D7 ⚑3 km (2 miles)
N of Dickwella ⏰6am–
midnight daily

The Wewurukannala Vihara temple is best known for its gargantuan 50-m- (164-ft-) high seated Buddha, which was constructed in the late 1960s and gazes serenely onto the road. A seven-storey building behind the statue allows visitors to climb up, past cartoon-strip-style depictions of scenes from the Buddha's life, to the statue's head, from where there are good views of the temple complex.

Nearby, the temple's main image house, dating from the late 19th century, contains numerous statues, while next door a gruesome "chamber of horrors" is filled with life-size models portraying various tortures inflicted in Buddhist hell. Look out for the figures being immersed in boiling cauldrons and disembowelled.

11

Weligama

D7 ⚑9 km (6 miles) N
of Midigama 🚌

Persistently overlooked in favour of nearby Mirissa *(p120)* and Unawatuna *(p123)*, Weligama is one of the south's most appealing, and under-rated, destinations. The beach here is among the finest on the coast, with its sweeping arc of largely deserted sand stretching around the sparkling waters of Weligama bay. An immensely photogenic selection of pastel-painted fishing boats bob up and down in the bay. The town is a popular spot with surfers, especially beginners, as the waves here are fairly reliable.

Out in the bay it's hard to miss minuscule Taprobane Island, which is covered in a dense canopy of trees and home to an elegant mansion built by the self-styled French "Count" de Mauny-Talvande in the 1930s. The count later sold it to American novelist

Did You Know?

The Wewurukannala Buddha is the largest on Sri Lanka.

Paul Bowles. The island is now owned by the Sun House in Galle, from whom the property can be rented. Recent visitors have included Kylie Minogue, who wrote a song about it.

On the western edge of town, just north of the railway line, stands the striking Kustha Raja Gala ("Rock of the Leper King"). Dating from between the 6th and 9th centuries AD, the 3-m- (10-ft-) high statue is said to commemorate an anonymous Sinhalese monarch who was miraculously cured of leprosy after eating an exclusive diet of coconut milk for three months. An alternative, more prosaic, theory suggests that the statue carved into the rock represents the *bodhisattva* Avalokitesvara, who embodies divine compassion.

12

Matara

D7 ⚑45 km (28 miles)
SE of Galle 🚉🚌

The second-largest town on Sri Lanka's south coast, Matara is a major regional transport and economic hub, as well as being home to the south's leading university. Despite this eminence, Matara sees relatively few visitors and its hectic streets can come as quite a shock after experi-encing the quiet beaches that surround it.

← A golden Buddha in the image house of Wewurukannala Vihara

One of several quiet and attractive beaches at Dickwella ↑

The Nilwala Ganga divides Matara into two parts, namely the Old Dutch Town and the New Town. The Old Town lies to the south of the river and is home to a fort built by the Dutch in the 18th century. Its eastern side is bound by ramparts that encompass a gateway dated 1780, and there is also a British clock tower, which was added later. The streets behind the ramparts hide dilapidated yet imposing colonial buildings. Head for the Dutch Reformed Church, which is one of the oldest colonial churches in Sri Lanka. Read the names on the tombstones paving the floor.

North of the river, the New Town boasts the hexagonal Star Fort. It was built by the Dutch in 1763, and is believed to have been erected to defend the main fort area after a Sinhalese rebellion in 1760. The structure has now been restored and houses a small museum. Stroll over the working drawbridge and walk around the ramparts for views over the modern town.

On the northeastern edge of the town, the village of Weherahena is home to another super-sized brightly painted Buddha, similar to that at Wewurukannala.

⓭
Dickwella

🅐D7 🅐15 km (9 miles) NE of Dondra ⬛

Located between Matara and Tangalla, the town of Dickwella straddles the coast, fringed by a series of attractive and pleasantly quiet beaches. Dickwella is also one of the island's major lace-making centres (a trade introduced by the Dutch). Dickella Lace cooperative – on the road towards Dondra – sells locally made cloth. Take some time to watch the local artisans busily stitching here before buying some delicate lace to take home.

Some 2 km (1 mile) east of Dickwella, Hiriketiya has emerged as Sri Lanka's newest off-the-beaten-track destination, with a few guesthouses clustered behind an idyllic palm-fringed cove beach with golden sand. Nothing disturbs the peace and quiet bar the sound of crashing waves.

 HIDDEN GEM
Secret Surfing

On the eastern edge of Matara, the suburb of Medawatta is a favourite haunt with in-the-know surfers. Come here to ride the impressive waves at the aptly named Secret Point.

STAY

Dots Bay House
The surf and social hub of Dickwella's Hiriketiya Beach is located right on the sand. Take your pick from its quaint little cottages and cabanas.

🅐D7 🅐Hiriketiya Beach, Dickwella
☎(077) 793 5593

💲💲💲

The Green Rooms
Set on the beach in Weligama, this ecolodge offers its guests surf and yoga lessons.

🅐D7 🅐New Bypass Road, Weligama
🆆thegreenrooms srilanka.com

💲💲💲

Taprobane Island
Sri Lanka's only privately owned island has five elegant bedrooms. The property is easily reached from Weligama.

🅐D7 🅐Weligama
🆆taprobaneisland.com

💲💲💲

↑ Visitors descending the stairs from Raja Vihara, one of the cave temples of Mulgirigala

14 ⊕ ⊛

Mulgirigala

△D7 **◯22 km (14 miles) northeast of Dickwella** **▤ ◯6am–6pm daily**

The magical cave temples of Mulgirigala are one of the south's most interesting religious sites. Carved out of a huge rock outcrop, the temples are arranged over four levels and connected by steep steps. It's worth the climb for the fine views from the top.

The temples originally date back to the 2nd century BC,

but were comprehensively remodelled by the kings of Kandy, who commissioned the interesting murals which can be found in several of the chambers. You might notice similarities with the paintings at the Dambulla Cave Temples (p180), which were created at the same time.

The third terrace is the most interesting. It's home to no fewer than four shrines, including the Naga (Cobra) Temple, named for the fearsome snake which is said to have once lived here. Also on this level is the Raja Vihara temple, where scholar George Turnour, and his teacher, discovered a bundle of ola-leaf manuscripts which proved to be the key to his translation of the Mahavamsa, a historical poem detailing the story of Sri Lanka.

Beyond this temple, sharp stairs continue to the summit, where a small, final terrace provides one of the south coast's most memorable views. As you look south, over a sea of palms, you'll catch a glimpse of the glinting Indian Ocean, while the craggy peaks of the Hill Country punctuate the vistas to the north.

15

Dondra

△D7 **◯9 km (6 miles) SE of Matara** **▤ ▦**

At the southern tip of the island is the small town of Dondra, also known as Devi Nuwara (City of the Gods). Formerly an important religious centre, the town was once home to a revered temple dedicated to Vishnu before it was destroyed by the Portuguese in 1588. All that remains of the original structure is a small shrine, known as the Galge, which is believed to date back to the 7th century, making it the oldest surviving stone building in Sri Lanka.

Today, the flamboyant **Devi Nuwara Devale** temple is modern Dondra's principal place of worship. Located next to the main road, this bright-blue building is hard to miss, especially as a huge statue of the Buddha stands outside the colourfully painted image house. A major festival – the Devi Nuwara Perahera – is celebrated here in early July or late August.

TRANSLATION OF THE MAHAVAMSA

The Mahavamsa (Great Chronicle), written in the Pali language, was long considered to be untranslatable. In 1836, however, George Turnour (1799–1843), a British civil servant and scholar, who was born in Sri Lanka, published 20 chapters of the chronicle with an English translation, and more followed in 1837. Turnour's work paved the way for further translations.

→ The Devi Nuwara Devale, the main temple in the little town of Dondra

> **A few kilometres to the east of Dondra, serene Talalla Beach is one of the south's most idyllic and unspoiled coastal destinations.**

Around 1 km (half a mile) south of the temple is Dondra Head Lighthouse, a striking octagonal-shaped structure that was completed in 1890. Standing at 49 m (160 ft) tall, it is the tallest of the island's various lighthouses and sports an impressively rugged exterior, which is clad in granite specially imported from Cornwall and Scotland in the UK. The lighthouse is also significant because it marks the southernmost point of Sri Lanka. Looking south, the nearest landfall is in Antarctica, almost 8,050 km (5,000 miles) away.

A few kilometres to the east of Dondra, serene Talalla Beach is one of the south's most idyllic and unspoiled coastal destinations. It has a 2-km (1-mile) sweep of golden sand backed by lush vegetation. A cluster of guesthouses and restaurants cater to a mix of surfers, yoga students and beach lovers.

Devi Nuwara Devale
🏠 Tangalla Road
🕐 5am–7pm daily

16
Polhena
🅰 D7 🏠 5 km (3 miles) S of Matara

Between Mirissa and Matara is Polhena. This beachside suburb offers a complete change of pace to Matara, with a handful of modest hotels and guesthouses half lost in an endless sea of palms. Swim, snorkel or try your hand at surfing on the breaks of Madiha, at Polhena's western end.

17
Hoo-maniya Blowhole
🅰 D7 🏠 7 km (4 miles) E of Dickwella 🕐 8am–6pm daily

The Hoo-maniya Blowhole earned its name from the "hoo" sound it supposedly

↑ Hoo-maniya Blowhole, especially impressive in the monsoon season

makes just before spouting water into the sky. A magical natural phenomenon, the blowhole is the result of water being forced upwards through a narrow crevice in the coastal rocks as waves crash against the shore.

Hoo-maniya is at its most impressive during the monsoon season, especially in June, when the waves are at their strongest and the water jets can rise more than 15 m (49 ft) high. At other times, it can be underwhelming, so time your visit carefully. Unfortunately there is a lot of waste in the area.

18

Tissamaharama

🅰 E7 **🚗 27 km (17 miles) NE of Hambantota** 🚌

Founded in the 3rd century BC, "Tissa" was the capital of the southern province of Ruhunu. Today, it serves mainly as a base for the Yala (p116) and Bundala (p130) national parks, although it does have a few attractions of its own.

A large tank called the Tissa Wewa, 1 km (half a mile) north of the town, dates from the 3rd century BC. It attracts a huge diversity of birdlife. To the west of the tank are other reminders of Tissa's rich history. Dating from the 2nd and 3rd century BC, Menik Wehera and Yatala Wehera are thought to be part of what was once a monastery complex. The latter is a white *dagoba*

surrounded by a wall, which is decorated with sculpted elephant heads. Between the tank and the town lies the Tissa Dagoba. It is said to have been built by King Kavan Tissa, father of King Dutugemunu, and is thought to enshrine a forehead bone of the Buddha.

19

Hambantota

🅰 E7 **🚗 43 km (27 miles) NE of Tangalla** 🛍🍴🚌

The largest coastal town to be found to the west of Matara, scruffy Hambantota sees relatively few tourists, although it makes a convenient base for trips to Bundala National Park and is also the slightly unlikely location for a glitzy Shangri-La hotel.

↑ The large white dome of the Tissa Dagoba, in Tissamaharama

Hambantota was originally settled by Muslims from China and Southeast Asia (the name Hambantota itself is said to derive from "sampan", a type of Chinese boat). It is best known nowadays as the home town of former president Mahinda Rajapaksa, who earmarked the area for two controversial, Chinese-funded mega-developments in an attempt to revive the area's economic fortunes (and put money in the pockets of his cronies, according to critics). The first, the vast new Hambantota international port, has been mired in practical and financial difficulties, while the second, the Mattala Rajapaksa Airport, has been even more disastrous. Intended to provide the country with a second international airport, the development has proved deeply unpopular with both airlines and travellers, and currently sits empty and virtually unused.

Despite these controversial attempts at development, fishing and salt remain the traditional trades here, with dazzling white saltpans dotting the coast. The town also served as the main local

---

LEONARD WOOLF

Best remembered nowadays as the husband of Virginia Woolf, Leonard Woolf *(right)* also has his own unique claim to literary fame as the author of *The Village in the Jungle* (1913). The classic novel of life in British-era Ceylon, *The Village* is based on Woolf's four years' experience as a colonial official in Hambantota. His writing shows a rare understanding of and sympathy for the sufferings of the people under British rule.

EAT

Yala Peace Cottage

Traditional home-cooked rice and curries in Tissamaharama.

⟨A⟩E7 ⟨🏠⟩43 Sandagirigama Road, Tissamaharama
⟨📞⟩(077) 109 9588

$⟨$⟩$⟨$⟩$⟨$⟩

Chef Lady Restaurant

Tissamaharama's best seafood restaurant.

⟨A⟩E7 ⟨🏠⟩92 Sadagiripura, Tissamaharama
⟨📞⟩(077) 109 9588

$⟨$⟩$⟨$⟩$⟨$⟩

centre in British times, and a cluster of atmospheric old colonial-era buildings can still be seen, crumbling quietly, on the hill above town. Elsewhere, the viewing platform opposite the bus station offers a good spot from which to enjoy the town's bustling fish market and the old port.

20 Rekawa Beach

⟨A⟩D7 ⟨🏠⟩10 km (6 miles) NE of Tangalla

Rekawa Beach is one of the most important sea-turtle nesting sites in Sri Lanka. It can be reached from Tangalla via Tangalla Road. The beach is visited by five species of sea turtle that come ashore at night to lay their eggs in the sand. Although turtles lay eggs all year round at Rekawa, the busiest months for turtle nesting are between March and September, with April and May seeing the most activity. The ideal time to turtle-watch is around the full moon, when there is natural light and they emerge out of the ocean onto the beach in large numbers .

Turtle watches are usually held from 8pm onwards, when locals spread out along the sand. Keep your distance and try not to disrupt the turtles in any way. Flash photography is a definite no-no as the light disturbs the turtles and confuses any hatchlings trying to make their way to the sea.

Boats on Rekawa Beach, and *(inset)* a sea turtle ↓

21 Tangalla

⟨A⟩D7 ⟨🏠⟩13 km (8 miles) NE of Dickwella 🚌

Visitors come to the town of Tangalla mainly for the superb beaches that are located to the east and west. The town is also well placed for day excursions in the surrounding area, including turtle-watching at nearby Rekawa Beach.

East of Tangalla are the beaches of Medilla and Medaketiya. Dotted with guesthouses and restaurants, these beaches are the busiest and also the most developed. Around 4 km (2 miles) north-east is Marakolliya, which offers more secluded stretches of sand backed by the Rekawa Lagoon.

Immediately southwest of the town are the tranquil Pallikaduwa and Goyambokka beaches, with rocky coves and a series of bays.

Did You Know?

The country's national bird is the Sri Lankan junglefowl (*Gallus lafayettii*).

22

Kalametiya Bird Sanctuary

E7 **26 km (16 miles) NE of Tangalla**

An area of coastal wetland with saltwater lagoons, mangrove swamps and scrub jungle, the Kalametiya Bird Sanctuary is an excellent place for bird-watching. Among the birds that can be commonly sighted here are spot-billed pelicans, painted storks and crested fish eagles, as well as egrets, lapwings and plovers. A greater variety of birdlife can be spotted during the warm winter months, from November to March, when the area is visited by a large number of migratory birds. The sanctuary also features a beautiful strip of beach.

It is possible to arrange bird-watching tours at the village of Hungama, which lies 6 km (4 miles) southwest of the bird sanctuary.

23

Bundala National Park

E7 **15 km (9 miles) E of Hambantota** **6am-6pm daily**

A quieter alternative to nearby Yala West (Ruhuna) National Park (*p116*), Bundala National Park offers ample bird-watching opportunities. The park extends along the coast for 20 km (12 miles) and is made up of scrub jungle and coastal dunes that are punctuated by brackish lagoons and salt pans.

Among the 200-odd bird species that can be seen here are brown-capped babblers, egrets, ibis, painted storks, whiskered terns and spot-billed pelicans. Bird numbers swell between September and March with the arrival of the migrants – many waders also visit during these months. In addition, Bundala is known for its many peacocks and large flocks of visiting flamingos. The number of these pink-hued birds, however, has dropped considerably in recent years. This decline has been attributed to changes in the salinity of the lagoons.

Along with birds, there are also many mammals here, including elephants, jackals, mongooses, wild pigs and monkeys. Crocodiles can be seen around the lagoons, and the beaches are nesting sites for turtles.

The park is rich in plant life, too. Nearly 400 species of plant have been recorded, including water lilies, various herbs and acacia trees.

You will need a jeep and driver to explore the park. These can be hired from the park's entrance or from the local guesthouses.

> An area of coastal wetland with saltwater lagoons, mangrove swamps and scrub jungle, the Kalametiya Bird Sanctuary is an excellent place for bird-watching.

↑ Bundala National Park, a haven for many species of birds and animals

BIRDS OF SRI LANKA

Sri Lanka is a popular and rewarding bird-watching destination due to its diverse range of habitats, which include coastal wetlands, rainforests and the Hill Country. More than 400 species of birds have been recorded in Sri Lanka, of which 33 species are believed to be endemic.

WHEN AND WHERE TO GO

Most of the resident species are found in the southwestern part of the country. Among these are the yellow-eared bulbul and the junglefowl. Migrant birds arrive from Europe and other parts of Asia every year and add to the number of residents. A trip to a national park will usually yield some good sightings. Home to tanks, or reservoirs, the parks attract a large number of water birds. The best time for bird-watching in Sri Lanka is from November to March, but sightings can occur throughout the year.

SRI LANKAN BIRDS

Around lagoons and along the coast, you'll find a wide variety of shore and seabirds, including sandpipers, terns, egrets and storks. Other common species that are frequently sighted around forests and water bodies include parakeets, warblers, thrushes and brightly coloured kingfishers. A less frequent sight is the lesser adjutant - a large bird with a yellow bill and head, and thin grey down. It is listed as an endangered species but it can sometimes be seen near water bodies or paddy fields in the low country dry zone.

Away from the coast and lagoons, you're very likely to see the yellow-eared bulbul in areas 1,300 m (4,265 ft) above sea level. The crested-serpent eagle is much more difficult to spot as it is found amid thick forest cover. Look out for a flash of its bold black-and-white patterned wings. You can't miss the male Indian peafowl's distinctive train, or plumage. This gregarious bird can often be seen foraging in the undergrowth.

① The lesser adjutant is much larger than other shore birds.

② The crested-serpent eagle has a dark body, making it difficult to spot when its wings aren't spread.

③ The Indian peafowl is found in reserves in the low country.

④ The yellow-eared bulbul is named for its distinctive yellow ear tufts.

KANDY AND THE HILL COUNTRY

The story of Sri Lanka's Hill Country is essentially a tale of two halves. The history of the north is dominated by Kandy, which was founded by Wickramabahu III of Gampola (r 1357–1374) after the fall of Polonnaruwa. The city rose to prominence as the capital of Sena Sammatha Wickramabahu's kingdom (r 1473–1511) and its reputation was further cemented with the arrival of the Tooth Relic in 1592. As the rest of the island fell first under Portuguese and then Dutch control, the kingdom of Kandy obstinately retained its independence, protected by its location amid dense jungle and huge hills at the heart of the island. In 1814, the kingdom was taken by the British, thanks partly to the unpopularity of the tyrannical Sri Wickrama Rajasinghe, who was exiled to India. Kandy soon became an important centre for trade, with a railway line linking it to Colombo. Today, it is Sri Lanka's second city.

The history of the southern Hill Country, by contrast, is a largely colonial affair. A remote backwater for much of the island's history, the region was irreversibly changed by the arrival of European tea planters in the late 19th century. Huge swathes of jungle were cleared and replaced with the orderly plantations you see today, accompanied by a string of British settlements – most notably the elegant town of Nuwara Eliya. The arrival of tea also dramatically changed the Hill Country's population thanks to the arrival of tens of thousands of Tamil tea pickers from India, brought in to compensate for the lack of local labour. Their colourful-sari-clad descendants can still be seen working on the plantations today.

THE CULTURAL TRIANGLE
p158
Wariyapola
Ibbagamuwa
Kurunegala
Matale
Mimure
KNUCKLES RANGE
Narammala
Mawathagama
5
Knuckles
1,864 m
(6,115 ft)
Polgahawela
Rangala
1 KANDY
PERADENIYA BOTANICAL GARDENS 7
Hunasgiriya
Kegalle
6 CEYLON TEA MUSEUM
Victoria Reservoir
Ambepussa
THREE-TEMPLES LOOP 8
Dedigama
Galaha
Bible Rock
798 m (2,618 ft)
Gampola
Hanguranketa
CENTRAL
Bulathkohupitiya
Pussellawa
Nawalapitiya
DAMRO LABOOKELLIE TEA LOUNGE
Ramboda
Karawanella
KITULGALA
16
14
Pidurutalagala
2,524 m (8,280 ft)
Kelani Ganga
Dimbulla
NUWARA ELIYA 12
13 PEDRO TEA ESTATES
Kalu Ganga
Nanu Oya
9
THE WEST COAST
p86
Hatton
HAKGALA BOTANICAL GARDENS
Eheliyagoda
Castlereagh Reservoir
Dalhousie
HORTON PLAINS NATIONAL PARK AND WORLD'S END 2
Palabaddale
4
ADAM'S PEAK
21
Ingiriya
Maha Saman Devale
BAMBARAKANDA FALLS
Kalu Ganga
Belihul Oya
23 RATNAPURA
Bulathsinhala
Kalthota
Balangoda
SABARAGAMUWA
Pelmadulla
Kuda Ganga
Rajawaka
Agalawatta
Kalawana
Madampe
Koswatta
Uda Walawe Reservoir
Moragala
Weddagala
Pallebedda
Kudawa
Gin Ganga
20 SINHARAJA FOREST RESERVE
Udawalawe
Pelawaththa
Deniyaya
Embilipitiya
0 kilometres 20
0 miles 20
N
SOUTHERN
A6
A10
A1
A5
A26
B492
B364
B457
A21
B132
B67
B445
A7
A4
B222
A8
B339
B477
B160
A18
A17
B115

THE EAST
p190

KANDY AND THE HILL COUNTRY

Must Sees

❶ Kandy

❷ Horton Plains National Park and World's End

❸ Ella

❹ Adam's Peak

Experience More

❺ Knuckles Range

❻ Ceylon Tea Museum

❼ Peradeniya Botanical Gardens

❽ Three-Temples Loop

❾ Hakgala Botanical Gardens

❿ Dunhinda Falls

⓫ Badulla

⓬ Nuwara Eliya

⓭ Pedro Tea Estate

⓮ Damro Labookellie Tea Lounge

⓯ Dambatenne Tea Factory

⓰ Kitulgala

⓱ Haputale

⓲ Buduruwagala

⓳ Adisham Monastery

⓴ Sinharaja Forest Reserve

㉑ Bambarakanda Falls

㉒ Diyaluma Falls

㉓ Ratnapura

THE SOUTH
p102

The city of Kandy, sprawling up the hills from Kandy Lake ↑

❶

KANDY

D5 **134 km (83 miles) E of Colombo** **In the Kandy City Centre shopping complex**

A charming, culturally vibrant city, Kandy was the seat of government of the last Sinhalese kingdom, until it was taken over by the British in 1815. Today, it attracts tourists and pilgrims alike who come here to visit the Temple of the Tooth, the sacred Buddhist shrine.

①
Kandy Lake

The centrepiece of the city, Kandy Lake (known locally as Kiri Muhuda – literally "Sea of Milk") was created by Sri Wickrama Rajasinghe, the last king of the Kandyan kingdom, in the 19th century. The island in the centre was used as the king's pleasure house before the British converted it into an ammunition store. The lake is best appreciated by walking along the southern shore, from where there are beautiful views of the Temple of the Tooth and the striking white two-storey Queens' Bath (Ulpange), on the opposite bank. This building once served as a bathing pavilion for Sri Wickrama Rajasinghe's various wives and concubines.

②
St Paul's Church

For services only
stpaulschurchkandy.lk

Completed in 1825, this Neo-Gothic church's distinctive, terracotta brickwork offers a welcome splash of colour against the uniform whiteness of the surrounding buildings. Inside, the time-warped interior seems straight out of Victorian England.

③
Devales

Kandy is popularly believed to be protected by four gods: Pattini, Natha, Vishnu and Kataragama. Each of these guardian deities has a *devale* (temple) dedicated to them in the city, exemplifying the intermingling of Hindu and Buddhist beliefs in Kandy.

The Natha Devale is the oldest of the four, dating from the 14th century. Nearby stands the Pattini Devale, a simple shrine devoted to Pattini, the Buddhist goddess of chastity. Opposite Natha Devale is the Vishnu (or Maha) Devale, which features a *digge* (drummers' pavilion). The main shrine at the Kataragama Devale is surrounded by shrines dedicated to Hindu and Buddhist deities.

④
Malwatte Vihara

Founded around the 16th century, the Malwatte Vihara is an important temple and

> **GREAT VIEW**
> **Arthur's Seat**
>
> Directly above Malwatte Vihara, on Rajapihilla Mawatha hill, is one of Kandy's best viewpoints, popularly known as Arthur's Seat. It offers a bird's-eye view of the Temple of the Tooth.

⑤ Kandy National Museum

🕐 9am–5pm Tue–Sat
🌐 museum.gov.lk

Housed in a white building that was once the Queen's Palace, the Kandy National Museum explores life in the city before the arrival of the Europeans. Among the displays are weapons such as bows and arrows, knives and daggers, as well as jewellery, traditional costumes and everyday items such as nut-crackers shaped like people.

⑥ International Buddhist Museum

📍 Behind the Audience Hall
🕐 8am–7pm daily 🌐 ibm.sridaladamaligawa.lk

Housed in a Neo-Classical building, this museum explores the history of Buddhism in Sri Lanka, and also has exhibits on Buddhism in other Asian countries, such as India, Pakistan, China and Japan. Shoes must be removed before entering the museum.

Did You Know?

Kandy is called Mahanuwara in Sinhalese, meaning "The Great City".

is home to over 300 Buddhist monks. The Ordination Room, with its magnificently painted ceiling, is worth a visit. The monastery also has a modest museum that contains Buddhist artifacts.

STAY

Helga's Folly
Sri Lanka's wackiest hotel is plastered in a riot of colourful murals and stuffed with outlandish bric-a-brac.

📍 65a Rajapihilla Mawatha 🌐 helgasfolly.com

$$$

Elephant Stables
A country-house-style hotel, with just six lavish rooms, a pool and sweeping views.

📍 46 Nittawela Road 🌐 elephantstables.com

$$$

The Kandy House
This boutique hotel is set in a stunning 19th-century manor house.

📍 Amunugama Road 🌐 thekandyhouse.com

$$$

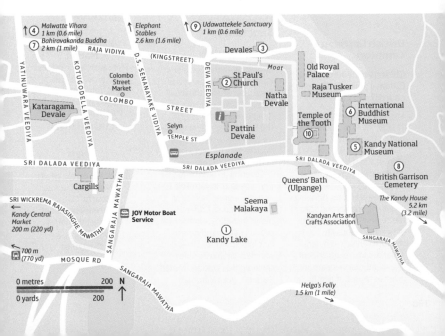

↑ The Royal Pond, surrounded by forest, in Udawattekele Sanctuary

Bahiravakanda Buddha

⌂ Sri Dharmarama Road
🕐 8am–5pm daily

Perched on a hill overlooking the town, this modern, white, seated Buddha statue is hard to miss. At the base of the huge statue is a temple, from where there are superb views over Kandy. It is possible to walk to the site or to take a tuk-tuk up to the temple by following the road that leads to the Topaz Hotel.

British Garrison Cemetery

⌂ Garrison Cemetery Road
🕐 8am–7pm daily 🌐 stpauls churchkandy.lk

This cemetery was founded in 1817 as the final resting place for deceased British colonialists. Today, it is a well-tended and tranquil spot, despite the many monkeys cavorting around the place.

There are around 195 graves of varying shapes and sizes in the cemetery, giving an idea of how hazardous life was in the 19th century – cholera, malaria, sunstroke, accidents and infant mortality are all given as causes of death.

If there is time, take a guided tour of the grounds with the caretaker, who can point out the most interesting tombstones and help to decipher the weathered inscriptions. Visitors are likely to come across the grave of John Spottiswood Robertson, the last-known European to have been killed by a wild elephant in Sri Lanka in 1856. The caretaker's cabin at the entrance has a register that contains a record of all the graves in the cemetery.

Udawattekele Sanctuary

🕐 7am–6pm daily

Stretching to the north of Kandy Lake, this forest was once reserved for the royal family. After the fall of the Kandyan kingdom in 1815, the British began felling trees for their own use, but they declared it a protected area in the mid-19th century.

Covering an area of 104 ha (257 acres), Udawattekele is home to a great variety of flora and fauna. Endemic plants include a number of orchid species and other epiphytes, such as ferns. Birdwatchers should be able to catch sight of golden-fronted leafbirds, yellow-fronted barbets and the yellow-browed bulbul, among other species. There are also butterflies, squirrels, monkeys and reptiles to look out for.

Explore Udawattekele by following one of the numerous trails, most of which are named after British governors' wives. The 5-km (3-mile) Lady Horton's Drive is one such path that takes in a good portion of the forest, including the pond where royalty once bathed. According to legend, gold coins lie beneath the surface of the pond, guarded by a red-eyed serpent.

ESALA PERAHERA

This 10-day festival, celebrated in honour of the Tooth Relic, attracts thousands of pilgrims and tourists to Kandy in July or August. Expect drummers, dancers and a party atmosphere, but be aware that elephants are exploited during the festival.

The *perahera* (festival) took shape in the 18th century during the reign of King Kirti Sri Rajasinghe, when Buddhist monks visiting from Thailand expressed their disapproval at the Hindu nature of the festival, with parades in reverence of Natha, Pattini, Vishnu and Kataragama from the four *devales* in the city. The king, therefore, ordered that the Tooth Relic *(p140)* be carried at the head of the four processions, hence incorporating the Temple of the Tooth parade into that of the *devales*.

Esala Perahera begins with the Kap Tree Planting Ceremony, followed by the Kumbal Perahera that marks the first five days of the festival. The last five days, known as Randoli Perahera, are when festivities become more spectacular. Every night there are processions, featuring dancers, drummers and acrobats, as well as heavily decorated elephants. The water-cutting ceremony, the concluding ritual of the festival, takes place before dawn on the last day of the *perahera*.

↑ The glittering Tooth Relic, which is paraded through the city

INSIDER TIP
Just the Spot

The *perahera* usually begins between 8 and 9pm. Be sure to arrive hours before that, though, to find a spot on the pavement next to the route. It's also possible to reserve one of the special window or balcony seats.

↑ Spinning rings of fire in a parade during the festival

↑ Thammattam players performing during the Esala Perahera

TEMPLE OF THE TOOTH

🏠 Palace Square, Kandy 🕐 Temple: 5am–8pm daily; Sri Dalada Museum: 9am–5pm daily 🌐 sridaladamaligawa.lk

Jutting into the lake and juxtaposed against the forested hills of the Udawattekele Sanctuary, this golden-roofed temple is an arresting sight. As you might expect from its position at the heart of the city, the Temple of the Tooth, or Sri Dalada Maligawa, houses Sri Lanka's most important Buddhist relic, the Buddha's tooth.

Built in the 16th century, the original temple stood at the heart of the Royal Palace complex. The main shrine was originally constructed during the reign of Vimala Dharma Suriya I (r 1590–1604), but it was rebuilt by King Rajasinghe II (r 1634–1686) following the Dutch incursion of the city in 1765, when they plundered the palace and its temple. The palace was renovated in the 19th century by Sri Wickrama Rajasinghe, the last king of Kandy, who built the moat and replaced the earlier entrances with a massive stone gateway. The temple's trials didn't end there. An LTTE bombing badly damaged it in 1998, but the temple has since been restored. Having survived these challenges, the tooth has only become more sacred.

THE STORY OF THE BUDDHA'S TOOTH

Legend states that after the Buddha was cremated in India in 543 BC, his remains were divided into eight. During the 4th century AD, the Tooth Relic was brought to Sri Lanka from Kalinga in India, concealed in the hair of Princess Hemamala *(below)*. To keep it safe, the tooth was moved around Sri Lanka, but it has been kept in Kandy since it arrived in 1592.

Royal Palace

The Raja Tusker Museum is dedicated to Raja, the elephant that carried the Tooth Relic casket during the Esala Perahera (p139) for 50 years.

The Maha Vahlkada, or Great Gate, marks the entrance to the temple. The moonstone here is visibly new; the original was destroyed in the bomb blast in 1998.

Did You Know?

Temples of the Tooth were built in Anuradhapura, Polonnaruwa and Yapahuwa.

The buildings making up the Temple of the Tooth complex ↑

① The Temple of the Tooth occupies a beautiful position on Kandy Lake.

② The Octagonal Tower is home to the library, which houses a number of ancient *ola*-leaf manuscripts.

③ Drummers and elephant tusks line the way to the entrance to the main shrine.

The treaty that ended the sovereignty of the Kandyan kingdom, and ceded power to the British, was signed in the Audience Hall in 1815.

The Drummers' Courtyard is where most people congregate before the puja.

A series of paintings around the Alut Maligawa's walls depict the story of the Tooth Relic, explaining how it arrived in Kandy.

The main shrine is a two-storey structure with decorated walls and doors, as well as a gilded canopy dating from the 1980s.

The furthest section in the Tooth Relic Chamber, Vadahitina Maligawa houses the sacred relic, which is kept in a bejewelled gold casket.

Pallemaluwa, a shrine room, has a large Buddha statue and colourful murals.

The Octagonal Tower

The view from World's End,
a precipice in Horton Plains
National Park

② ✏️ 🖥️

HORTON PLAINS NATIONAL PARK AND WORLD'S END

🄰 D6   🏠 32 km (20 miles) S of Nuwara Eliya   🚉 Ohiya station, then taxi
ℹ️ Farr Inn (on site); (070) 522 042; 6am–4pm daily (last entry 2:30pm)

Horton Plains is unlike any other place in the country and is often compared to the Scottish Highlands, for its windswept landscape and cool, wet climate. Apart from the wildlife, the park's key attraction is World's End, a sheer precipice offering panoramic views of the island.

The park is named after Sir Robert Wilmot-Horton, the British governor of Ceylon from 1831 to 1837. Formerly a wildlife sanctuary, the area was declared a national park in 1988. At an elevation of more than 2,000 m (6,562 ft), the park is situated on the highest plateau in Sri Lanka, with its terrain characterized by undulating grasslands interspersed with dense cloud forests, rocky outcrops and waterfalls.

Unlike other national parks in Sri Lanka, Horton Plains can be explored on foot and without a guide, provided visitors stick to the marked trails. While there are several trails in the park, the majority of people follow the Loop Trail. This 9-km- (6-mile-) long circular trail begins at the visitor centre near the entrance and takes in World's End before returning to the centre. The round trip takes three to four hours. A stunning escarpment plunging more than 880 m (2,887 ft) into the lowlands below, World's End offers breathtaking views. On a clear day, it is possible to see as far as the island's southern coast from here. On other days, the view may be limited to the nearer Uda Walawe National Park *(p112)*. The trail also takes in Baker's Falls, a beautiful 20-m- (66-ft-) high waterfall that was discovered by British explorer Samuel Baker in 1845. Reached by a steep forest path, the waterfall is an arresting sight.

↑ An axis deer in the grasslands of Horton Plains National Park

↑ Baker's Falls, tumbling over rocks, near the entrance to the national park

💬 INSIDER TIP
Early Birds

Aim to arrive as early as you possibly can, ideally by 7am, to allow plenty of time to reach World's End before 10am, before clouds roll in and the view is obscured from the escarpment. It'll be chilly in the morning, but it warms up quickly, so wear sunscreen. Be aware that the last stretch of the Loop Trail, between Baker's Falls and the entrance, offers no shade.

③

ELLA

A E6 **⌂** 21 km (13 miles) S of Badulla 🚂🚌

One of the Hill Country's most popular destinations, Ella is best known for its curries and hikes. The village is endlessly picturesque, perched above the Ella Gap, a cleft in the escarpment where the land drops a dizzying 1,100 m (3,609 ft) to the plains below.

① Ella Rock

Keen hikers might consider tackling Ella Rock. It's a stiff, four-hour return trip, with a confusing variety of routes to the top (ask at your guesthouse for directions), but you'll be rewarded with increasingly fine views the higher you climb. One possibility is to follow the railway track south of town, before striking up the rock.

② Little Adam's Peak

The most rewarding short walk from Ella is the hike up Little Adam's Peak, a landmark hill to the east of the village. The final ascent will leave you breathless, but it's more than worth it. Head down Passara Road and follow the signs to embark on this two- to three-hour return hike.

③ Newburgh Tea Factory

⌂ Passara Road **⏰** 8:30am-5pm Mon-Sat

Easily combined with the walk up Little Adam's Peak is a visit to this green tea factory, which offers short factory tours. After touring Newburgh Tea Factory, continue on to Demodara Bridge and then follow the railway all the way back to Ella for a satisfying three- to four-hour walk.

④ Demodara Bridge

Known as "Nine Arches Bridge", Demodara Bridge was built in the early 1920s to carry the railway line north of Ella. Walk through the forest

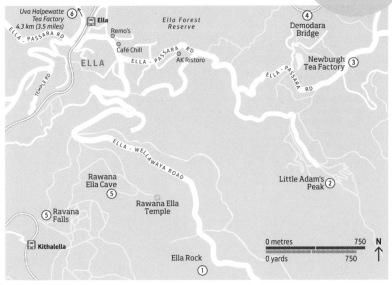

Uva Halpewatte
Tea Factory
4.3 km (3.5 miles) ⑥

🚉 Ella

Remo's

Café Chill

Ella Forest Reserve

④ Demodara Bridge

ELLA - PASSARA RD

AK Ristoro

ELLA

TEMPLE RD

Newburgh
Tea Factory ③

ELLA - PASSARA RD

ELLA - WELLAWAYA ROAD

Rawana
Ella Cave
⑤

Rawana Ella
Temple

Little Adam's
Peak ②

⑤ Ravana
Falls

🚉 Kithalella

Ella Rock
①

0 metres   750
0 yards   750

N ↑

---

from Art Café Umbrella for a breathtaking view of this viaduct bridge, surrounded by tea plantations and green hills.

---

⑤
Ravana Falls and Ravana Ella Cave

About 4 km (2 miles) south of Ella, 600 steep steps lead up to the diminutive Ravana Ella Cave where Hindu goddess Sita is said to have been held captive by the god Ravana. The cave itself isn't terribly exciting, although the views justify the climb. Continuing 5 km (3 miles) further south, the majestic Ravana Falls tumble 90 m (295 ft) over a cliff right next to the main Wellawaya road. It's especially photogenic after rain.

---

⑥ 🏵 🅼 🖳
Uva Halpewatte Tea Factory

🏠 Badulla Road ⏰ 8am-4pm Mon-Sat 🌐 halpe tea.com

Some 6 km (4 miles) outside Ella, the Uva Halpewatte Tea Factory is an essential visit if you love the drink. The tour of this 1940s factory is the best on the island and you can sip tea on the terrace afterwards, while taking in the view.

←

Little Adam's Peak, soaring above hilly tea plantations near Ella

---

EAT

AK Ristoro
Unexpectedly chic eatery, serving Italian and Japanese fare alongside curries.

🏠 Passara Rd 📞 057 205 0676

$ⓢ$ⓢ$ⓢ

Café Chill
This funky chill-out café on the main drag is Ella's go-to after-dark destination.

🏠 Main St 📞 077 180 4020

$ⓢ$ⓢ$⑤

Remo's
Ella is famous for its curry, and Remo's serves up delicious dishes at rock-bottom prices.

🏠 7 Main St 📞 077 409 9231

$ⓢ$⑤$⑤

Sunrise over Adam's Peak,
taken from the top, and *(inset)*
prayer flags at the summit ↑

④ Ⓜ ▭

ADAM'S PEAK

🅐 D6 🏠 52 km (32 miles) SE of Kitulgala 🚉 To Hatton, then bus to Dalhousie 🚌

Towering above the southern hill country, the 2,243-m (7,359-ft) Adam's Peak is easily Sri Lanka's most dramatic mountain and the breathtaking view from the summit at sunrise is reason enough to make the night-time hike. On top of this, the peak is one of the island's most sacred sites, attracting pilgrims of all faiths.

Known locally as Sri Pada ("Sacred Footprint"), the peak is revered by all of Sri Lanka's faiths thanks to an impression on a rock at its summit. While Buddhists believe the mark to be an imprint of the Buddha's foot, Hindus associate it with Shiva, Muslims with Adam and Christians with St Thomas. The peak is, however, primarily a Buddhist site.

The easiest and shortest route up the mountain is from Dalhousie, where the majority of visitors base themselves. The 7-km (4-mile) ascent consists of around 5,500 steps. The climb is traditionally made at night – most people set off at 2am and take about 4 hours to reach the peak to watch daybreak. Pilgrimage season lasts from December to May. During this period, the steps leading to the peak are illuminated, and there are little stalls along the route offering tea and snacks.

At the summit, check out the footprint and ring one of the bells to mark your ascent. As dawn breaks, the sun sometimes casts a unique triangular shadow of the peak that seems to hang in mid-air in front of the mountain.

> 💬 INSIDER TIP
> **Off-the-Beaten Path**
>
> The route up the peak from Ratnapura offers a tougher, but much quieter, ascent, and a real taste of Sri Lanka in the wild. Guesthouses in Ratnapura can arrange a guide.

↑ The path from Ratnapura to Adam's Peak, illuminated for the night-time ascent

Looking out at ↑
the verdant Knuckles
Range or Dumbara Hills

EXPERIENCE MORE

⑤
Knuckles Range

🅐 D4 🕒 25 km (16 miles) NE of Kandy 🚌 Hunnasgiriya

Also known as Dumbara Hills, the Knuckles Range was so named by the British for its resemblance to the knuckles of a clenched fist. It consists of five main peaks and several smaller ones. The highest is over 1,800 m (6,000 ft).

A UNESCO World Heritage Conservation Area, the mountains support a wide range of flora and fauna. With vegetation varying from dry evergreen forests to wet grasslands, these ecosystems support numerous animal species, such as deer, wild boar, langurs and slender loris, as well as a variety of birds.

The Knuckles Range is popular with hikers. Hiring an experienced guide is vital, as there are few trail markers. Local hotels and guesthouses can recommend a good guide.

> 🔍 **HIDDEN GEM**
> **On the Knuckle**
>
> One of Asia's most beautiful golf courses, the Victoria Golf and Country Resort lies east of Kandy in a stunning location between the Knuckles Range and the Victoria Reservoir (www.golfsrilanka.com).

⑥
Ceylon Tea Museum

🅐 D5 🕒 5 km (3 miles) S of Kandy 🕗 8:30am-3:45pm Tue-Sat, 8:30am-3pm Sun 🌐 ceylonteamuseum.com

Located in the Hantane Estate, the Ceylon Tea Museum occupies a former four-storey tea factory dating from 1925. Exhibits on the ground floor include drying furnaces, grinders and sorters used in the 19th century. Look out for the miniature working model of a tea factory and an 80-year-old tea bush.

The first floor contains displays on two of Sri Lanka's greatest tea pioneers: James Taylor and Thomas Lipton. There is a small collection of Taylor's personal articles, which includes his books and walking stick.

The third floor has small shops selling tea, and on the top floor is a café, where you can enjoy a free cup of the beverage while admiring the glorious Knuckles Range.

⑦
Peradeniya Botanical Gardens

🅐 D5 🕒 6 km (4 miles) SW of Kandy 🚌 From Kandy 🕗 7:30am-5:30pm daily 🌐 botanicgardens.gov.lk

Originally laid out for the Kandyan royalty in 1371, the royal park was turned into botanical gardens in 1821 (the British had dethroned the last Kandyan king, Sri Wickrama Rajasinghe, in 1815). A useful map at the entrance helps visitors explore some of the 60 ha (148 acres) of foreign and endemic plants and trees. Check out the giant bamboo, palmyra palms and tailpot palms, as well as the 300 varieties found in the Orchid House. Then, follow your nose to the spice garden, which teems with a wealth of plants such as clove, cinnamon, vanilla and nutmeg.

Lined with exotic varieties of trees, the attractive avenues provide a pleasant stroll. When you're ready to rest, the cool shade provided by the sprawling branches of a gargantuan Javan fig tree makes the Great Lawn a perfect place for a picnic.

8
Three-Temples Loop

🅰D5 🕐11 km (7 miles) SW of Kandy 🚌 From Kandy

Among the many Kandyan-era temples in this area, the **Gadaladeniya**, **Lankatilaka** and **Embekke Devale** temples are exceptional. You can easily explore all three on foot, but tuk-tuks are also available along the way if you get tired.

Situated atop a rock, the Gadaladeniya Temple complex was built during the reign of King Bhuvanekabahu IV in 1344. The main stone temple is adorned with carvings of dancers and drummers and two small elephant sculptures

guard the steps leading to the entrance. Inside, a serene golden Buddha sits under a *makara torana* (ceremonial arch) decorated with murals.

Located 2 km (1 mile) southwest, the bright-white Lankatilaka Temple is probably the most impressive of the three shrines and its highlight is the Buddhist image house. Flanking the doorway to the chamber are two guardian *gajasinghas* (elephant-lions). Inside, there is a seated Buddha statue under a *makara torana* surrounded by Kandyan-era paintings on the walls and ceiling.

Dedicated to the guardian deity Kataragama, the Embekke Devale lies 2 km (1 mile) southeast of the Lankatilaka Temple. The shrine is famous for the richly carved wooden pillars of its *digge* (drummers' pavilion), portraying flowers, dancers, soldiers and wrestlers, among other themes.

Gadaladeniya Temple
♿ 🏛Gadaladeniya Road 🕐8am–6pm daily

Lankatilaka Temple
♿ 🏛Lankatilaka Vihara Road 🕐8am–6pm daily

Embekke Devale
♿ 🏛Embekke Pilimatalawa Road 🕐8am–6pm daily

The outstanding Lankatilaka Temple, near Kandy ↓

9

Hakgala Botanical Gardens

🅰D6 🅰10 km (6 miles) SE of Nuwara Eliya 🚌 🕐8am–5:30pm daily 🌐botanicgardens.gov.lk

These gardens were originally laid out in 1861 to cultivate cinchona, the bark of which is a source of the anti-malarial drug quinine. Today, rather than cinchona, Hakgala is famous for its roses, which bloom from April to August. Spread over 27 ha (67 acres),

the garden is divided into different sections, including a Japanese garden, a fernery and a rock garden. The beds here host a diverse range of flowers, from sunflowers and pansies to orchids. The plants and trees labelled in red are indigenous to Sri Lanka.

After exploring the gardens, why not check out the Sita Amman Temple, which is just 2 km (1 mile) to the east? Dedicated to Sita, wife of Lord Rama, the shrine is thought to mark the spot where she was held prisoner by Ravana.

→

Nuwara Eliya's grand post office, with its striking clock tower

EAT

Hill Club

Live out your grandiose fantasies at this time-warped restaurant in Nuwara Eliya. Formal attire required.

🅰D6 🅰29 Grand Hotel Road, Nuwara Eliya 📞(052) 222 4132

$⑤$⑤$⑤

Sri Ambaal

Cheap and tasty South Indian and Sri Lankan vegetarian classics are served on banana-leaf plates at this Nuwara Eliya eatery.

🅰D6 🅰New Bazaar Street, Nuwara Eliya 📞(052) 223 5281

$⑤$⑤$⑤

Grand Indian

Part of Nuwara Eliya's Grand Hotel, the Grand Indian serves up a range of curries on *thalis* (round platters).

🅰D6 🅰Grand Hotel, Nuwara Eliya 🌐grandhotel nuwaraeliya.com

$⑤$⑤$⑤

10

Dunhinda Falls

🅰E5 🅰6 km (4 miles) N of Badulla 🚌From Badulla

Fed by the Badulla Oya river, the 63-m- (210-ft-) high Dunhinda Falls are one of the island's most impressive water-falls, spouting an enormous volume of water into the pool below amid a cloud of spray. It's a pleasant 1-km (0.6-mile) walk from the road to the falls, passing the lower and wider Kuda Dunhinda Falls en route. Stalls selling drinks and snacks line the path, but watch out for thieving monkeys when taking a break and soaking up the scenery. The falls are particularly busy at weekends and on public holidays.

11

Badulla

🅰E6 🅰125 km (78 miles) E of Kitulgala 🚉🚌

The capital of Uva Province, Badulla is thought to be one of the oldest towns in Sri Lanka. Today, it is an important transport hub and visitors are only likely to pass through Badulla while travelling between the Hill Country and the East Coast.

The highlight here is the **Kataragama Devale**, a Hindu

↑ The torrential flow of Dunhinda Falls, a thundering waterfall

temple that was built in the 18th century. The Kandyan-style main shrine houses an image of Kataragama, flanked by statues of Saman and Vishnu. The shrine's outer walls are painted with murals depicting a *perahera*. Some fine carvings of human figures, animals and floral motifs can be seen on the pillars and in other areas of the temple.

Kataragama Devale
⌂ Lower Street ◷ 6am–6pm daily

---

⑫

Nuwara Eliya

⌂ D6 ⌂ 88 km (55 miles) SW of Mahiyangana ▣▦

Established by the British in the 19th century, Nuwara Eliya is often referred to as Sri Lanka's "Little England". Set in a wooded valley beneath the 2,524-m (8,281-ft) Pidurutalagala or Mount Pedro (the tallest peak in the country), it is the highest town on the island. With a cool though unpredictable climate, the town provides a welcome relief from the hot and humid lowlands.

Perennially popular, the town becomes particularly busy in April during the Sinhalese and Tamil New Year holidays, when Sri Lankans flock here in droves. A festive atmosphere prevails during this period – many horse- and motor-racing events are organized and stalls line the streets – and accommodation prices tend to be higher.

At other times of the year, you can take a quiet walk around the town. In the centre is the well-maintained 18-hole Golf Club, which was founded in 1889. Behind the Club House are the remains of a British Cemetery, where the infamous elephant hunter Major Thomas William Rogers is buried. Also in the town centre is the pink colonial-era post office with an eye-catching clock tower. Nearby, the charming **Victoria Park** offers some excellent bird-watching and also has a play area for children near the entrance. A little further on, there is an interesting covered market on New Bazaar Street, where vendors sell a wealth of fruit and vegetables.

To the east of the centre stands the Anglican Holy Trinity Church, which was consecrated in 1852. Further east lies Lake Gregory, where you can rent pleasure boats and pedaloes or simply take a stroll along the shore.

Where better to stay in "Little England" than one of Nuwara Eliya's elegant colonial-era hotels? There's the Hill Club, which seems to have been transported to Sri Lanka from the home counties, and the half-timbered Grand Hotel, located further north along the Grand Hotel Road. Non-guests can visit for a drink, or simply to admire the period exteriors and colourful flower gardens.

Victoria Park
⊛ ◌ ◷ 7am–6pm daily

> **Did You Know?**
>
> Nuwara Eliya means "City on the Plain" or "City of Light".

↑ Workers picking tea on the corduroyed hills of the Pedro Tea Estate

13 ⊗ ⊗ ⊡ ⊡

Pedro Tea Estate

🅰D6 🚗3 km (2 miles) E of Nuwara Eliya ☎(052) 222 2016 📧 🕐8am–5pm daily

Established in 1885, this small, suburban tea estate runs guided tours of its factory. The tea produced here is very light, so processing happens at night when it's colder. Get to the estate before 8am if you want to see the processing in action. The factory handles about 2,500 kg (5,511 lbs) of tea every day. After the tour, savour a complimentary cup of tea in the café overlooking the plantation.

14 ⊗ ⊗ ⊡ ⊡

Damro Labookellie Tea Lounge

🅰D5 🚗17 km (10 miles) N of Nuwara Eliya 📧 🕐8:30am–6:30pm daily 🌐damrotealounge.com

This expansive, 415-ha (1,025-acre) tea estate is set in a lovely location. In addition to a brief guided tour of the factory, it is possible to join the tea pluckers on the slopes and help to pick the leaves. The tour ends with a free sampling of the tea.

The nearby **Bluefield Tea Gardens** offers excellent free tours of its factory. Afterwards, dine in the restaurant, browse the shop and amble through the surrounding tea bushes.

Bluefield Tea Gardens
⊗⊗⊗ 🚗23 km (14 miles) N of Nuwara Eliya 🌐blue fieldteagardens.com

---

15 ⊗ ⊗

Dambatenne Tea Factory

🅰E6 🚗10 km (6 miles) E of Haputale 📧 🕐8am–6pm Mon–Fri

The Dambatenne Tea Factory was built by Sir Thomas Lipton in 1890. Guided tours take in everything from drying and rolling through to grading.

Located 7 km (4 miles) east is the Lipton's Seat lookout, which is reached via a 2-hour climb that winds through lush tea plantations. Be sure to reach the lookout early as mist rolls in by mid-morning. Why not take a taxi up and walk back down?

THOMAS LIPTON

Sir Thomas Lipton was born in Glasgow in 1850. In 1871 he opened his first grocery shop and soon Lipton had a chain of around 400 shops across Great Britain. In 1889, he started buying tea at auctions in London and went on to sell 10 million pounds of tea within two years. His tea empire reached new heights in 1890 when he bought several tea estates in Ceylon. Upon returning to Scotland, he marketed Ceylon tea with his usual panache and eventually became synonymous with the beverage.

TEA IN SRI LANKA

Sri Lanka is one of the largest exporters of tea in the world. The country produces a wide range of varieties, including grades of the traditional black tea, flavoured teas, organic teas and green tea.

The first tea plants, brought from China, were grown in Peradeniya Botanical Gardens (p148) in 1824, but it was not until 1867 that the first commercial tea plantation was established near Kandy. Before the cultivation of tea began on the island, coffee was the principal plantation crop. However, when the coffee trees were decimated by disease in the 1870s, tea became a profitable alternative. Today, the tea industry is of great importance to Sri Lanka's economy. The country's tea estates attract visitors from around the world and offer tours of tea factories, stays in plantation bungalows and picturesque views of rows of tea bushes.

↑ A huge pile of tea being packed into sacks, for auctions in Colombo

FROM BUSH TO CUP

Tea production is labour-intensive. Tea leaves are still plucked by hand, mostly by women. The majority are descendants of the Tamil labourers who were brought from South India to work in the plantations by the British in the 1870s. Their wages are low and living conditions are poor – they often live in barrack-style buildings comprising only one room.

After the leaves have been collected, they are delivered to the factory where they are processed using either the traditional or the CTC (crush, tear and curl) method. In the former, the leaves are dried, crushed and then left to ferment before being fired in an oven. The CTC method is much faster as the fresh leaves are passed through a series of cylindrical rollers that crush, tear and curl the tea. The ground-up leaves are then rolled into little pellets and oxidized. After this, the tea is ready to be sent for auction to make its way onto shop shelves.

Female workers plucking tea on a plantation near Nuwara Eliya ↑

STAY

'T En Zal
The Dutch owner of this one-of-a-kind guesthouse collected crafts from across Sri Lanka to furnish his Haputale hotel.

E6 **Welimada Road, Haputale** **tenzal.com**

$$$

Jetwing St Andrews
A graceful Edwardian building, set amid immaculate lawns, this Nuwara Eliya hotel is committed to sustainability. Luxurious and guilt-free.

D6 **St Andrew's Drive, Nuwara Eliya** **jetwinghotels.com**

$$$

↑ Market stalls in the town of Haputale, on the southern edge of the Hill Country

16
Kitulgala
D5 **73 km (45 miles) NW of Nuwara Eliya**

Surrounded by low wooded hills, the small village of Kitulgala is perhaps best known for being the location where David Lean filmed *The Bridge on the River Kwai* (1957). A path signposted from the main road leads to the banks of the Kelani river, where the filming site can be seen. Those familiar with the Oscar-winning film will recognize some of the riverside scenery and the remains of the bridge's concrete foundations.

Today, Kitulgala serves as a base for a range of adventure activities, such as whitewater rafting. Most hotels in the area can also arrange rock climbing, cycling, abseiling and overnight river trips. A boat trip across the Kelani Ganga river leads to the **Kitulgala Forest Reserve**, where you can trek in lowland rainforest, searching the trees and sky for birds. Among the many feathered creatures that can be spotted here are the grey hornbill, the yellow-fronted barbet and various kingfishers.

Kitulgala Forest Reserve
Colombo-Avissawella-Hatton Road

17
Haputale
E6 **47 km (29 miles) NW of Buduruwagala**

This market town clings to a narrow ridge, corduroyed with tea plantations, on the southern edge of the Hill Country. Many of Haputale's mainly Tamil population still work in the tea plantations nearby. While the town does not have much in the way of sights, if you venture a short walk away from the centre of town, you'll be rewarded with superb vistas. On a clear day, it is possible to see all the way to the south coast. Be aware that the views are obscured by clouds around midday, when it often rains.

To make the most of Haputale's scenic position, take a walk in the surrounding hills. One of the best hikes is the 10-km (6-mile) route through beautiful tea estates to the Dambatenne Tea Factory (p152).

North of the town centre on a small hill is the Anglican St Andrew's Church, a pretty Neo-Gothic building that speaks of the town's colonial past. Memorial plaques and gravestones of 19th-century tea planters can still be seen in the small churchyard.

WHITEWATER RAFTING
The stretch of Kelani river around Kitulgala is considered to be the best place for whitewater rafting in Sri Lanka. The main rafting stretch is about 4 km (2 miles) long and the rapids vary from Grade 3 to 5 depending on rainfall. The best time for a trip is from April to November when the water level is higher. A typical route covers a range of major and minor rapids, and usually includes a swimming stop. Experienced rafters can arrange for more challenging trips. Rafting excursions can be organized on arrival in Kitulgala. Be sure to book with a reputable operator and check the quality of the gear.

18

Buduruwagala

E6 **37 km (23 miles) SE of Ella** **Dawn–dusk daily**

Increasingly popular with tourists, Buduruwagala boasts seven colossal rock-cut figures that are said to date from the 10th century. Carved in low relief, the impressive sculptures belong to the Mahayana school of Buddhism, which enjoyed royal patronage between the 3rd and 10th centuries AD.

In the centre is a 16-m-(52-ft-) high standing Buddha in the *abhaya mudra (p187)*, flanked on either side by a group of three sculptures. The central of the three figures to the Buddha's right is thought to represent Avalokitesvara, the *bodhisattva* of compassion in Mahayana Buddhism. He can be identified by the image of the meditating Buddha on the crown he wears. The figure still bears orange paint around the head and white stucco on the body; all the other sculptures may originally have been decorated in a similar fashion. The female figure to the right is thought to be the Mahayana goddess, Tara.

Among the group of figures to the left of the Buddha, the one in the centre is believed to be Maitreya, the fifth and future Buddha. The sculpture to his left depicts the Tibetan *bodhisattva* Vajrapani (or Sakra), holding a thunderbolt symbol, while the figure to his right is thought to be Vishnu.

19

Adisham Monastery

E6 **3 km (2 miles) W of Haputale** **9am–4:30pm Sat, Sun & *poya* days** **adisham.org**

Set in tranquil surroundings, a little west of Haputale, this monastery has an interesting history. It started life as a stately stone mansion, built in the 1930s by Sir Thomas Villiers, a British tea planter. Villiers named the place after the village in Kent where he was born. In the 1960s, the house was bought by the Sylvestro-Benedictine monastic order, and has functioned as a monastery ever since.

Visitors are permitted to see only a section of the monastery, which comprises the well-preserved living room and the library. The property is surrounded by orchards and features a well-manicured garden full of many varieties of orchids and roses. There is also a small shop on site that sells jams, cordials and jellies made by the monks.

> HIDDEN GEM
> ## Walk the Line
>
> A well-hidden walk follows the railway line from Haputale, past Adisham Monastery, to the ridgetop above Idalgashinna, where you can soak up breathtaking views. Ask locally for directions.

Ancient Buddhist statues carved in the rock at Buduruwagala ↓

← Visitors to the Sinharaja Forest Reserve, and the endemic Ceylon blue magpie *(inset)*

SRI LANKAN RAINFORESTS

Known as the wet zone, the southwestern lowlands of Sri Lanka are home to the last remaining rainforests in the country. The largest tract of rainforest in the area is Kanneliya-Dediyagala-Nakiyadeniya (KDN; *p122*), but human activities such as logging have had a serious impact on it. As a result, Sinharaja, albeit smaller, is considered the primary remnant of rainforest on the island, harbouring rare birds, insects and reptiles, as well as endemic mammals and butterflies.

20 🚫 Ⓜ️

Sinharaja Forest Reserve

🅐 D6 🚗 108 km (67 miles) SE of Ratnapura 🚌 From Ratnapura, then change at Kalawana to reach Kudawa ⏰ By guided tour only; 6am–6pm daily

The largest undisturbed rainforest in Sri Lanka, this reserve stretches over an area of 89 sq km (34 sq miles) and is bounded by the Gin Ganga river to the south and the Kalu Ganga river to the north. Sinharaja, meaning "Lion King", is believed by some to be the home of the mythological Sri Lankan lion from whom the Sinhalese trace their descent. Others believe it was once a royal reserve, when it covered an even larger expanse of the island's lowlands. What we know for certain is that the forest became the property of the British Crown in 1840. It suffered damage from logging in the early 1970s, until it was recognized as a reserve in 1977 and as a World Heritage Site by UNESCO in 1989. Careful management of the reserve aims to balance the needs of wildlife with those of the surrounding villages, whose inhabitants are still allowed to access the forest reserve to collect wood and tap kitul palms for making jaggery and palm wine.

Sinharaja receives up to 599 cm (236 inches) of rainfall annually and the climate inside the rainforest is hot and humid. The forest is a treasure trove of unique flora and fauna. Of the 211 tree species found here, over 60 per cent are endemic. The reserve supports a thriving bird population, with as many as 21 endemic species. These include the crested goshawk, Sri Lankan spurfowl, yellow-fronted barbet and the Ceylon blue magpie. A wide variety of rare butterflies, amphibians and reptiles, such as the rough-nose horned lizard, can also be glimpsed in this forest.

There are two entrances to the reserve, geographically close, but widely separated by road. Visitors approaching

> **Sinharaja, meaning "Lion King", is believed by some to be the home of the mythological Sri Lankan lion from whom the Sinhalese trace their descent.**

from Ratnapura should head for the Kudawa entrance. From the south coast, it is easier to reach the reserve via Deniyaya. Kudawa has a slightly better selection of accommodation, but Deniyaya is easier to reach by public transport.

The best time to visit Sinharaja is during the dry months, which extend from January to early April and August to September. It is compulsory to hire a guide to get around the forest. There are trails of varying lengths in the reserve, ranging from 5 km (3 miles) to 14 km (9 miles). Most tourists follow the 8-km (5-mile) Moulawella Trail, which begins at the Kudawa Conservation Centre and winds through the rainforest to the Moulawella Peak. There are a number of observation points along the trail, which offer great opportunities for wildlife-watching. Leeches abound because of the abundant rainfall so be sure to wear appropriate footwear.

㉑ Bambarakanda Falls

Ⓐ D6 **Ⓑ** 35 km (22 miles) W of Haputale **Ⓒ** To Kalupahana, then a three-wheeler to the falls

The Bambarakanda Falls, in the village of Kalupahana, are the highest on the island, at 240 m (787 ft). The falls are especially impressive after a spell of heavy rainfall, when they cascade down the rocks;

in the dry season, however, they can be reduced to little more than a trickle.

㉒ Diyaluma Falls

Ⓐ E6 **Ⓑ** 30 km (19 miles) SE of Haputale **Ⓒ**

The attractive Diyaluma Falls are the second-highest in Sri Lanka at 170 m (557 ft). A circuitous walk leads to the top of the falls, where it is possible to swim in one of the large natural bathing pools.

The hike to the pools begins at the bottom of the falls, from where it winds a few hundred metres east to the estate track that cuts through rubber plantations. Upon reaching the small rubber factory, bear left and head uphill on an indistinct and rough path. The climb takes about an hour each way. It is also possible to get a tuk-tuk to the half-way point and then to walk the last 30 minutes.

㉓ Ratnapura

Ⓐ D6 **Ⓑ** 92 km (57 miles) SW of Haputale **Ⓒ**

Ratnapura is best known as Sri Lanka's gem capital, and is surrounded by mines. The busy town is home to numerous gem museums, where visitors can see local precious stones as well as exhibits related to gem mining. At the heart of the town lies the clock tower, the area around which is the best place to watch locals buying and selling gems, including sapphires, zircons, garnets, rubies and cat's eyes.

Located 4 km (2 miles) west of Ratnapura, the **Maha Saman Devale** is dedicated to Saman, one of the island's guardian deities. There has been a temple on this site since the 13th century, although it was damaged by the Portuguese in the 16th century. The shrine was then restored during the Dutch era. As you enter, look for the carving that depicts a Portuguese invader killing a Sinhalese soldier.

Maha Saman Devale
Ⓐ Horana Road **Ⓑ** 6am–9pm daily

→ Buddhist devotees at the Maha Saman Devale, near Ratnapura

THE CULTURAL TRIANGLE

Home to five UNESCO World Heritage Sites, the Cultural Triangle was for many centuries the island's richest and most powerful region. It was in these northern plains in around 500 BC that early Sinhalese settlers founded the city of Anuradhapura, which would go on to dominate the island for well over a thousand years.

Much of this time was centred on Buddhism, which was adopted as the state religion in 246 BC. In fact, Mihintale, not far from Anuradhapura, is said to be where Mahinda introduced Buddhism to Sri Lanka. The kings of Anuradhapura saw themselves as protectors of the faith, building the vast monasteries and monuments whose remains can still be seen today. At the same time, they constructed a vast irrigation system, gradually transforming the arid surrounding plains to provide food to support the city's burgeoning population, which included thousands of monks.

Recurrent invasions from South India increasingly blighted Anuradhapura's fortunes, however, culminating in the devastating attack by Chola monarch Rajaraja in AD 993, during which the city was sacked and destroyed. A new capital was established at Polonnaruwa, to the southeast, during which early Sinhalese civilization enjoyed a magnificent second flowering before the Indians returned yet again in 1215. Monasteries were abandoned, irrigation works fell into disrepair, and the focus of Sri Lankan history shifted decisively south, never to return.

Palampiddy

Ambatta
Iluppaikulam

Madhu

Omanthai

Padaviya

A16

**JAFFNA AND
THE NORTH**
p206

A30

Vavuniya

*Padawiya
Tank*

B211

A9

A29

*Wahalkada
Tank*

Kebitigollewa

Nelumwila

A16

Medawachchiya

Rathmalgahawewa

Horowpotana

B283

B282

A12

Pemaduwa

A9

Hamillewa

Oyamaduwa

A20

Kahatagasdigiliya

**NORTH
CENTRAL**

*Wilpattu
National Park*

ANURADHAPURA
3

MIHINTALE
4

*Nuwara
Wewa*

Nochchiyagama

A12

Anuradhapura

A13

Galkulama

B133

**HURULU
ECO PARK**
12

Maragahawewa

Talawa

A28

*Nachchaduwa
Wewa*

Gal Oya

Saliyawewa

B563

Tambuttegama

B213

Yoda Ela

Eppawala

A9

*Ritigala Strict
Natural Reseve*

RITIGALA
16

A12

Meegalewa

B213

**THE WEST
COAST**
p86

AUKANA
15

HABARANA
10

A11

*Minneriya
Wewa*

Galgamuwa

SASSERUWA
17

*Kala
Wewa*

SIGIRIYA
1

B79

Anamaduwa

**JATHIKA NAMAL
UYANA**
8

B326

Saliyagama

A6

DAMBULLA
6

**POPHAM
ARBORETUM**
7

A10

Nikaweratiya

Daladagama

Maho

Madagalla

5

**DAMBULLA
CAVE
TEMPLES**

Bakamuna

YAPAHUWA
13

**NORTH
WESTERN**

Aluthgama

Elahera

A28

Kumbukgete

Aluthgama

NALANDA GEDIGE
22

Hiripitiya

ARANKELE
19

A6

CENTRAL

A9

Padeniya

Wariyapola

B423

Ridigama

B409

Palapatwela

Pallegama

14
**PANDUWAS
NUWARA**

A10

RIDI VIHARA
20

Kurunegala

ALUVIHARE
21

Mawatagama

MATALE
18

A10

0 kilometres   20

0 miles   20

N

**KANDY AND THE
HILL COUNTRY**
p132

Pulmoddai
Kuchchaveli
B424
Irakkandi
Gomarankadawala
A12 B424
Trincomalee
A6

Bay of Bengal

Mutur
A15

THE EAST
p190

Serunuwara

Alut Oya
A6

11 KAUDULLA
NATIONAL PARK

Minneriya **Hingurakgoda**
Hingurakgoda

9 MINNERIYA
NATIONAL PARK

Welikanda

2 POLONNARUWA
Parakrama Samudra
A11

Amban Ganga

Mahaweli Ganga

Wasgomuwa National Park

AB44 Aralaganwila

B517

Dehiattakandiya

Maduru Oya Reservoir

Madurd Oya National Park

Girandurukotte
A5

Padiyathalawa

A26

Mahiyanganaya

THE CULTURAL TRIANGLE

Must Sees

1 Sigiriya
2 Polonnaruwa
3 Anuradhapura
4 Mihintale
5 Dambulla Cave Temples

Experience More

6 Dambulla
7 Popham Arboretum
8 Jathika Namal Uyana
9 Minneriya National Park
10 Habarana
11 Kaudulla National Park
12 Hurulu Eco Park
13 Yapahuwa
14 Panduwas Nuwara
15 Aukana
16 Ritigala
17 Sasseruwa
18 Matale
19 Arankele
20 Ridi Vihara
21 Aluvihare
22 Nalanda Gedige

THE CULTURAL
TRIANGLE

❶ 🏊 🅜

SIGIRIYA

🅓D4 **🅐28 km (17 miles) NE of Dambulla** 🚌 **🕐6:30am–6pm daily (last entry around 5pm)**

Declared a UNESCO World Heritage site in 1982, the ancient citadel of Sigiriya (Lion Rock) sits atop a giant gneiss rock rising 200 m (656 ft) above the surrounding countryside. Ascend perilously perched stairs to discover legends, ancient frescoes *(p164)* and an amazing view at the summit.

There are conflicting theories about the history of Sigiriya, but according to the *Mahavamsa* King Kasyapa killed his father, King Dhatusena, in AD 477 to inherit the throne. Fearing retribution from his half-brother, Mogallana, Kasyapa built an impregnable palace-fortress on the summit of the rock between AD 477 and 485. The site is thought to have been occupied for millennia, but much of what can be seen here today is attributed to the time of King Kasyapa. The ruins were first discovered by British archaeologists in the early 20th century, and excavations have continued here ever since. Get here early to avoid the crowds.

KING KASYAPA

King Dhatusena initially chose Mogallana, Kasyapa's brother, as his successor. Enraged, Kasyapa rebelled, driving Mogallana into exile and executing his father (according to legend, by sealing him inside a brick chamber and leaving him to die). Established as king, Kasyapa constructed Sigiriya, his "fortress in the sky", but, when Mogallana returned to the area with an army, Kasyapa chose to abandon his impregnable citadel and engage him on the plains below, where he was promptly killed.

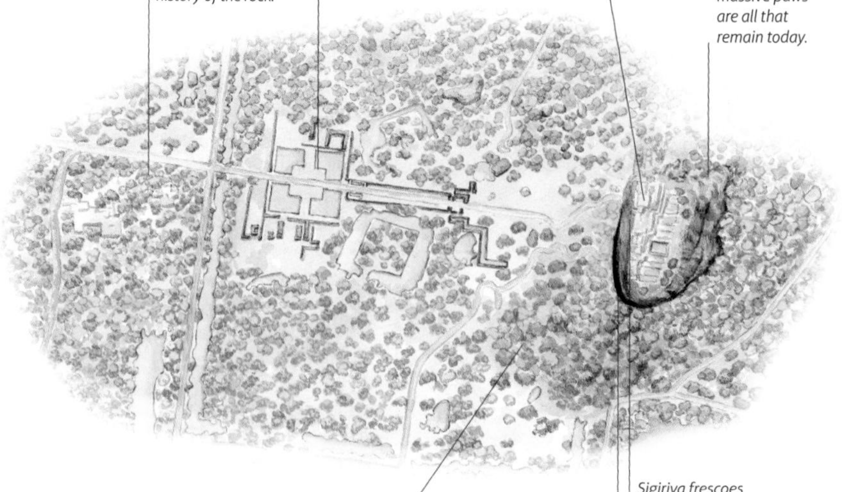

The landscaped Royal Gardens are divided into water, boulder and terrace gardens. The water gardens, with their brick-lined pools, form an avenue to the rock.

Nearly 2 ha (4 acres) in extent, the summit was once covered with buildings. Today, only the foundations can be seen. The main attraction here is the spectacular view over the water gardens and beyond.

At one time, a colossal brick lion guarded the stairway leading to the top of the rock. The lion's massive paws are all that remain today.

The Sigiriya Museum details the history of the rock.

Cistern and Audience Hall rocks

Cobra Hood Cave has a drip ledge with a Brahmi inscription dating from the 2nd century BC.

Sigiriya frescoes

The towering rock and majestic gardens that make up Sigiriya

An orange-clothed monk walking towards the soaring Sigiriya Rock ↑

Did You Know?

Beehives cling to the rock, from which swarms emerge to attack unwary visitors.

SIGIRIYA FRESCOES

One of the highlights of a visit to Sigiriya are the beautiful frescoes that can be seen in a sheltered gallery in the western rock face. Of the estimated original 500 frescoes, only 21 remain today, but they are remarkably well preserved, in part because of the protection afforded by the stone ledge. Dating from around the 5th century, the paintings were initially thought to depict Kasyapa's concubines but are now believed to be portraits of *apsaras* (celestial nymphs) with their attendants. However, a theory suggested by Dr Raja de Silva claims that these are actually depictions of the Mahayana goddess, Tara. Whatever the truth, they are one of the island's most iconic images.

STYLE AND TECHNIQUE

The paintings of the damsels are naturalistic in style, with each of the figures possessing a distinct character. The girls are mostly bare chested and adorned with jewellery. Guides are able to point out the errors made by the painter, such as the girl with three hands, or the one with three nipples. These errors only add to the frescoes' charm.

The principal colours used to paint these frescoes were red, yellow and brown; green was used only very occasionally. The colours were derived from natural materials, which were dried and crushed into pigment. The frescoes were then painted on wet plaster. As the paintings dried, the colours became permanently incorporated into the plaster.

↑ The towering outline of Sigiriya, home to the frescoes

↑ The vibrant frescoes on the wall of one of Sigiriya's caves

↑ The rickety spiral staircase leading up to the frescoes

DAMAGE AND RESTORATION

Some of the frescoes were defaced by a vandal in 1967. Italian restoration expert Luciano Maranzi was then brought in to help restore the damaged paintings. Since then, the frescoes have been damaged by exposure to the sun and by the insects that have nested beneath the plaster. There has been much discussion over their fading colours and how to counter this, as well as accusations of neglect.

APSARAS AND ATTENDANTS

An *apsara* is a celestial or water spirit in Hindu and Buddhist mythology. Painted on the ceilings of caves and temples, as well as carved on pillars and in bas-reliefs, these voluptuous mythical beings are often pictured dancing, attending to the gods or even hovering above the Buddha. The Sigiriya damsels are believed to be *apsaras*, and the figures carrying platters of flowers and fruit *(below)* are thought to be their attendants. This is attributed to their slightly darker skin tone and covered torsos.

2 ⌖

POLONNARUWA

⚠E4 🏠57 km (35 miles) E of Sigiriya 🚌 ☎(027) 222 4850 🕖7:30am–6pm daily (last entry at 5pm)

The ruins of Polonnaruwa are often considered the highlight of the Cultural Triangle and the city was the centrepiece of the Sinhalese kingdom established by King Vijayabahu I. Abandoned in 1293 and quickly consumed by the jungle, Polonnaruwa was excavated in the 20th century and declared a UNESCO World Heritage site in 1982.

①

Gal Vihara

One of the highlights of Polonnaruwa, Gal Vihara (the "Rock Monastery") houses four large Buddha statues

painstakingly carved from a single granite outcrop. Dating from the 12th century, the carvings were originally housed within brick shrines but now stand in the open air, protected from the elements

only by a rather ugly corrugated iron canopy.

Pride of place goes to the 14-m- (46-ft-) long reclining carving, depicting the Buddha at the moment of his entering nirvana. The figure's serene features, flecked with streaks of black sediment, rest on a pillow that is so skilfully carved that it looks soft enough to squeeze. Rising alongside is a 7-m- (23-ft-) high standing Buddha, which is posed in the unusual *paradukkha dukkhitha* ("sorrow for the sorrow of others") *mudra*, with its arms

←

Meditative Buddha statues, carved out of stone, at Gal Vihara

↑ An aerial view of the ruins at Polonnaruwa, an ancient city

③ Tivanka Patamaghara

Marking the northern edge of the ruins, the impressive Tivanka Patamaghara is one of the most flamboyant shrines found in the city. Indian influence is unmistakable in the richly decorated – although seriously eroded – exterior, which is covered in carvings. Look for the depictions of the *vimanas* (celestial abodes) of the gods, as well as assorted dwarfs and lions. Inside stands a headless Buddha in the unusual tivanka ("thrice-bent") posture, bent at the shoulder, waist and knee, after which the shrine is named. The walls are covered in an array of exceptionally fine murals – although the dim light and faded paintwork makes them difficult to see.

④ Demala Maha Seya

Located down a small side track at the far northern end of the site is the Demala Maha Seya, the remains of an ambitious attempt to build the world's largest stupa. Begun by King Parakramabahu, the structure was built by Tamil prisoners of war – hence the name, which means "Great Tamil Stupa."

Building work was never finished, which might not surprise you given the scale of the design – the circumference of the base alone measures a staggering 613 m (2,011 ft). Subsequently taken over by jungle, the stupa is slowly being excavated.

crossed across its chest. The statue is usually thought to depict a mourning Ananda – the Buddha's closest disciple – but it could also represent the Buddha himself. Two large, and much more ornate, seated Buddhas complete the gallery.

② Rankoth Vihara

Towering over the north of the ancient city is the gigantic Rankoth Vihara ("Gold-Pinnacled Shrine"). At 50 m (164 ft) tall, it's the fourth-largest stupa in Sri Lanka, surpassed only by the three great stupas of Anuradhapura. The *dagoba* was modelled on the great Ruwanwelisaya Dagoba at Anuradhapura, but subsequent renovations flattened the imitation's outline and reduced its original height somewhat. The plaster which originally covered the structure has also vanished, exposing the great hemisphere of bricks within.

Rankoth Vihara was built by Tamil prisoners of war, who were brought to the city by King Nissankamalla (r. 1187–96). An inscription on the left side of the entrance path attests to their struggle.

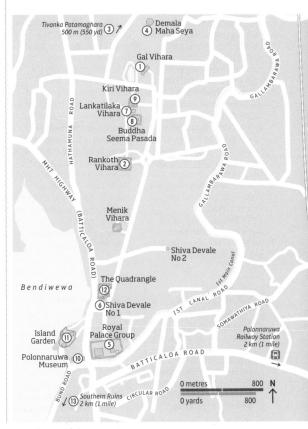

↑ Exploring the Royal Palace Group, the remains of a brick construction

⑤ Royal Palace Group

At the centre of the ancient city is the Royal Palace Group, where King Parakramabahu's grand palace, also known as Vejayanta Prasada, and other buildings were once protected by heavy fortifications. The palace is believed to have originally stood seven storeys high with a thousand rooms, although all that remains today is a three-storey building made of brick. Despite its diminished proportions, it's still possible to imagine the palace's former glory. The palace's great hall had a roof supported by 30 columns, and visitors can still see the holes in the walls that held the beams in place.

To the east of the palace is the Council Chamber, or Audience Hall, where the king would have met with his advisors and various officials. The roof of the chamber is long gone, but the base still remains, decorated with friezes depicting dwarves, lions and elephants. The staircase leading up to the landing has a fine moonstone at its base, ornamented balustrades, and two lions flanking the top step.

Towards the east of the Council Chamber are the unusual geometric-shaped Royal Baths. It is thought that this area may have been a pleasure garden with trees and flowers surrounding the baths. Nearby are the remains of what was probably a bathhouse, where the royals would have probably got changed before and after submerging themselves in the water. It, too, is decorated with the usual lions and moonstone.

---

⑥ Shiva Devale No 1

Located north of the Royal Palace Group, this is one of the many shrines at Polonnaruwa dedicated to Lord Shiva. The temple is thought to have been built during a period of South Indian occupation of Polonnaruwa in the 13th century. Peculiarly, no mortar was used in the construction of the shrine, instead the stones fit together perfectly. Look out for the *lingam* (a phallic symbol representing Shiva) in the inner sanctum. Some very fine bronze statues that were found here are now on display in the Colombo National Museum (*p66*).

---

⑦ Lankatilaka Vihara

One of the tallest buildings to survive from ancient Sri Lanka, this image house was built by Parakramabahu I. The towering walls of the shrine enclose a huge, albeit headless, standing Buddha statue. Do not miss the bas-relief on the exterior walls, which shows elaborate multistorey *vimanas* (palaces).

---

⑧ Buddha Seema Pasada

Situated near Lankatilaka, Buddha Seema Pasada was

> **INSIDER TIP**
> **It's Wheelie Good Fun**
>
> Thanks to the flat terrain, lack of traffic and modest distances involved, the most pleasant way to explore Polonnaruwa is on two wheels. Hire a bike from a nearby guesthouse.

→ Walking around the Kiri Vihara, the white *dagoba* surrounded by bricks

> *Kiri* means milk in Sinhalese, and the *dagoba* was named after the bright white lime plaster covering it, which was found in perfect condition when the building was discovered.

a large chapter house within a monastery complex. It is said that, due to the thickness of the remaining supporting walls, the original structure that stood here was as tall as 12 storeys. The upper levels would have been constructed from wood, which quickly rotted away.

Monks' cells surround a pillared hall with a raised platform at its centre, which is thought to have been reserved for the highest-ranking member of the monastery. The hall is connected to the inner courtyard by four entrances, each decorated with a moonstone.

---

⑨

Kiri Vihara

Towards the north of Lankatilaka lies the Kiri

Vihara, a *dagoba* very similar in style to the Rankoth Vihara (*p167*). It is believed to have been dedicated to one of King Parakramabahu's wives, Subhadra. *Kiri* means milk in Sinhalese, and the *dagoba* was named after the bright white lime plaster covering it, which was found in perfect condition when the building was discovered after seven centuries shrouded in under-growth. The base of Kiri Vihara is encircled by shrines that seem straight out of English author Rudyard Kipling's novel *The Jungle Book* (1894).

---

⑩

Polonnaruwa Museum

🕑 7:30am–5:30pm daily

The museum exhibits artifacts recovered from the site, including beautiful bronze statues. Look for

the figure of the god Shiva performing a cosmic dance on the head of a dwarf. This dwarf symbolizes ignorance and nonsensical speech. These statues of Hindu deities show the influence of South Indian beliefs on the ancient city's culture. Alongside these illuminating religious objects, you'll find scale models showing how the city's buildings would have looked in their heyday. These reconstructions make the museum a good starting point for your visit to Polonnaruwa. You'll see how the buildings looked in their prime before setting out to explore the modern reality. It's amazing that so much of the original city remains.

Did You Know?

Many of Polonnaruwa's Buddhist kings married Hindu wives from South India.

⑪ Island Garden

Just behind the Polonnaruwa Museum lie the ruins of Nissankamalla's royal palace, which was built on the site of Parakramabahu's pleasure gardens. The complex comprises the remains of several buildings, but the most interesting structure is the Council Chamber. Although the roof has now gone, the plinth, and four rows of columns that presumably balanced the roof, survive. At the southern end of the plinth is a large granite lion, most likely marking the position of Nissankamalla's throne. The columns nearest to the lion have inscriptions identifying dignitaries, such as the prime minister, the record keeper and members of the chamber of commerce, who sat next to them during meetings with the king.

Towards the south of the Council Chamber is a stone mausoleum, possibly the site of Nissankamalla's cremation. The remains of the Royal Baths, fed by underground pipes from the Parakrama Samudra, are nearby. Also close to the Council Chamber is a mound where the remains of King Parakramabahu's Summer House can be found.

---

⑫ The Quadrangle

North of Shiva Devale No 1 (p168) is the Quadrangle. This complex is home to a number of fascinating buildings,

The Council Chamber in the Island Garden, and *(inset)* the granite lion on the plinth ↓

PICTURE PERFECT Polonnaruwa Photo

Arrive early, or stay late, when the long shadows emphasize the site's sculptural details to great effect. The richly decorated buildings of the Quadrangle are particularly striking.

including the Vatadage –one of the most beautiful sights in Polonnaruwa. A relic house built by Parakramabahu, the Vatadage comprises a central *dagoba* set on a raised terrace, surrounded by a brick wall.

Located opposite the Vatadage, the Hatadage is a Tooth Relic temple built by Nissankamalla, which was originally a two-storey building. A beautiful moonstone adorns the entrance, and inside the shrine are three Buddha statues. Adjacent lies the Atadage that was built by Vijayabahu I to house the

Tooth Relic when Polonnaruwa was made the capital of the kingdom. Only a few pillars and the base remain.

On the other side of the Hatadage is Gal Pota, a large granite slab that weighs over 25 tons (28 tonnes) and is over 8 m (26 ft) long. The inscriptions on it relate the works of King Nissankamalla. Beside Gal Pota is the Satmahal Prasada, which was built to a stepped design.

Close to the gate west of the Vadatage is Nissankalata, also known as the Lotus Mandapa. This small *dagoba* is set on a platform, encircled by stone pillars that are shaped like thrice-bent lotus buds on stalks. It is believed that Nissankamalla used this platform to listen to the chanting of religious texts.

The last of the Quadrangle's shrines is the Thuparama, set in the southwest corner. An image house that dates to the time of Vijayabahu, this ancient structure houses eight Buddha statues, some of which date from the

Brightly clothed monks walking from the Vatadage, an ancient relic house

Anuradhapura period. The thick walls of the shrine have loopholes that allow sunlight to penetrate inside, enabling the limestone crystals in the Buddha statues to sparkle.

⑬
Southern Ruins
A short distance away from the rest of the ruins is Polonnaruwa's southern site. Visitors can either take a pleasant walk or cycle along the bank of the Parakrama Samudra to reach these ruins. Here lies the well-preserved Potgul Vihara, a monastery complex comprising, among other ruins, four *dagobas* that surround a circular brick building. The central structure, with its thick walls, is thought to have housed a library of sacred books. Some believe that it was built by Parakramabahu as a place where he could listen to a great Brahmanical sage named Pulasti.

To the north of Potgul Vihara is a large 4-m- (12-ft-) high statue of a bearded figure carved from a rock. It is notable for being less stylized than the other sculptures in Polonnaruwa. It is said by some that the statue is that of King Parakramabahu I himself. Others believe that it is a representation of a sage, possibly Kapila or Pulasti.

Did You Know?
Parakrama Samudra translates as "Sea of Parakrama".

Must See

171

ANURADHAPURA

Ⓐ D3 **⬀ 70 km (43 miles) NE of Yapahuwa** 🚉🚌 **☏ (025) 222 7640**
🕐 **7:30am–6pm daily (last entry 5pm)**

Founded in the 5th century BC, Anuradhapura was one of Sri Lanka's greatest centres of political and religious power until it fell to the Cholas in the 10th century. The ancient city is home to temples, immense *dagobas*, pools and ruined palaces, all of which hint at the splendour of the place at the height of its power during the 9th century AD.

①
Ruwanwelisaya Dagoba

At the centre of Anuradhapura is the majestic Ruwanwelisaya Dagoba, also known as the Maha Thupa or "Great Stupa", despite being smaller than the other great stupas. At 55 m (180 ft) high, this is one of the ancient city's most prominent landmarks, and it serves as a useful navigational aid when exploring the city.

Ruwanwelisaya is the oldest and most revered of the city's three great stupas. It was constructed by the legendary Sinhalese king Dutugemunu after his victory over the Tamil general Elara in around 161 BC. Look for the weatherbeaten statue in a glass case, which is believed to represent Dutugemunu himself.

According to legend, the *dagoba* was originally built in the shape of a bubble but subsequent restorations have changed its appearance. It still stands on an enormous raised platform, however, supported by a striking wall, formed of a frieze of elephants. Four smaller stupas mark the corners of the platform and elaborate shrines *(valkahadas)* are attached to its base.

> 💬 INSIDER TIP
> **Take a Tuk-Tuk**
>
> Cycling is a great way to explore Anuradhapura, but some people prefer to take a tuk-tuk, given the distances involved and how easy it is to get lost. Be aware that some drivers overcharge.

②
Jetavana Monastery

East of the Ruwanwelisaya stretches the second of ancient Anuradhapura's three great monasteries: Jetavana. At the centre of the complex is the Jetavanaramaya Dagoba, whose gigantic red-brick outline is visible from across the city.

Did You Know?

Anuradhapura's Queen Anula (r 47–42 BC) is thought to be Asia's first female head of state.

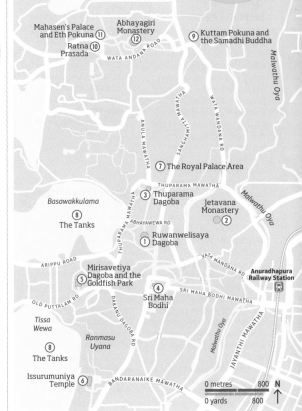

① Ruwanwelisaya Dagoba

② Jetavana Monastery

③ Thuparama Dagoba

④ Sri Maha Bodhi

⑤ Mirisavetiya Dagoba and the Goldfish Park

⑥ Issurumuniya Temple

⑦ The Royal Palace Area

⑧ The Tanks

⑨ Kuttam Pokuna and the Samadhi Buddha

⑩ Ratna Prasada

⑪ Mahasen's Palace and Eth Pokuna

⑫ Abhayagiri Monastery

WATA ANDANA ROAD

ANULA MAWATHA

SANGHAMITTA MAWATHA

WATA WANDANA RD

Malwathu Oya

THUPARAMA MAWATHA

Basawakkulama

ABHAYAWEWA RD

ARIPPU ROAD

OLD PUTTALAM RD

Tissa Wewa

DAKANU DAGOBA RD

Ranmasu Uyana

BANDARANAIKE MAWATHA

VATA MANDANA RD

SRI MAHA BODHI MAWATHA

Anuradhapura Railway Station

Malwathu Oya

JAYANTHI MAWATHA

0 metres 800
0 yards 800

N

The stupa originally reached a height of 120 m (394 ft), making it the fourth-tallest structure in the ancient world after the two great pyramids of Giza and the *pharos* (light-house) of Alexandria. Time and later renovations have significantly reduced its size, although the *dagoba* still reaches an impressive 70 m (230 ft) and it is thought to be the largest structure in the world built entirely of bricks – an astonishing 90 million were used in its construction.

Scattered all around the parkland surrounding the stupa are the foundations of the former monastery buildings, which once housed around 3,000 monks. Many finds recovered from the area are displayed at the interesting Jetavana Museum, including beautiful carvings, some exquisite jewellery, and an interesting urinal pot – the ultimate in fifth-century bathroom luxury.

Immediately north of the museum, look out for the finely preserved bathing pool and the so-called "Buddhist Railing", an unusual kind of stone fence.

③

Thuparama Dagoba

A short walk north of the Rawanwelisaya sits the modest Thuparama, one of the smallest but most revered of Sri Lanka's major stupas. The original Thuparama is

←

Jetavanaramaya Dagoba, and *(inset)* a fresco on the stupa's ceiling

believed to have been built by King Devanampiya Tissa following his conversion to Buddhism in 247 BC, making it the oldest in Sri Lanka, but most of what you see today is the result of an 1862 recon-struction. The picturesquely lopsided pillars that surround the *dagoba* would originally have supported a sloping roof and are the work of King Aggabodhi II (r 598–608).

Stretching between Thuparama Dagoba and Ruawanwelisaya Dagoba are the extensive remains of Mahavihara, the oldest and most prestigious of Anuradhapura's three great monasteries. Worth a look is the magnificent moonstone, around 100 m (328 ft) south of Thuparama, which is one of the most beautiful in the city.

④
Sri Maha Bodhi

South of the Ruwanwelisaya Dagoba is the Sri Maha Bodhi, or "Sacred Bo Tree", which has a fair claim to being the most holy tree on Earth. Offering a direct link to the Buddha himself, the tree is said to have been grown from a cutting taken from the bodhi (bo) tree in Bodhgaya, in northern India, beneath which the Buddha himself attained enlightenment some time in around 450 BC. The tree is believed to have been transported to Sri Lanka by Princess Sangamitta, the sister of Mahinda, the monk who brought Buddhism to Sri Lanka.

The original Indian tree perished not long after this event, but its Sri Lankan descendant is still going strong today, albeit partly propped up on iron crutches. Festooned in prayer flags, and surrounded by an elaborate series of golden-railed platforms, the tree attracts a steady stream of pilgrims. Dressed in traditional white robes, these visitors sit quietly around Sri Maha Bodhi in quiet prayer and meditation, while large crowds descend during poya days, particularly during Poson Poya in June.

HIDDEN GEM
Stop Write Now

South of Issurumuniya Temple are the little-visited remains of the Vessagiriya Monastery. Look for the ancient characters carved onto the rocks dotting the site. They are some of the oldest inscriptions in Sri Lanka.

⑤
Mirisavetiya Dagoba and the Goldfish Park

Due west of the Sri Maha Bodhi, the imposing white Mirisavetiya stupa was the first structure to be built here by King Dutugemunu. He is said to have built it on the site where his spear stuck in the ground. It looks rather like a trial run for the later and larger Ruwanwelisaya, with which it shares many similarities. The remains of many monastic buildings lie scattered around the dagoba.

Further south lie the remains of the former royal pleasure gardens, known as the Goldfish Park after the fish which were once kept in the twin pools here. These baths are decorated with quaint elephant friezes.

↑ The colourful reclining Buddha in the striking Issurumuniya Temple

⑥
Issurumuniya Temple

Squeezed between a striking pair of rock outcrops on the shores of Tissa Wewa, the small and intimate Issurumuniya Temple offers a complete change of scale to the grandiose monuments further north. Dating back to the reign of Sri Lanka's first Buddhist monarch, King Devanampiya Tissa, the temple is best known for its reclining Buddha and celebrated carvings. The latter are housed in a small museum on the site. Highlights of the collection include The Lovers, showing a man and a woman sat beside each other. The stone relief most likely represents a bodhisattva and his consort, but popular legend claims that the pair are Prince Saliya, son of King Dutugemunu, and his wife Asokamala. In order to marry a woman from a low caste, Saliya had to renounce the throne. It's an incredibly romantic story.

↑ Buddhist pilgrims at the entrance to Sri Maha Bodhi

Outside the museum, steps lead up to a viewing platform that overlooks the lake and assorted stupas. Look out for the base of the giant Sandahiru Seya ("Stupa of Triumph"), which is currently under construction. The first *dagoba* to be built in Anuradhapura for over 2,000 years, this stupa was commissioned in 2010 by President Mahinda Rajapaksa to commemorate the soldiers who were killed while fighting the LTTE in the Civil War. The stupa will be 95 m (312 ft) tall when it is finished, but it's still some way off completion.

← Carving of the demon Bahirawa on the guard-stone of the Royal Palace

⑦
The Royal Palace Area

The area north of Jetavana Monastery is where the city's royal precinct was once located. It's hard to imagine this former majesty when you survey the disorientating jumble of ruins that now stand here. The palace was commissioned by Vijayabahu I after his victory over the Cholas in 1070. Only the terrace survives, its steps flanked by two exceptionally fine guardstones. This carved pair of obese dwarves actually represent the Buddhist demon Bahirawa. A few flecks of paint on a wall of the terrace are all that remains of the palace's original frescoes.

Opposite the palace are the scattered remains of the Mahapali Refectory. Check out the stone trough, which would have been filled with rice on a daily basis by the citizens of Anuradhapura for the benefit of any monk in need of nourishment.

STAY

Palm Garden Village Hotel
Serene rural retreat, with low-slung bungalows and a sensationally large pool.

🏠 Puttalam Road
🌐 palmgarden village.com

$$$

———

The Sanctuary at Tissawewa
Anuradhapura's most atmospheric lodgings occupy a rambling colonial mansion, which was once home to the local British governor.

🏠 Old Puttalam Road
🌐 tissawewa.com

$$$

———

Milano Tourist Rest
A great money-saving option, Milano Tourist Rest is also home to one of the best restaurants in town.

🏠 Harischandra Mawatha 🌐 milano touristrest.com

$$$

↑ Kuttam Pokuna bathing pool, and (inset) the nearby serene Samadhi Buddha

⑧ The Tanks

Anuradhapura stands at the centre of one of the ancient world's greatest irrigation systems, with hundreds of reservoirs (or "tanks", as they're locally known). Some of these tanks are many miles wide and they are connected by an intricate system of canals and conduits. It was these reservoirs that helped transform Sri Lanka's arid northern plains into a huge rice bowl, funding the construction of Anuradhapura and providing food for the enormous community of monks who filled the ancient city's monasteries.

Anuradhapura itself lies nestled between three major tanks: the Basawakkulama, Tissa Wewa and Nuwara Wewa. The largest of these tanks is Nuwara Wewa, which

lies to the east and is spread over an area of 120 sq km (46 sq miles). Built around 20 BC, it was expanded by later kings. To the south lies the 160-ha (395-acre) Tissa Wewa, which was built by King Devanampiya Tissa, and to the north is the city's oldest tank, the 120-ha (296-acre) Basawakkulama, which is said to date back to the 4th century BC. These tanks still provide the city with water, cooling breezes and some memorable views. Basawakkulama offers particularly fine panoramas of the Ruwanwelisaya and Mirisavetiya *dagobas* rising above the placid blue waters.

The tanks play as essential a role in modern-day life as they did during the Anuradhapura period as they provide essential washing facilities for local laundry ladies and housewives. They can be seen pummelling dirty clothes into submission at many places around the tanks.

⑨ Kuttam Pokuna and the Samadhi Buddha

To the east of Abhayagiri Dagoba are the elegant Kuttam Pokuna bathing pools. Although known as the "twin ponds", these two pools differ significantly in size. While the northern pond measures 40 m (131 ft) in length, the one to the south is 28 m (92 ft) long. They were built in the 8th century, and were probably used by the monastery's monks for ritual ablutions, as there are steps from each side leading into the water. The tanks used an ingenious hydraulic system whereby water was pumped from the ground into the smaller tank, before being fed into the second, larger tank.

A short walk southeast of the pools is the serene Samadhi Buddha. Dating from the 4th century AD, this limestone sculpture of the meditating Buddha is a classic example of early Sinhalese sculpture. Three companion statues once sat alongside, but all have now vanished, save for a single pair of legs.

a royal dwelling). The moonstone here is perhaps the most beautiful one in Anuradhapura. It dates from around the 8th century, and features five circles representing the journey to Nirvana.

Due south of Mahasen's Palace, it's a short stroll through beautiful woodland to the vast Eth Pokuna ("Elephant Pool"). The largest pool in the ancient city, this might also be considered one of the world's biggest bathtubs, built to provide washing facilities for the Abhayagiri Monastery's 5,000 monks.

---

⑫

Abhayagiri Monastery

North of the Royal Palace Area are the sprawling remains of the Abhayagiri Monastery. The ruins here are the most varied in the city, magically scattered around large swathes of sylvan forest. It's easy to get lost amid the winding woodland paths. As at the Jetavana Monastery, Abhayagiri has a dedicated museum housing an

impressive collection of artifacts recovered during excavations, including some fine sculptures.

The third of Anuradhapura's great stupas, the Abhayagiri Dagoba, marks the site of the ancient monastery. Built in 88 BC by Vattagamini Abhaya, the *dagoba* formerly stood at 115 m (377 ft) tall. When the structure lost its pinnacle, however, it was reduced to a height of 70 m (230 ft). The monastery is known for its unusual urns, which symbolize abundance and plenty. The entrance is flanked by statues of the dwarfish deities Padmanidhi and Samkanidhi.

Did You Know?

Elements of Tantric Buddhism were taught at the Abhayagiri Monastery.

⑩

Ratna Prasada

Founded on the outskirts of the city, this monastery dates from the 8th century. The monks who lived in this monastery were known for giving sanctuary to those in need. Check out the extraordinary guardstone next to the entrance. The stone's convoluted sculptural design features a *nagaraja* (snake god) standing on a dwarf. The god is sheltered by a cobra with seven heads, resembling both animals and humans.

---

⑪

Mahasen's Palace and Eth Pokuna

Another exquisite, although somewhat less surreal, piece of carving can be found at the nearby Mahasen's Palace (actually a shrine rather than

→

The steps leading up to Abhayagiri Monastery, a great stupa

④ 🏛

MIHINTALE

🅐D3 🚗15 km (9 miles) E of Anuradhapura 🚌From Anuradhapura 🕐6am–6pm daily

The sacred hill of Mihintale is where Mahinda, son of the Indian King Asoka, converted King Devanampiya Tissa to Buddhism in the 3rd century BC. Exploring the site involves long climbs, so it is a good idea to visit it early in the morning or late in the afternoon.

① Hospital Ruins

The ruins of a 9th-century hospital built during the reign of King Sena II can be seen near the car park. Upon entering the ruins, visitors will come across a stone trough with its interior carved in the shape of a human form. This is thought to have been used as a medical bath where patients were immersed in healing oils.

② Stairway

Shaded by frangipani trees, the stairway leading to the summit of Mihintale comprises 1,840 rock-cut steps inter-spersed with terraces that allow visitors to catch their breath. While the first flight of stairs is broad and shallow, the ones higher up are narrower and steeper.

③ Kantaka Chetiya

At the first small landing, steps lead off on the right to the remains of the Kantaka Chetiya Dagoba, the oldest at Mihintale. Originally over 30 m (98 ft) high, the *dagoba* now stands at a height of only 12 m (39 ft). Look for the carvings of geese, elephants, flowers and birds on the *dagoba's* doors and columns. South of here is an enormous boulder bearing an ancient inscription in early proto-Brahmi script.

④ Refectory Terrace

Situated on the left side of the second landing, the refectory has big stone troughs that would have been filled with food such as rice or porridge for the monks. On the terrace directly above is the image house, the entrance to which is flanked by two large stone

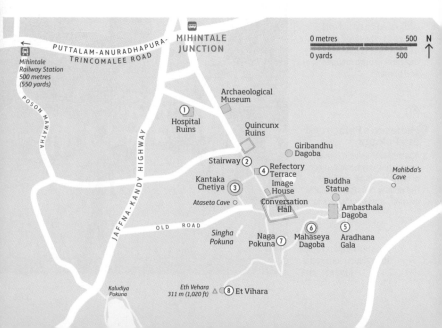

↑ The view over Mihintale from Aradhana Gala

slabs inscribed in Sinhalese. Erected during the reign of King Mahinda IV (r 975–991), these tablets detail the rules and responsibilities for monks in the monastery. A short distance to the south lie the ruins of the Conversation Hall, where the monks would meet.

To the right of the terrace is the small Singha Pokuna (Lion Pool), which is named after the weathered sculpture of a lion whose mouth served as the waterspout. The frieze above the lion sculpture is decorated with fine carvings of dancers and elephants.

---

⑤
Aradhana Gala

A set of steep stairs leads up to the upper terrace, where visitors have to buy a ticket and remove their shoes and hats. At the centre of the terrace is the Ambasthala Dagoba, which is believed to mark the spot where Mahinda met King Devanampiya Tissa. Next to it is a stone carving of the Buddha's footprint surrounded by railings and with coins offered by pilgrims

scattered all over it. The ancient headless statue nearby is said to be of King Devanampiya Tissa. On the opposite side of the terrace are steps leading up to the big white seated Buddha statue.

East of the Ambasthala Dagoba, a flight of rock-cut steps leads to Aradhana Gala (Meditation Rock), from where there are great views of the surrounding countryside and the grand Mahaseya Dagoba.

A path from the upper terrace leads down to Mahinda's Cave – a space beneath a huge boulder with a large flat stone believed to have been his bed.

---

⑥
Mahaseya Dagoba

From the southwest corner of the terrace, steps lead up to the summit where the 14-m- (45-ft-) high Mahaseya Dagoba stands. The *dagoba* is clearly visible from a distance and is where Mahinda's relics are said to be interred. There are wonderful views stretching southwest to the *dagobas* of Anuradhapura from here.

⑦
Naga Pokuna

After seeing the Mahaseya Dagoba, visitors retrace their steps to pick up their shoes and head down the stairs from the Ambasthala Dagoba. A path leads off to the left to Naga Pokuna (Snake Pool). This peaceful spot was named after the five-headed cobra carved on the rock face of the pool. This pool supplied water to the monastery below.

---

⑧
Et Vihara

A flight of around 600 steps leads to the ruins of the Et Vihara *dagoba*, located at the highest point in Mihintale.

Did You Know?

The name Mihintale is a contraction of *Mihinda Tale* – "Mahinda's Hill".

DAMBULLA CAVE TEMPLES

D4 **Off Kandy-Jaffna Highway, 47 km (29 miles) N of Matale** **(066) 228 3605** **7am–7pm daily**

At Dambulla, a network of caves is the incongruous setting for five beautifully painted temples, filled with statues of the Buddha in various sizes and *mudras*.

INSIDER TIP
Just the Ticket

When visiting the cave temples, be sure to buy your tickets from the office in the Golden Temple at the bottom, close to the main road. From the ticket office, it's a steep 15-minute walk up to the five cave temples themselves.

The caves are carved out of a granite outcrop that towers 100 m (350 ft) above Dambulla (*p182*). Inside, the temples date back to the 1st century BC, when King Valagambahu (r 103 BC and 89–77BC) sought refuge here after being exiled from Anuradhapura. When the king regained his throne, he converted the caves into temples in gratitude to the monks who had offered him sanctuary. The walls and ceilings are adorned with murals, dating from between the 2nd century and 18th century AD, depicting religious and secular themes.

The vibrantly painted interior of Cave II, the largest of Dambulla's cave temples →

↑ The entrance to the cave temples, under an overhanging rock

Did You Know?

The caves are man-made – built beneath an over-hanging rock.

Cave Highlights

Cave I (Devaraja Viharaya)

The highlight here is a 14-m- (46-ft-) long reclining Buddha, carved out of solid rock. A statue thought to be of Ananda, the Buddha's loyal disciple, stands at his feet. The paintings on the walls and ceiling of this cave are faded by smoke from incense.

Cave II (Maharaja Viharaya)

The largest and the most impressive, this cave contains a painted wooden statue of King Valagambahu and another statue of King Nissankamalla (r 1187–96), in addition to a large number of Buddha statues. The murals here depict the life of the Buddha, as well as scenes from the history of Sri Lanka.

Cave III (Maha Alut Viharaya)

▷ King Kirti Sri Rajasinghe (r 1747–82) converted this cave from a storeroom in the 18th century. The reclining Buddha by the left wall *(right)* is carved out of rock, as is the Buddha figure facing the entrance. The frescoes here are largely painted in the Kandyan style.

Cave IV (Pascima Viharaya)

Relatively small in size, this cave contains a *dagoba* in the middle that was broken into by thieves who thought it contained some of the jewels of Queen Somawathie, wife of King Valagambahu. The cave also contains a splendid seated Buddha under an elaborate makara torana, along with several larger seated Buddhas.

Cave V (Devana Alut Viharaja)

◁ This cave is the newest and smallest of the temples. Unlike the statues in the other caves, some of which are carved out of rock, the images here are built of brick and plaster. The cave features a 10-m (33-ft) reclining Buddha *(left)*, and on the wall, behind his feet, are paintings of the Hindu deities Vishnu and Kataragama.

EXPERIENCE MORE

6

Dambulla

D4 47 km (29 miles)
N of Matale

A small town situated in the
heart of the Cultural Triangle,
Dambulla lies at a junction of
the Kandy-to-Anuradhapura
and Colombo-to-Trincomalee
roads. There are several accommodation options in town and
in the surrounding countryside, so Dambulla serves as a
good base for exploring sights
in the nearby area. While
most visitors come here to
see the famous Dambulla Cave
Temples *(p180)*, the town's
museums are also worth
checking out.

The imposing golden
Buddha statue at the foot of
the steps leading up to the
Dambulla Cave Temples is hard
to miss. This 30-m- (98-ft-)
high image portrays the
Buddha in the *dharmachakra*
(wheel-turning) pose. At the
base of the statue lies the
**Golden Temple Buddhist
Museum**, the entrance to
which is through the mouth
of a kitsch-looking dragon.
Exhibits on display include
Buddha statues from Thailand,
Myanmar, Korea and Japan,

panels illustrating the story
of the Buddha's life, *ola*-leaf
manuscripts, many paintings
of drummers and *peraheras*
(religious festivals), as well
as a number of artifacts.

A short distance south of
the Golden Temple Buddhist
Museum stands **Dambulla
Museum** which traces the
history of Sri Lankan art from
cave paintings to the colonial
era. The museum exhibits
accurate canvas repro-
ductions of both well-known
and lesser-known frescoes
and murals from all over the
island. It's a great way to see
art that would otherwise
remain inaccessible.

On the first floor is an
excellent exhibition detailing
the history of mural painting
in Sri Lanka. The seven rooms
here are in chronological order
and begin with the rock and
wall paintings of the Veddahs,
before moving through to the
frescoes of Sigiriya, the 12th-
century wall paintings at
Polonnaruwa, and works from
the prolific Kandyan period.
The exhibition finishes with
reproductions of early 20th-
century paintings. The
museum also explains
the 21st-century
tradition of

painting scenes on Buddhist
shrines depicting the tortures
inflicted in hell.

Golden Temple Buddhist Museum

In the Dambulla Cave
Temples complex (066)
228 3606 6:30am–
7pm daily

Dambulla Museum

Main Road (066)
228 4760 8:30am–
4:30pm daily

7

Popham Arboretum

D4 Kandalama Road,
3 km (2 miles) E of Dambulla
 (077) 726 7951 6am–
10pm daily

Founded in 1963 by British
tea planter and dendrologist
(someone who studies shrubs)
Sam Popham, this is the only
dry-zone arboretum in Sri
Lanka. When Popham bought
this abandoned piece of land,
it was covered with scrub. After
clearing the scrub vegetation,
he noticed that the indigenous
trees, which were unable to
grow previously owing to the
dense cover, were starting to

STAY

Heritance Kandalama

Designed by Geoffrey Bawa, the Kandalama is one of Sri Lanka's great hotels, half-hidden under a lush canopy of jungle, near Dambulla.

D4 **Dambulla** **heritancehotels.com**

$$$

Back of Beyond Dehigaha Ela

Nestled in pristine jungle, this eco-retreat near Sigiriya offers tree houses, as well as more traditional options.

D4 **Dehigaha Ela, near Sigiriya** **backof beyond.lk**

$$$

↑ Pink quartz hills and Na trees in rarely visited Jathika Namal Uyana forest reserve

thrive. Following this observation, he developed the "Popham Method", an experiment in reforesting that involved selectively clearing a scrub jungle so that native trees could seed and grow.

Spread over an area of 14 ha (35 acres), the arboretum has around 200 species of trees and shrubs, including many endemic ones. Among the tropical trees here are satinwood, ebony, tamarind and ironwood, which in turn provide habitat for a number of small mammals and a variety of birds such as the endemic Sri Lankan jungle fowl, the grey hornbill and the blue-tailed bee eater.

Designed by Geoffrey Bawa, the visitor centre

←

The Golden Temple Buddhist Museum with the Golden Buddha statue behind

of the arboretum used to be Popham's home before he left Sri Lanka in the 1980s and headed back to the UK.

There are three colour-coded trails, all beginning at the visitor centre, that meander through the arboretum grounds. Visitors can explore these trails independently, or arrange for a guided walk. It's also possible to book an hour-long evening walk (starting at 6:45pm), when there is a chance of sighting elusive nocturnal mammals in the park, including slender loris, spotted deer and pangolin.

---

8 🖊️

Jathika Namal Uyana

D4 **7 km (4 miles) NW of Dambulla** **(025) 325 3816** **From Dambulla** **6am– 6:30pm daily**

Seldom visited by tourists, Jathika Namal Uyana, in Ulpathgama, is the perfect destination for those who enjoy walking and wildlife-watching. Covering an area of more than 105 ha (260 acres), it is said to be the largest Na tree, or ironwood, forest in Asia. The forest is home to diverse flora as well as a wide range of birds, butterflies, lizards and mammals, such as monkeys and giant squirrels. It is believed that the forest

was planted by King Devanampiya Tissa in the 3rd century BC. However, another legend states that the forest was a sanctuary for Buddhist monks in the 8th century. These monks offered refuge to people in need, and all those who took shelter here had to plant a tree and tend to it, which eventually resulted in the large forest that can be seen today. The area is dotted with various monastic remains, and there are also the ruins of a stupa near the entrance, backing up the myth.

Besides Na trees, Jathika Namal Uyana is also famous for a range of pink quartz hills, which is made up of seven peaks and is thought to date back more than 550 million years. A small, pink Buddha statue stands on the summit of the lowest hill, and can be reached by following a gently rising forest trail, crisscrossed with streams. There are great views of the surrounding countryside from the top.

Did You Know?

The hills at Jathika Namal Uyana are pink because of traces of manganese, titanium and iron.

A herd of Sri Lankan elephants at Minneriya National Park

9

Minneriya National Park

🅐D4 🏠32 km (20 miles) E of Habarana 📞(027) 327 9243 🚌 ⏱6am–5pm daily

Along with the Kaudulla National Park towards the north and Wasgomuwa National Park in the south, Minneriya forms part of the elephant corridor that connects the protected areas located within the Cultural Triangle and facilitates elephant migration.

The large Minneriya Wewa tank, which is the focal point of the park, was built by King Mahasena in the 4th century AD and covers an area of 30 sq km (11 sq miles). Between the months of August and October, at the height of the dry season, elephants congregate at this watering hole. Their numbers peak during September – as many as 300 elephants have been recorded here at this time. This annual event is popularly known as "The Gathering," when the animals come to Minneriya to look for mates and for water, as well as fresh shoots of grass, which grow on the lake bed as the waters recede.

Elsewhere, the park has a wide variety of habitats, ranging from wetland to tropical forest. Aquatic and forest birds can both be sighted here, as well as macaques, sambar deer, wild buffaloes, land monitors, and elusive leopard and sloth bears.

Hotels and guesthouses can arrange safaris to the park. The best time to visit is between June and October. Note, however, that at the time of "The Gathering" it can become very busy, and some concerns have been raised about the number of tourist jeeps and their effect on elephant movement.

10

Habarana

🅐D4 🏠11 km (7 miles) NW of Sigiriya 🚉🚌

A small and laid-back village, Habarana sits on an important tourism route that connects the cities of Anuradhapura and Polonnaruwa. It is a major transport junction, with roads leading north towards Trincomalee and Jaffna, as well as south towards Kandy and Colombo.

Other than an attractive lake, which is great for a leisurely evening stroll, Habarana does not boast many attractions. It is a convenient base, however, from which to explore the Cultural Triangle as it offers easy access to almost all important sights, such as Sigiriya, Anuradhapura, Polonnaruwa and Dambulla. A safari to Minneriya or Kaudulla national parks, or Hurulu Eco Park, to observe elephants and other wildlife can also be easily arranged from Habarana. There is a decent choice of relatively upmarket accommodation. You can even find places offering personalized Ayurvedic treatments in the village – perfect for those looking to relax after a long day's sightseeing.

> **This annual event is popularly known as "The Gathering," when the animals come to Minneriya to look for mates and for water, as well as fresh shoots of grass.**

INSIDER TIP
Follow the Herd

Elephants migrate freely along the "elephant corridor" that connects Minneriya and Kaudulla national parks. Check their latest movements with local guides before deciding which of the two parks to visit.

11

Kaudulla National Park

E4 **22 km (14 miles) NE of Habarana** **(027) 327 9735** **6am–6pm daily**

Established in 2002, Kaudulla is part of the elephant corridor. Like Minneriya, it has a tank as its centrepiece, which attracts a large number of elephants during the dry season. The park is also similar to Minneriya in the fact that its varied habitats support the same range of wildlife, although rusty spotted cats are also found here. Where Kaudulla differs is that, outside the dry season, much of the park is underwater, and the elephants migrate to the surrounding jungles. As you would expect from this watery landscape, the park is home to a wide variety of aquatic bird species, including spot-billed pelicans and cormorants.

Hotels and guesthouses can arrange trips to the park, as well as boat trips on the lake. When on a safari, be aware that jeeps do not venture too close to the animals. It is always best to maintain a safe distance from elephants, as they may charge.

12

Hurulu Eco Park

D3 **10 km (6 miles) NE of Habarana** **6am–6:30pm daily**

Part of the Hurulu Biosphere Reserve, Hurulu Eco Park opened to visitors in 2008. Hurulu is often suggested as an alternative when Minneriya and Kaudulla are too wet for any wildlife-spotting. Although the park does not have a large tank – it has small waterways that intersect – it attracts a good number of elephants and birds as well as other mammals such as deer, water buffaloes and monkeys. There are plans underway to merge the smaller abandoned tanks within the park to create one large tank. To take a closer look at the progress of this project, walk up to the viewpoint above the tanks. As with the other parks, trips to Hurulu can be arranged by local hotels and guesthouses.

13

Yapahuwa

D4 **45 km (28 miles) SW of Aukana** **7:30am–6pm daily**

This rock fortress, rising 90 m (295 ft) above the surrounding plains, was the centre of a short-lived Sinhalese capital established by King Bhuvanekabahu I during the 13th century. The king brought the Sacred Tooth Relic here to protect it against invasions from South India. However, after Yapahuwa fell to the Pandyan army of South India in 1284, it was abandoned and taken over by Buddhist monks.

Although there are remnants of the palace and the ancient city around the base, the real attraction here is a steep staircase that leads up to a natural rock terrace. The initial section of the staircase is plain but the top part is beautifully decorated with intricate carvings and impressive statues. There are large ornate sculptures of lions and elephants flanking the stairs, as well as an imposing porch with pillars and carved window frames on either side. Panels around the base and sides of the stairs depict dancers and musicians. You may notice that these carvings have a very distinctive South Indian influence.

A rocky path at the rear left side of the terrace leads up to the summit, and there are panoramic views of the beautiful countryside to be enjoyed from here.

→

The stone staircase leading up to the rock fortress of Yapahuwa

14

Panduwas Nuwara

C5 **91 km (56 miles) NW of Matale** **6am-6pm daily**

Dating back to the 12th century, Panduwas Nuwara was used as a temporary royal capital before King Parakramabahu I built his citadel at Polonnaruwa (p166). The remains of the city are scattered over a sprawling site stretching for several square kilometres. The main attraction is the royal palace, which is enclosed within the citadel. An inscription inside the palace building records a visit by King Nissankamalla. Beyond the royal complex is a renovated tooth temple, which is open to visitors.

15

Aukana

D4 **37 km (23 miles) W of Habarana** **7am-7pm daily**

The village of Aukana is best known as the site of a 12-m- (40-ft-)

GREAT VIEW
Rise and Shine!

Early birds are rewarded at Aukana, when the east-facing statue catches the rays of the rising sun. This light brings out the finest details in the statue's mineral-flecked crystalline stone.

high standing Buddha statue carved from solid rock. It is an elegant, imposing sculpture, with some intricately carved details, such as the folds of the Buddha's robes. The Buddha stands in the *asisa mudra*, which is a variation of the *abhaya mudra*.

16

Ritigala

D4 **21 km (13 miles) NW of Habarana** **7am-6pm daily**

A forest monastery complex now protected within the Ritigala Strict Nature Reserve, Ritigala is an enigmatic archaeological site. In the

9th century, the jungle-covered, monastic caves were inhabited by monks of the Pansakulika Order, who were sworn to a life of extreme austerity and were attracted to the area's remote location.

It may be possible to hire a guide at the reserve's visitor centre, which also has some information panels about the area. Beyond the entrance of the ruins is a path running around the periphery of the Banda Pokuna bathing tank, which has been partially restored. In the far corner are steps leading up to a walkway that links all of the complex's major buildings, including a library and hospital. Up ahead in the first clearing is one of the double platform structures that Ritigala is known for, linked by a stone bridge. It is believed that the structures were used by the monks for meditation purposes and that the area underneath was flooded with water to keep the place cool.

17

Sasseruwa

D4 **12 km (7 miles) W of Aukana** **6am-6pm daily**

The Buddha statue at Sasseruwa is similar to the one at Aukana in height and posture, albeit rather clunky in appearance. A favourite legend surrounding the statues states that the one at Aukana was carved by a master and the one at Sasseruwa by his student. Aukana was completed first and to a higher standard so the student abandoned his sculpture in dismay.

Along with the Buddha statue – accessed via a flight of about 50 steps – there is a bo tree and a couple of nondescript cave temples.

←

The impressive Buddha statue, carved from solid rock, at Aukana

BUDDHIST MUDRAS

In Buddhism, a *mudra* is defined as a gesture or a posture that has symbolic significance. In Sri Lanka, the Buddha is depicted in three main postures, namely standing, seated and reclining. The seated and standing statues are characterized by gestures of the hand, which represent key events in the life of the Buddha, such as the moment of enlightenment and his first sermon at Sarnath. The Buddha's *parinirvana*, or final release, is represented by the reclining pose. The Buddha is most frequently portrayed either in the *dhyana mudra*, which is the meditation pose, or in the reclining *mudra*. The *mudras* seen in Sri Lanka are outlined below.

THE RECLINING BUDDHA
This pose is symbolic of the Buddha's *parinirvana*, having attained nirvana at the time of his death. However, there are two types of reclining pose, the sleeping pose and the actual *parinirvana* pose. In the former, the toes of the Buddha are in a straight line.

THE ABHAYA MUDRA
The "fearlessness" gesture shows the Buddha with his right hand raised to shoulder height, arm bent and the palm facing outwards. It is understood to mean "have no fear".

THE BHUMISPARSHA MUDRA
This *mudra* depicts the Buddha touching the ground with the fingertips of his right hand, while his left hand rests in his lap. The gesture commemorates the Buddha's resolve in the face of the demon Mara's temptations and distractions.

THE DHYANA MUDRA
When in the meditation pose, the Buddha sits in the lotus or half-lotus position with both hands in his lap, and the right hand resting on the left.

THE VITARKA AND DHARMACHAKRA MUDRAS
The "explanation" and the "turning of the wheel" poses are characterized by the Buddha's index finger touching his thumb to form a circle, symbolic of the wheel of *dharma* (law and order). This is said to convince listeners of the truth of *dharma*.

1 This reclining Buddha is in the sleeping pose.

2 The *abhaya* is fearless.

3 The *bhumisparsha mudra* symbolizes resolve.

4 *Dhyana mudra* is the meditation pose.

5 The *vitarka mudra* is shown by this Buddha.

⓲
Matale

🅰D5 🚗150 km (92 miles)
NE of Colombo 🚆🚌

This busy town does not have many attractions of its own, but serves as an entry point to Sri Lanka's ancient cities. Tourists en route to Kandy or Dambulla often make a stopover in Matale to visit the **Sri Muthumariamman Thevasthanam** – an attractive *kovil* dedicated to the goddess Mariamman.

About 2 km (1 mile) north of the temple is the **Matale Heritage Centre**, where you can watch artisans producing intricate batik. After seeing the artisans at work, explore the centre's sprawling gardens and then pile your plate high with curry at the Aluvihare Kitchens.

Sri Muthumariamman Thevasthanam
⊛ 📍King's Street
🕐6am–6pm daily

Matale Heritage Centre
🏠🛈 📍33 Sir Richard Aluvihare Mawatha 📞(066) 222 2404 🕐8:30am–4pm Mon-Sat

⓳
Arankele

🅰D4 🚗48 km (30 miles) W of Matale 🕐6am–6pm daily

Isolated and heavily forested, this 6th-century hermitage is home to a community of monks, who have devoted themselves to an austere and meditative lifestyle.

Stroll along the meditation walkway, a long paved path interspersed with small flights of steps. En route to a small shrine devoted to the Buddha, you will see the ruins of medi-tation chambers, bathing ponds and the remains of the principal monk's residence.

⓴
Ridi Vihara

🅰D5 🚗36 km (22 miles) NW of Matale 🚌 🕐7am–10pm daily

The little-visited Ridi Vihara, or Silver Temple, was founded by King Dutugemunu on the spot where a vein of silver ore was discovered. The temple complex comprises rock-cut

📷 PICTURE PERFECT
Walk This Way

The meditation walkways at both Ridi Vihara and Arankele offer all sorts of unusual photographic possibil-ities, with the paths cutting directly through the tangled surrounding jungle.

shrines, hermitages and *dagobas*. The highlight of the complex, however, is the traditional Kandyan frescoes.

The main temple, Pahala Vihara, houses a golden seated Buddha and a large reclining Buddha. A platform in front of the reclining statue is inset with blue and white Dutch (Delft) tiles, depicting biblical scenes. There is a beautifully carved door frame inlaid with ivory right next to the entrance.

The nearby Uda Vihara was built by King Kirti Sri Rajasinghe. A Kandyan-era moonstone, flanked by large elephants with intricate carvings under their trunks, can be seen by the entrance. The main chamber has a

seated Buddha statue as well as some very beautiful 18th-century frescoes.

21

Aluvihare

🅰️ D5 🚗 4 km (2 miles) N of Matale 🚌 🕐 7am–6pm daily

Comprising a series of caves carved out of rock, the Aluvihare monastery complex is an atmospheric site. It marks the spot where the *Tripitakaya* – the Theravada Buddhist canon – was first penned in the 1st century BC. Prior to this, the Buddha's diverse teachings were passed orally from one generation to the next. The *ola*-leaf manuscripts, transcribed from the Pali language by 500 monks, remained safe here until the mid-19th century, when they were destroyed by British troops during an attack on the temple.

The monastic caves are linked to each other by a flight of steps and small paths between the rocks and boulders – triangular shapes have been carved into the stone to act as holders for

The ancient carved stone building of Nalanda Gedige, near Matale

lamps. The first cave temple has a 10-m- (32-ft-) long reclining Buddha and colourful lotus-flower paintings adorning the ceiling. Some steps up, the second cave is also home to a reclining Buddha statue. The most striking aspect of this cave, however, is the graphic murals on the walls of the cave depicting sinners being tortured in hell. They are beheaded, impaled or their skulls are cut open.

The cave opposite this one has life-size plaster figures enduring similar torments. A gap in the rock between the first two cave temples leads to a smaller cave with a brightly painted exterior. This cave is dedicated to the Indian scholar, Buddhaghosa, known for his work on the *Tripitakaya* (Buddhist scriptures). From here, steps lead up to a bo tree, a *dagoba* and a terrace that offers lovely views of the surrounding hills.

To the left of the temple complex is the International Buddhist Library and Museum. Inside is a display detailing how palmyra leaves become *ola*-leaf manuscripts.

←

The Sri Muthumariamman Thevasthanam Hindu Temple in Matale

22

Nalanda Gedige

🅰️ D4 🚗 20 km (12 miles) N of Matale 🚌 🕐 7am–5pm daily

Named after the famous Buddhist university in northern India, Nalanda Gedige is a unique structure built in the South Indian architectural style. Despite looking like a Hindu temple, complete with a *mandapa* (pillared porch), the *gedige* (image house) bears no signs of any Hindu gods and it is thought to have only ever been used by Buddhists.

Constructed entirely of stone, the *gedige* is believed to have been built between the 7th and 11th centuries, and once stood amid low-lying paddy fields. It was moved to its present site in the 1980s to make way for a man-made lake.

Much of the original building has been reduced to ruins. The carvings on the exterior walls may be aged, worn and weather-beaten, but it is still possible to make out details such as faces, a carving of a god on the south side and a row of miniature buildings carved on the entrance arch-way. Look out for the tantric carving on the southern side of the base plinth.

THE EAST

Remote and largely undeveloped, Sri Lanka's east coast offers a striking contrast to the brash and populous west. It was not always so. The superb deepwater natural harbour at Gokana (modern-day Trincomalee) was home to a major trading port from the Polonnaruwa period right through to the Second World War, while Batticaloa, further south, was the site of the Dutch's first fort. In the 20th century, the east began to decline as trade was diverted to first Galle and then Colombo. As the island's economic focus shifted decisively westwards, the east was relegated to the margins of Sri Lanka's modern history.

Ethnically, this is one of the most diverse parts of the island. It's here, around Maduru Oya National Park, that the Veddahs – the original inhabitants of the island – still try to maintain their traditional way of life. Beyond the park, most of the coast is occupied by Tamils and Muslims, while the areas inland are largely Sinhalese. As such, the region suffered greatly during the Civil War, with endless clashes between the Tamil LTTE and the Sinhalese Sri Lankan Army further contributing to its isolation. Post-war reconstruction has been modest, with the newly constructed resorts at Passekudah the only manifestation of the headlong developments that are overtaking other parts of the island.

THE
EAST

THE EAST

Must See

① Trincomalee

Experience More

② Nilaveli

③ Uppuveli

④ Kanniya Hot Wells

⑤ Passekudah and Kalkudah

⑥ Batticaloa

⑦ Velgam Vehera

⑧ Maligawila

⑨ Gal Oya National Park

⑩ Lahugala National Park

⑪ Monaragala

⑫ Arugam Bay

⑬ Maduru Oya National Park

⑭ Kumana National Park

⑮ Okanda

⑯ Panama

⑰ Kudumbigala Hermitage

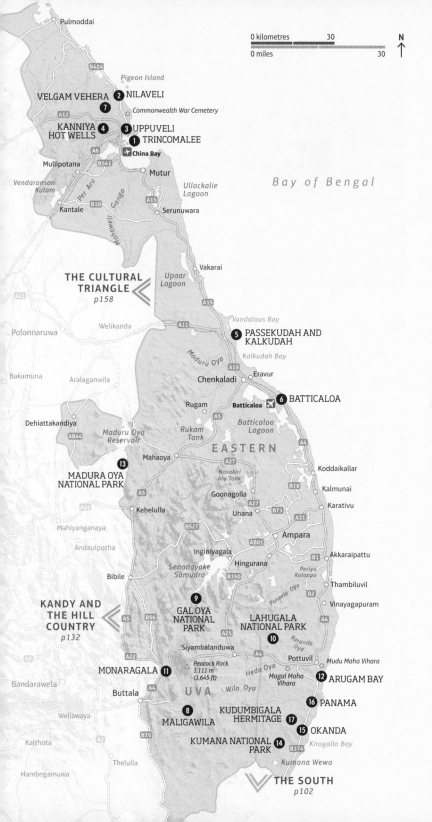

0 kilometres 30
0 miles 30

N

Pulmoddai

B424

Pigeon Island

VELGAM VEHERA ② NILAVELI
⑦
A12   Commonwealth War Cemetery

KANNIYA ④   ③ UPPUVELI
HOT WELLS   ① TRINCOMALEE

A6   ✈ China Bay

Mullipotana   B541

Vendaransan
Kulam   Mutur

Kantale   B10   Ullackalie
                                Lagoon
                    A15
                           Serunuwara
         Per Aru

Bay of Bengal

THE CULTURAL   Upaar
TRIANGLE   Lagoon
p158 ≪   Vakarai

          Welikanda   A15
                              Vandalous Bay
Polonnaruwa   A11

Bakamuna   ⑤ PASSEKUDAH AND
                        KALKUDAH
Aralaganwila   Kalkudah Bay

Dehiattakandiya   Chenkaladi   Eravur

AB44   Batticaloa ✈ ⑥ BATTICALOA
        Maduru Oya   Rugam
        Reservoir   A5   Batticaloa
                     Rukam   Lagoon
    ⑬   Tank
MADURA OYA   Mahaoya   EASTERN   A4
NATIONAL PARK   Koddaikallar
          A27   Navakiri
         A5   Aru Tank   B18   Kalmunai
  Kehelulla   Goonagolla   A27
Mahiyanganaya   Uhana B73   Karativu
                              A31
Andaulpotha   B527   AB01   Ampara

           Inginiyagala   Hingurana   B1   Akkaraipattu
  Bibile   Senanayake   Periya
           Samudra   B350   Kalappu B2 Thambiluvil
KANDY AND   Vinayagapuram
THE HILL   ⑨   ⑩
COUNTRY   GAL OYA   LAHUGALA
p132 ≪   NATIONAL   NATIONAL
  A5 B56   PARK   PARK Karanda
      A22   Oya
      A25   Siyambalanduwa   A4   Pottuvil
         Peacock Rock   Mudu Maha Vihara
MONARAGALA ⑪ 1,111 m   Heda Oya   ⑫ ARUGAM BAY
Bandarawela   (3,645 ft)   Magul Maha
     Buttala A4   Wila Oya Vihara
Wellawaya   UVA   ⑯ PANAMA
        ⑧   KUDUMBIGALA ⑰
Kalthota MALIGAWILA HERMITAGE ⑮ OKANDA
   A2 B35   Kiragalla Bay
      KUMANA NATIONAL ⑭
Thelulla   PARK   B374
        Kumana Wewa
Hambegamuwa   THE SOUTH
         ⋁ p102

❶
TRINCOMALEE

🅰E3 📍269 km (167 miles) NE of Colombo 🚆🚌

The capital of Sri Lanka's Eastern Province, "Trinco" is famous for its deepwater natural harbour. Most visitors come for the beaches that lie to its north, but the town has a charm of its own, with faded colonial buildings, a picturesque seafront and vibrant *kovils*.

①
Fort Frederick

🏛**Konesar Road** 🕐**Daily**

The main attraction in Trinco is Fort Frederick, which sits on a strip of land that juts out into the Indian Ocean. Built by the Portuguese in 1623, the fort passed through Dutch and French hands before being finally taken over by the British in 1795. It remained under British control until Sri Lanka's independence in 1948. During this period, its name was changed from Fort of Triquillimale to Fort Frederick, after the Duke of York, the second son of King George III.

The fort is still in military use, but can be visited. Inside, there are several colonial buildings interspersed with old, wide-canopied trees. One of these buildings is Wellesley Lodge, where Arthur Wellesley, who went on to become the Duke of Wellington, is said to have stayed in 1800.

_____

②
Koneswaram Kovil and Lover's Leap

🏛**Konesar Road** 🕐**Daily**

At the highest point of Swami Rock, a steep cliff that drops about 130 m (426 ft) to the sea, is Koneswaram Kovil, one of the five most sacred *Shaivite* (dedicated to Lord Shiva) sites in Sri Lanka. A shrine is thought to have stood at this spot for about 2,500 years until it was destroyed by the Portuguese in the 17th century. Today, a huge blue statue of Shiva, outside, dwarfs the brightly coloured temple and *gopuram* (gateway), which was built here in 1952.

To the right of the temple is a tree with wooden cradles hanging from its branches, left by families praying for children. Nearby is another tree that clings precariously to the cliff, its branches covered with prayer flags. This spot is known as Lover's Leap. It marks a spot where a Dutch woman, Francina van Rhede, supposedly jumped off the cliff in 1687 when her lover abandoned her and sailed away. It's a romantic story, although somewhat spoiled by the government records showing that Francina was still alive and well eight years later. She either survived the fall or, according to some sources, never jumped at all.

> **This spot is known as Lover's Leap. It marks a spot where a Dutch woman, Francina van Rhede, supposedly jumped off the cliff in 1687.**

↑ The melange of buildings lining Trincomalee's bay

③
Commercial Centre

West of Fort Frederick lies the town's commercial centre, which comprises three parallel streets: Main Street, Central Road and North Coast (NC) Road. At the confluence of NC Road and Central Road stands the clock tower, next to which is the busy fish market, stocked from Trinco's famous harbour. The market is worth a quick visit, as is the fruit and vegetable market nearby.

A short distance south of the clock tower is the large Kali Kovil with a colourful *gopuram* on Dockyard Road. The late-afternoon *puja* here is a lively affair with drums and ringing of bells.

A couple of minutes' walk southeast, the town's overgrown and increasingly dilapidated General Cemetery is a reminder of Trinco's colonial history. Beneath the undergrowth, you'll find the tombs dating back to the early 19th century, including the final resting places of those who died mainly from malaria and other tropical diseases. English author Jane Austen's brother, Rear Admiral Charles John Austen, who died of cholera in Burma in 1852, is thought to be buried here.

④
Dutch Bay

Bounding the eastern side of town, the half-moon-shaped Dutch Bay is a popular place at dusk when locals come to walk along the breezy seafront and relax in the sand. Roughly halfway along the bay is the Maritime and Naval History Museum. The museum occupies a beautifully restored building, dating from 1602, which was once the residence of the Dutch naval commander. Exhibits feature a mildly interesting mishmash of artifacts, both naval and maritime. The collection ranges from Chinese ceramics, recovered from the waves, to a large cannon.

Just south of here, St Mary's Cathedral, which is buried amid verdant gardens, is another survivor from colonial times, as are the little pastel-painted villas which line the surrounding streets. Dyke Street is particularly pretty.

> 🔍 HIDDEN GEM
> **Hoodwinked**
>
> Hidden deep inside the city's high-security naval base, the small Hood's Tower Museum offers an interesting glimpse inside one of Sri Lanka's biggest harbours. You need to show your passport.

Must See

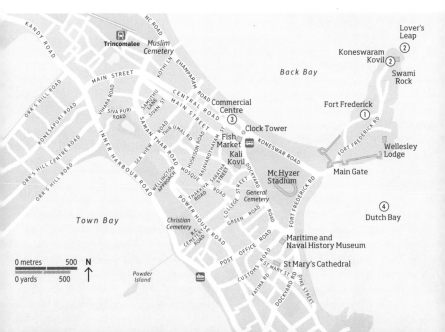

EXPERIENCE MORE

② Nilaveli

A E3 **□** 15 km (9 miles) NW of Trincomalee
🚌 From Trincomalee

North of Trincomalee lies the sleepy village of Nilaveli, harbouring a modest selection of hotels and guesthouses. Strung out along kilometres of white-sand beach tickled by palm trees, this is one of Sri Lanka's ultimate get-away-from-it-all destinations. Diving, water sports and whale- and dolphin-watching excursions are all available in season.

Also popular are boat trips to **Pigeon Island National Park**. Named after the blue rock pigeons that nest here, the island is a marine national park. It has two small beaches and the shallow water of its curving bays makes it one of Sri Lanka's best places to snorkel. Check out the live coral on the seaward side of the island and tropical fish on the beach-facing side. Blacktip reef sharks and turtles can also be seen.

Pigeon Island is very popular at weekends and during public holidays. It is a good idea to arrive early as the island becomes crowded by lunchtime in high season, which extends from May to September.

Pigeon Island National Park

🚭🚭 **□** 1 km (0.6 miles) NE of Nilaveli **🚌** **○** 8am–5pm daily

③ Uppuveli

A E3 **□** 4 km (2 miles) NW of Trincomalee
🚌 From Trincomalee

Just north of Trincomalee, the village of Uppuveli is blessed with one of Sri Lanka's finest

↓ Pigeon Island National Park, and *(inset)* below the waterline

beaches, with clear waters, a generous swathe of white sand and the outline of Trincomalee's Swami Rock rising in the distance.

Battered first by the Civil War and then the tsunami, Uppuveli has had more than its fair share of misfortunes, although this has also helped preserve the beach's largely undeveloped atmosphere and sense of remoteness. Even now the whole place feels resolutely low-key, despite the presence of cafés and restaurants on the beach and several largish hotels, including the sprawling Trinco Blu resort.

As with Nilaveli, Uppuveli's main activities are lounging, beachcombing and wave-gazing, although there are also a number of local diving and water sports operators, while whale-watching trips can be arranged in season.

Within walking distance of the village is the moving and immaculately main-tained **Commonwealth War Cemetery**, housing the graves of 362 service personnel who died in Sri Lanka during World War II. In April 1942,

Trincomalee – a major Allied base at the time – suffered Japanese air raids that also sank several British and Australian ships in the Indian Ocean. Among the ships sunk were the Royal Navy aircraft carrier HMS *Hermes* and the escort Australian destroyer HMAS *Vampire* (p199).

Organized in rows, each of the headstones bears symbols that identify the deceased as seamen or part of the air crew. The symbols also denote the nationality: gravestones of those from New Zealand, for example, are engraved with the silver fern. The moving epitaphs here are a grim reminder of the horrors of World War II. One such epitaph is that of a nurse called Joan Barker, which reads, "A short but tremendously useful life".

Those who wish to have a look at the register of the graves can contact the warden, who is usually on site and has maintained the cemetery for decades. There is no fixed entry fee to the cemetery, but a donation is appreciated.

Commonwealth War Cemetery

🏛 200 m (219 yards) N of Uppuveli Nilaveli Road ⏰ Dawn–dusk daily

Kanniya Hot Wells

📍 E3 🏛 20 km (12 miles) W of Uppuveli ⏰ 6am–6pm daily

The Kanniya Hot Wells comprise seven warm natural springs enclosed in seven square-shaped wells. The spring water is thought to have therapeutic properties; those with skin problems or ailments such as arthritis and rheumatism come here looking for relief. Since the wells are too small to bathe in, locals and pilgrims use buckets to pour water over themselves – tourists are encouraged to join in, too. The temperature of the water varies in each of the wells.

The wells are only 1 m (3 ft) deep, but this does not mean that they are without their mysteries. There are two legends associated with the wells. One of these claims that Lord Vishnu created the wells when he appeared to Ravana, the king of Lankapura, on this spot. It is believed that when Lord Vishnu struck the ground with his sword, water poured forth. The other maintains that King Ravana created the wells so that he could conduct the funeral rites for his beloved mother.

↑ The Kanniya Hot Wells, said to have therapeutic properties

STAY

Amaranthé Bay
Stylish Uppuveli resort, with white villas set around a gorgeous palm-shaded pool.

📍 E3 🏛 Alles Garden, Uppuveli 🌐 amaranthe bay.com

$$$

Nilaveli Beach Hotel
This attractive resort in Nilaveli is straight out of paradise.

📍 E3 🏛 11th mile post, Nilaveli 🌐 nilaveli. tangerinehotels.com

$$$

Jungle Beach
This super-stylish little boutique resort, 10 km (6 miles) north of Nilaveli, is nestled between the sea and the lagoon.

📍 E2 🏛 Pulmoddai Road, Kuchchaveli 🌐 ugaescapes.com

$$$

EAT

Café on the 18th

Expect Western comforts at this surprisingly stylish Uppuveli café – try the paninis. Good veggie and vegan options.

🅰E3 🏠18 Alles Garden, Uppuveli 📞(077) 978 8814

$$$⑤

Ubay Restaurant

A rustic little restaurant in Uppuveli, serving homemade Sri Lankan dishes, including crab and prawn curries.

🅰E3 🏠15 Beach Road, Uppuveli 📞(077) 713 3920

$$$⑤

Sri Kishna Café

This lagoon-side "Batti" eatery serves tasty vegetarian dishes.

🅰F4 🏠Lake Road, Batticaloa 📞(065) 222 8900

$$$⑤

❺
Passekudah and Kalkudah

🅰F4 🏠Passekudah: 28 km (17 miles) NW of Batticaloa; Kalkudah: 27 km (16 miles) NW of Batticaloa 🚌From Batticaloa

The east's twin beaches of Passekudah and Kalkudah provide a neat barometer of Sri Lanka's changing fortunes over the years. Prior to the Civil War, this was the east coast's most developed tourist destination, with a cluster of low-key resort hotels catering to vacationing Europeans. Soon after the outbreak of war, these hotels were abandoned, and subsequently blown up by the LTTE. After the resorts' destruction, the area returned to its former sleepiness and was seemingly forgotten.

This abruptly changed in the late 2000s when Passekudah was earmarked for massive development. A string of resorts was constructed, transforming the beach within just a couple of years from a hidden gem into one of the island's biggest package-tourism destinations. Despite these constructions, Passekudah is still one of Sri Lanka's most beautiful beaches, with milky white sand and clear, gently lapping waves. For those who balk at the idea of just lying on a beach all day, there is a range of water sports on offer, including sailing boat trips, jet skis, water-skiing and banana boat rides.

Kalkudah, by contrast, retains much of its former somnolence and charm, with a beautiful and almost completely undeveloped swathe of golden sand. The beach is backed by just one boutique hotel (with stylish and low-key tented rooms) and a couple of houses. The remaining 12km (7 miles) or so of sand is fringed by seemingly endless coconut plantations and cashew groves. The waves are rougher here than at Passekudah and there is a sharp seabed drop-off close to the shore, but you'll get the chance to see Tamil fishermen pulling in their huge nets in the morning as sea eagles swoop above – a splendid sight!

---

❻
Batticaloa

🅰F4 🏠138 km (86 miles) SE of Trincomalee 🚉🚌

The second-largest town on the east coast, Batticaloa (or "Batti", as it's usually known) makes up for what it lacks in headline attractions with its rich history, quirky charm and off-the-beaten-track appeal. The fact that it's seemingly located in the middle of a disorientating labyrinth of

↑ The beach of Kalkudah, one of the most beautiful in the country

> **INSIDER TIP**
> ## Go Batti
>
> East 'n' West On Board runs an enjoyable selection of local tours and activities around Batti, including cycling and guided walks, boat trips and cookery classes (*www. eastonboard.com*).

THE SINGING FISH OF BATTICALOA

The stretch of the Batticaloa Lagoon under the Kallady Bridge is home to Batticaloa's "singing fish". Between April and September, around the time of the full moon, the fish are said to make noises that are described as the twanging of a violin string. There have been a number of theories to explain the sounds, ranging from courting mussels to the movement of water at the bottom of the lagoon.

water – hemmed in as it is by the lagoon and the sea – only compounds Batti's lost-world beauty.

The fort is the town's main attraction. Originally built by the Portuguese in 1628, it was captured by the Dutch 10 years later, and was subsequently rebuilt. There isn't much to see inside the central courtyard, apart from some time-warped buildings, so head straight up to the top of the fort instead. Here, a couple of cannons sit beneath a shady canopy and there are fabulous views of the lagoon.

West of here, the town centre is strung out along the parallel Main and Bazaar streets, which are both lined with quaint little shops and cafés. In the shadow of the old-fashioned clock tower marking the centre of town is an incongruous statue of a boy scout. It was erected in 1998 to celebrate the 80th anniversary of the local Scout Movement.

The streets to the south of the clock tower are home to a rich assortment of colonial churches and colleges. Among these is St Michael's College, which is one of the largest schools in the Eastern

↑ The interior of St Mary's Cathedral, Batticaloa, and (inset) its colourful entrance

Province. It was founded in 1873 by Reverend Ferdinand Bonnel and was privately run until the 1970s. Directly opposite stands St Mary's Cathedral, with a powder-blue Neo-Classical exterior. The building was damaged by a cyclone in the 1970s, after which it was repaired, but underwent further restoration work in the late 1980s and 1990s. It was also where Tamil politician Joseph Pararajasingham was assassinated during Midnight Mass in 2005.

Separated from Batticaloa by the lagoon, and reached by the wrought-iron Kallady Bridge, the laid-back suburb of Kallady offers a strip of golden sand, several guest-houses and dive schools. Note that the water here is rough and not suitable for swimming.

Instead, the dive schools' boats make for the wreck of HMS Hermes, which lies off the coast. This Royal Navy aircraft carrier, and its escort, Australian destroyer HMAS Vampire, sank during an air raid by Japanese bombers in April 1942. Around 307 men lost their lives in the sinking. Lying 44 m (145 ft) below the water, the wreck is perfect for experienced technical divers, with good visibility, abundant marine life and a number of nearby wrecks to explore. Diving is possible only from March to October.

↑ One of the two enormous limestone Buddha statues at Maligawila

⑦ Velgam Vehera

E3 **9 km (6 miles) W of Uppuveli** ⏰ **Dawn-dusk daily**

The atmospheric remains of Velgam Vehera, just north of Kanniya Hot Wells (p197), are well worth a visit. Known to Hindus as Natanar Kovil, this Buddhist monastery is thought to have been built by King Devanampiya Tissa in the 3rd century BC. It escaped destruction in the 10th century when the Cholas from South India invaded Sri Lanka. Instead of destroying it as they did many other Buddhist shrines and temples, the Cholas renovated the building and also used it as a place of worship.

The extensive ruins here include an image house, a well-preserved standing Buddha and a dagoba. Tamil inscriptions dating from the 10th century can still be seen around the site. There is no entry fee to the temple, but a donation is appreciated.

Nearby stands a small museum devoted to an LTTE bombing in 2000 that killed around 26 civilians and Sinhalese soldiers. Filled with disturbing images of the bombing, this museum is not for the faint-hearted.

⑧ Maligawila

E6 **17 km (11 miles) S of Monaragala** 🚌 **From Monaragala** ⏰ **Dawn-dusk daily**

The village of Maligawila is home to two enormous Buddhist statues that stand hidden among the trees of the unspoiled lowland jungle. Carved out of limestone, the impressive figures date from the 7th century and are thought to have been part of a monastery. The statues, which had toppled over and lain in pieces for centuries, were raised to a standing position in the late 1980s and reassembled over the following years.

The site is reached by a path that begins at the car park and winds through the woods to a point where it splits into two. The left fork leads to the first of the two statues – an 11-m- (36-ft-) high standing Buddha. The image is supported by a brick arch at the back, which makes it possible to walk all the way around to admire the crafts-manship and marvel at its size.

The right fork takes visitors to the stairs that lead up to the *bodhisattva* statue, under a large canopy. To the left of the steps, under a protective covering, is a 10th-century pillar that bears an inscription from the reign of Mahinda IV. It details the work undertaken by the king to support the Buddhist order and some rules about the administration of Buddhist sites.

⑨ Gal Oya National Park

F5 **80 km (50 miles) SW of Batticaloa** 🚌 **From Batticaloa to Ampara, then taxi to Inginiyagala** ⏰ **6am–6pm daily**

Covering an area of 540 sq km (208 sq miles), the picturesque dry-zone reserve of Gal Oya is situated in a part of Sri Lanka little visited by tourists. At the centre of the park is the Senanayake Samudra, a vast reservoir that was created in 1948. The park itself was established in 1954 to protect the catchment area around this body of water. Dotted with many small islands, the

↑ The picturesque ruins of the Magul Maha Vihara temple, Lahugala National Park

The evocative ruins of **Magul Maha Vihara** are situated 6 km (4 miles) southwest of the park. Inscriptions found at the site suggest that the monastery complex was built by King Dhatusena in the 5th century AD and restored in the 14th century. Only a small section of the complex has been excavated, while the rest is still covered in thick jungle. Look out for the *dagoba*, the image house and the well-preserved moonstone ringed with the stone carving of a chain of elephants, accompanied by their *mahouts*. A donation is appreciated when you enter the site.

Magul Maha Vihara
⏰ Dawn–dusk daily

_____

reservoir is one of the largest lakes in Sri Lanka.

A number of water birds can be spotted around the reservoir, including the white-bellied fish eagle, the rare painted francolin, Layard's parakeet and Indian nightjars. Grey langurs, wild boar, water buffaloes and deer can also be seen in the park. If you're lucky, you may even catch sight of an elephant or two on one of the islands. It is possible to tour the park

in a jeep but travellers are recommended to take a boat trip to see the islands on the reservoir. Among the highlights is the appropriately named Bird Island – an ornithologist's paradise.

_____

10

Lahugala National Park

🗺 F6 📍 19 km (12 miles) NW of Arugam Bay on the Monaragala Road ⏰ 6am–6pm daily

Located within easy reach of Arugam Bay (p202), this small national park offers the chance to see a wide range of aquatic birds as well as elephants. Of the three reservoirs here, the Lahugala Tank is a good place to spot storks and pelicans. During the dry season (July and August), herds of elephants congregate at the tank to eat the *beru* grass, which grows in profusion around the water. You can get jeeps from outside the park entrance or organize a trip with guesthouses in Arugam Bay.

← A fisherman on Senanayake Samudra reservoir, Gal Oya National Park

11

Monaragala

🗺 E6 📍 151 km (94 miles) SW of Batticaloa 🚌

Meaning "the rock of peacock landing", Monaragala derives its name from the imposing and densely forested Peacock Rock that it nestles beneath. A typical Sri Lankan town, Monaragala is the starting point for some good nature walks through the surrounding countryside, which is surprisingly lush and home to elephants, buffaloes, peacocks and deer.

Monaragala is a good base from which to visit Maligawila and also serves as a gateway to Arugam Bay.

HIDDEN GEM
Rubber Route

One of the best hikes in Monaragala starts at the town's bus station. You pass a colourful Ganesh temple before reaching the town's ageing rubber factory. The path winds its way through a plantation of trees tapped for latex.

SHOP

Ecowave

Run by a local social enterprise (it also offers tours and cookery classes), this Arugam Bay store stocks a small selection of locally sourced spices.

🅰F6 🏠Main Street, Arugam Bay
🆆ecowave.lk

Rice and Carry

Souvenirs made from recycled sacks and discarded plastic bags in Arugam Bay.

🅰F6 🏠Main Street, Arugam Bay
🆆riceandcarry.com

Batticaloa Central Market

Old-fashioned stalls selling a good selection of fabrics, food and other colourful essentials in "Batti".

🅰F4 🏠Lloyds Avenue
🕗8am-6pm daily

---

⑫

Arugam Bay

🅰F6 🏠76 km (47 miles) E of Monaragala 🚌

The remote village of Arugam Bay (or "A-Bay", as it is known locally) remains the east coast's biggest draw, thanks to its laid-back atmosphere. The first tourists to arrive in the village were surfers, attracted by the area's world-class waves. Surfing remains the biggest single reason to make the trip, although there are still plenty of other attractions even if you have no intention of riding the waves. Note that the whole place is very quiet, and some businesses close down, during the low season, from November to April.

The village itself has a uniquely (for Sri Lanka) left-field appeal, exemplified by the landmark Siam View Restaurant, set in a Thai-style pavilion restaurant with an old British red telephone box outside. Large hotels and package tourists are notable by their complete absence. Most accommodation consists instead of homely guest-houses, quirky bamboo cabanas and the occasional tree house on enormous stilts. All of this backs onto an attractive beach where local fishermen and sunbathing foreigners happily coexist.

Surfing-wise, beginners should make for Pottuvil Point, while more experienced practitioners will be rewarded at Whiskey Point or Crocodile Rock (p205).

Aside from surfing, popular excursions from A-Bay include Kumana National Park (p204), Kudumbigala Hermitage (p205), Okanda (p205) and Pottuvil. The latter is a short distance to the north of Arugam Bay, on the opposite side of the Arugam Lagoon. This small town is where most of the buses for Arugam Bay arrive and depart from. It is well worth taking a trip on Pottuvil Lagoon to see the rich aquatic life of the mangrove swamp. In addition to water birds, it is possible to catch sight of monkeys, and even crocodiles.

Nearby on the coast, nestled among the sand dunes, are the atmospheric ruins of Mudu Maha Vihara. Standing amid the sand are the remains of the walls of an image house and a striking 3-m- (10-ft-) high standing Buddha sculpture, as well as images of two *bodhisattvas*.

A man selling ice cream from his bicycle on ↑ Arugam Bay's beach

SURFING IN SRI LANKA

Quality waves and the possibility of surfing year-round bring enthusiasts to Sri Lanka. Don your swim suit, grab a board and get ready to ride the swell.

The island boasts a number of superb places with breaks to suit every level of expertise. Hikkaduwa (p100) remains the favourite spot on the west coast owing to its relaxed atmosphere and buoyant nightlife. Further along the coast to the south, Midigama (p123) and Ahangama are better suited for the more serious surfer, with long walling lefts and plenty of coral and rock. Other surf hotspots along the south coast include Mirissa (p120) and Weligama (p124), which is a great place for beginners to take lessons. The best-known destination on the east coast is Arugam Bay, which has hosted several international surfing competitions, as well as the Sri Lanka Champion of Champions Surf Contest. The area around the village boasts a number of good surf spots including the Point, Pottuvil Point, Peanut Farm, Crocodile Rock and Okanda Point. The season on the west coast extends from November to April, and then the east coast takes over from May to October.

↑ Surfers walking along the beach with their boards in Weligama

SURF'S UP!

Surf schools in prime surfing destinations across Sri Lanka offer board hire and repair, surf tours to major surfing spots and professional lessons. Some guesthouses also run "learn to surf" packages for beginners.

Group or private surf lessons can be arranged at most beaches. Sri Lanka has some ideal surf spots for beginners, where the waves are smaller, usually around 1 m (3 ft) to 2 m (6 ft).

Riding a wave buffeting the western corner of Mirissa's beach ↑

13

Maduru Oya National Park

⚐E4 **⚑91 km (56 miles) N of Monaragala** **⏱6am-6pm daily**

Maduru Oya was designated a national park in 1983. The entrance to the park lies in the village of Dambana, where jeeps can be hired to explore the park. Madura Oya was created to protect the catchment areas of nearby reservoirs and attracts abundant birdlife as well as Sri Lanka's usual fauna of elephants, sambar deer and monkeys.

The indigenous people of the island, the Veddahs, live in an area known as Henanigala on the edge of the park. Be cognisant of the fact that the Veddahs were turfed out when Maduru Oya became a national park, and are only allowed to enter during the day if they have a permit. The rustic little village of Kotabakina offers a rare (if touristy) glimpse into the Veddahs' vanishing way of life. Visitors are presented with displays of traditional dancing, fire-making and archery and, most importantly, the chance to talk to some of the local Veddahs themselves.

14

Kumana National Park

⚐F6 **⚑120 m (131 yards) E of Okanda** **⏱6am-6pm daily**

The Kumana National Park was closed for a large part of the Civil War before reopening in 2010. Located on the pilgrimage route to Kataragama, the park is one of the five blocks of the Yala National Park (p116). Jeeps for exploring the park can be hired at Arugam Bay.

The 357-sq-km (138-sq-mile) park is noted for its impressive range of resident and migratory birds, which include painted storks, cormorants and Eurasian spoonbills – there have also been occasional sightings of the endangered black-necked stork. The park's most significant feature is the Kumana Villu, a huge mangrove-swamp lake fed by the Kumbukkan Oya river by way of a long, narrow channel. A range of water birds nest in these mangroves during May and June. Besides the wetlands, the park's thriving bird population is also supported by an array of lagoons and

> **💬 INSIDER TIP**
> **Pade Yathra**
>
> Time your visit to Okanda to coincide with the Pade Yathra, Sri Lanka's oldest, longest and most celebrated pilgrimage. In June and July, worshippers walk the entire length of the east coast.

salt marshes. A number of mammals, including elephants, wild boar, fishing cats and golden jackals, are known to inhabit the park. In addition, the place is a nesting ground for several species of turtles.

As well as the furry and feathered creatures seen through your binoculars, Kumana National Park is also home to some archaeological ruins. Among the highlights is the sacred site of Bambaragasthalawa, where you'll find ancient rock caves with fascinating inscriptions and a badly damaged 11-m- (36-ft-) tall Buddha statue dating from the 9th century. At Bowattegala, 13 km (8 miles) southwest, lie the remains of a rock temple dating from the 3rd century BC.

STAY

Samantha's Folly
This A-Bay guesthouse offers a choice of beachfront cabanas, or "follies", resembling thatched beach huts. There's a good restaurant on site.

⚐F6 **⚑Main Road, Arugam Bay** **📞(077) 338 7808**

↑ Maduru Oya National Park, a haven for birds, elephants, monkeys and sambar deer

⓯

Okanda

🅰F6 🔳18 km (11 miles) SW of Panama 🚍From Panama

Located just east of the entrance to Kumana National Park, Okanda is an important stop for those undertaking the epic Pade Yathra pilgrimage from Jaffna (p210) to Kataragama (p118). The town is home to the ancient Velayudha Swami Temple, which lies at the base of a rocky outcrop. Legend has it that this is the spot where Skanda and his consort Valli arrived in Sri Lanka in stone boats. Pilgrims stop at the shrine for a 15-day festival in July. The peak of the rock is crested by the Valli Amman Kovil, a simple shrine, in front of which is a natural spring.

A few minutes' walk east of the Velayudha Swami Temple is a beach that was a popular surfing spot before the Civil War made Okanda hard to access. However, intrepid enthusiasts are now returning here to ride the waves and also to escape the high season at Arugam Bay. Note that it is suitable only for experienced surfers, as it is very remote and there is no lifeguard on duty.

⓰

Panama

🅰F6 🔳12 km (7 miles) S of Arugam Bay 🚍

A tiny, isolated village, Panama offers a wide unspoiled beach that stretches east of the settlement. The sand dunes and rock boulders lend the beach a desert-island feel. Note that the sea here is rough and not suitable for swimming. The only other attraction is a white *dagoba* at the entrance to the village, which is hard to miss.

The road between Arugam Bay and Panama passes through a beautiful landscape of deserted beaches and coastal lagoons interspersed with a sequence of strangely shaped rock outcrops, most notably Crocodile Rock and Elephant Rock – named after their supposed resemblance to these creatures. Crocodiles can be found in many of the lagoons and can occasionally turn nasty – a British visitor was killed here by one in 2017.

⓱

Kudumbigala Hermitage

🅰F6 🔳14 km (9 miles) SW of Panama 🕐6am–5pm daily

Hidden away among thick jungle, the beautiful forest hermitage of Kudumbigala is a tranquil and atmospheric spot. Spread over an expanse of 47 sq km (18 sq miles), the hermitage consists of hundreds of shrines set in rock caves, some of which contain inscriptions in Brahmi – an Ancient Indian script, dating back to the 5th century BC. The site is said to date back to the 2nd century AD and was originally established as a refuge for Buddhist monks seeking isolation and a life of quiet reflection. Monks still come here to meditate. Visitors, meanwhile, come for the breathtaking views from the summit of the highest rock, crowned by a *dagoba*.

THE VEDDAHS

The Veddahs or *Wanniyala-Aetto* (forest people) are the original forest-dwelling inhabitants of Sri Lanka and are thought to have lived on the island for millennia. Over the years, many Veddahs have been assimilated into the local Sinhalese and Tamil communities, although there are some who have resisted government resettlement schemes and have tried to carve out a life that retains their traditional beliefs and customs - including ancestor worship and coexisting in harmony with nature - and the hunter-gatherer lifestyle of their forefathers. Colonization, land development, implementation of reserves and national parks, as well as the Civil War, have all affected the Veddah way of life and their traditional land is fast disappearing.

A cow being fed by a shopkeeper in Jaffna

JAFFNA AND THE NORTH

Much of the story of northern Sri Lanka has been shaped by its proximity to India. Exactly when the first settlers arrived here from southern India remains unclear, although there seems to have been a Tamil presence on the Jaffna Peninsula since as far back as the 3rd century BC.

By the 13th century AD, a powerful Tamil kingdom – Jaffnapatnam – had emerged here. Thanks to its control of the strategically important Palk Strait, connecting India's east and west coasts, Jaffnapatnam soon attracted the attentions of the Portuguese. These European invaders gained control of Jaffna in 1621, only to be evicted by the Dutch in 1658, who built Jaffna's massive star fort.

The North receded in importance during the British era but sprang back to tragic prominence with the outbreak of the Civil War. During the conflict, much of the region functioned as a self-contained state, ruled by the despotic LTTE. Repeated fighting reduced many of the region's towns and villages to rubble, and hundreds of thousands of landmines made large swathes of countryside uninhabitable. Reconstruction since the war's end in 2009 has been commendably swift, although many scars remain in the form of bullet-ridden buildings and a strong military presence. Today, visitors are drawn to this, Sri Lanka's empiest and least-developed region, to experience its natural, eerie beauty.

Palk Strait

Kankesanturai

Valvedditturai

Point Pedro

AB21

AB20

Karaitivu

Tellippalai

✈ Jaffna

Uppu Aru
Lagoon

Vallipuram

Karainagar

Puttur

JAFFNA
PENINSULA ❶

Manalkadu
Desert

JAFFNA
ISLANDS ❷

Kayts

Jaffna

Kodikamam

A9

Chavakachcheri

B371

Kayts

Valanai

Punkudutivu

AB19

Pallai

Nainativu

AB39

Kurikadduwan

Jaffna
Lagoon

Delft

Palaitivu

Pooneryn

A32

Kakerativu

Chempankundu

Mandekal
Aru

B375

Palk Bay

Mudkompan

Pallawarayankaddu

Akkarayan

Iranativu
North

Akkarayan
Kulam

Iranativu
South

Mulankavit

Vellankulam

B269

A32

Talaimannar

MANNAR
ISLAND ❺

Anthoniyarpuram

Vavuni
Kulam

A14

Vidattaltivu

Mannar

Periyamadu

Moondu
Murippu

Thiruketheeswaram

Gulf of
Mannar

A32

Adampan

Parappukadanthan

Palampiddy

Yodha
Wewa

Madhu

B299

A14

B378

A30

Ahathimurippu

Silavathurai

Mullikulam

**THE WEST
COAST**
p86

THE EAST
p190

THE CULTURAL
TRIANGLE
p158

JAFFNA AND THE NORTH

Must Sees
1. Jaffna Peninsula
2. Jaffna Islands

Experience More
3. Vavuniya
4. Kilinochchi
5. Mannar Island
6. Elephant Pass

Bay of Bengal

Maruthankerny

6 ELEPHANT PASS

A9

A35

Tharmapuram

4 KILINOCHCHI

Visuvamadu

Puthukkudiyiruppu

Thirumurikandy

Iranamadu Tank

A35

Nanthi Kadal Lagoon

Mullaittivu

Muthuiayankadu Kulam

Mulliyawalai

A9

A34

Oddusudan

B296

A34

Mankulam

B269

B334

Nayaru Lagoon

B297

Kokkuthoduvai

Kanakarayankulam

Nedunkerni

Tannimurippu Kulam

Kokkilai Lagoon

NORTHERN

B296

Nedunkerni

Puliyankulam

A9

Omantai

Padawiya Tank

B60

JAFFNA AND THE NORTH

3 VAVUNIYA

✈ Vavuniya

B211

A29

Pavatkulam Tank

NORTH CENTRAL

A14

A9

Medawachchiya

0 kilometres   20

0 miles   20

N

The Clock Tower, overlooking a cricket pitch, in Jaffna, the main town on the peninsula ↑

❶

JAFFNA PENINSULA

🅐D1 🅐385 km (246 miles) NE of Colombo 🚌

Located at the northernmost tip of Sri Lanka, the fertile Jaffna Peninsula is still fairly isolated from the rest of the country. Some evidence of the Civil War still remains in the form of roofless buildings and heavily militarized areas, but temples are being repainted and renovated, and houses are being rebuilt. Travel around this primarily rural peninsula to catch glimpses of a world that remains untouched by modernity.

①

Jaffna

🅐169 km (105 miles) NE of Mannar Island 🚌

The peninsula's main city, Jaffna, is very different from the rest of Sri Lanka, primarily because of the scars it bears from the long conflict of Civil War. Although there are very few tourist sights, it is still a fascinating place to visit.

Built by the Dutch between 1680 and 1792 on the site of an earlier Portuguese construction, the enormous Jaffna Fort suffered during the fighting – renovation efforts are ongoing. It is possible to walk around the ramparts and see some of the original coralline bricks used in the construction of the edifice. Other important sights in the town include the Jaffna Public Library, which was torched by Sinhalese mobs in 1981, and the Clock Tower, which was erected in 1875 to a design by British architect J G Smither.

All the main religions have their representative houses of worship in Jaffna, but the large Christian buildings are hardest to miss. The Main Street is lined with atmospheric churches, including St James Church and the enormous **St Mary's Cathedral**. The latter has a pleasant interior and shady grounds where visitors can rest for a while and take in the peace and quiet.

Jaffna's **Archaeological Museum** is situated west of the town centre. It contains 15th-century artifacts excavated from Kantharodai, along with Hindu and Buddhist antiquities. Jaffna also boasts a vibrant market towards the west of the bus station. Although it is stocked with many day-to-day items, palmyra bags and mats are among the most popular products for sale. There is also a covered produce market where vendors sell a wealth of fresh fruit and vegetables.

> **All the main religions have their representative houses of worship in Jaffna, but the large Christian buildings are hardest to miss.**

St Mary's Cathedral
🏠 Press Road ⏰ 8am–5pm daily

Archaeological Museum
🏠 Navaly Road ⏰ 8am–5pm Wed–Mon

---

②

Nallur Kandaswamy Temple

📍 2 km (1 mile) NE of Jaffna ⏰ 5am–7pm daily; inner sanctum: 6am–2pm & 4–7pm daily 🌐 nalluran.com

Dedicated to Skanda or Murugan, the original Nallur Kandaswamy Temple was destroyed by the Portuguese in the 17th century and the current building dates to the 19th century. The temple features a richly decorated interior, with an ornate ceiling. The temple is the centre of the 25-day-long Nallur Chariot Festival, held between July and September, which reaches its peak on the 24th day when a large carved wooden cart is paraded through the streets.

Men must remove their clothing from the waist up to enter the temple, while women must cover their knees and shoulders.

③

Kantharodai

📍 10 km (6 miles) N of Jaffna ⏰ Daily

An unusual and atmospheric spot, Kantharodai is an archaeological site comprising a cluster of squat miniature *dagobas*. These stupas are thought to be around 2,000 years old, but their exact purpose or significance remains a mystery. Some think that the *dagobas* enshrine the remains of monks, while others say that they were constructed and consecrated in fulfilment of prayers. Artifacts from the site are on display in Jaffna's Archaeological Museum.

---

④

Nilavarai Well

📍 10 km (6 miles) NE of Jaffna ⏰ Daily

According to legend, the Hindu god Rama created the Nilavarai Well to quench his thirst. It may not be much to look at, but the well is a natural phenomenon as the water at the top is fresh, while the deeper water is more saline.

EAT

Rio Ice Cream
One of Jaffna's favourite meeting spots, this colourful ice-cream parlour is a great place to cool down.
🏠 448 Point Pedro Road, Jaffna

$$$

Mango's
Expect a wide-ranging menu of North and South Indian vegetarian food at this Jaffna eatery.
🏠 359 Temple Rd, Jaffna
☎ (021) 222 8294

$$$

Malayan Café
South Indian-style café, offering an authentic taste of Tamil cuisine in Jaffna, with cheap rice and curries, served on banana leaf "plates".
🏠 36 Grand Bazaar, Jaffna

$$$

⑤ Valvedditturai

⌂ 30 km (19 miles) NE of Jaffna

A fishing town, Valvedditturai (often abbreviated to VVT) is most famous as the birthplace of the founder of the LTTE, Velupillai Prabhakaran. However, the elusive guerilla leader's childhood home was destroyed in 2010.

Valvedditturai has a couple of interesting temples, including the **Amman Temple** towards the east of the town. The temple's festival, in April, draws huge crowds. Behind this shrine is a temple dedicated to Shiva, and formerly owned by Prabhakaran's family.

Did You Know?

The Jaffna Peninsula is famed for its succulent mangos, in season from May.

Amman Temple

⌂ Commantharai Road
🕐 6am–6pm daily

---

⑥ Point Pedro

⌂ 33 km (21 miles) NE of Jaffna

Point Pedro is the peninsula's second-largest town and sits at Sri Lanka's northernmost point. The bustling town, known as PPD, doesn't have much in the way of sights, but you can check out the Theru Moodi Madam. This gateway, which shades the road, is thought to date from Dutch colonial times.

The point itself, 2 km (1 mile) northwest of the town centre, offers views of both sunrise and sunset. Point Pedro's main landmark is its lighthouse, which is located in a military base to the east of the centre, but can be photographed from the road with permission of the sentry. Fisherman's beach, located just east of the lighthouse, is attractive and worth a visit.

⑦ Manalkadu Desert

⌂ 11 km (7 miles) S of Point Pedro

Towards the south of Point Pedro is a modest stretch of white-sand coastal dunes, somewhat grandly called the Manalkadu Desert. The remains of St Anthony's Church, dating from the early 20th century, can be seen here, half-buried in the sand. From the church, you'll see an eerie group of seafront grave markers, mostly dating to the 2004 tsunami. There is also a beach lapped by bright blue water, and a small cluster of new houses built after the devastating tsunami.

---

⑧ Keerimalai Springs

⌂ 20 km (12 miles) N of Jaffna 🕐 Daily

Located at the peninsula's northern edge are the Keerimalai hot springs, one for men and one for women.

Colourful boats moored on Fisherman's beach, near Point Pedro's lighthouse ↓

The latter is walled but the men's pool has a good view of the sea.

According to local folklore, a 7th-century Chola princess had such a disfigured face that she resembled a horse, until she bathed in these waters and was cured of her affliction. In gratitude, she ordered the construction of the **Maviddapuram Kandaswamy Temple**, found south of the area.

The springs attract many visitors who come to immerse themselves in the therapeutic waters. There is another temple, the **Naguleswaram Siva Kovil**, nearby, which is dedicated to Shiva. The damage it sustained in the late 1990s is no longer apparent, and the interior has been repainted in a riot of colours.

Maviddapuram Kandaswamy Temple

⌂ Kankesanturai
⊙ 6am–6pm daily
Ⓦ mavaikandan.com

Naguleswaram Siva Kovil

⌂ Kankesanturai ⊙ 6am–6pm daily

↑ Women praying in Vishnu Kovil, the Hindu temple in Vallipuram

⑨
Vallipuram

⌂ 4 km (2.5 miles) S of Point Pedro

A sleepy town, Vallipuram's main attraction is **Vishnu Kovil**, dedicated to the Hindu god Vishnu, who is believed to have appeared here in the form of a fish.

Vishnu Kovil

⌂ Maruthankerny Road
⊙ 5am–5pm daily

2

JAFFNA ISLANDS

🅰 B/C1 🚗 380 km (236 miles) N of Colombo 🚢 Available for trips to Nainativu and Delft

Stretching out into the waters of the Palk Strait, this string of small islands can feel like the end of the earth – they are sparsely populated, with white sand, blue sea and palmyra trees. Kayts, Karaitivu and Punkudutivu are connected to the mainland by causeways, but the other islands can only be accessed by boat. For a relaxing day on the beach, Karaitivu or Kayts are the best options, while the more isolated Delft is the place for those seeking to get away from it all.

①
Delft

🚗 41 km (25 miles) W of Jaffna 🚢

Named after the famous Dutch city, and better known locally by its Tamil name Neduntivu, this island was occupied by all three colonial powers, despite being the most remote of Jaffna's inhabited islands. Delft is known for its wild ponies, descendants of horses first introduced by the Portuguese.

West of the ferry dock stand the ruins of a coral Dutch fort, while to the dock's south is an immense baobab tree, an unusual sight outside of Africa. The island also has some peaceful swathes of sand, which are perfect for lounging on.

Make the most of your trip to the island by hiring a tuk-tuk from the dock as soon as your ferry arrives from the mainland. Your driver will show you all the main sights and then can drop you at the beach for the rest of the day.

②
Nainativu

🚗 31 km (19 miles) SW of Jaffna 🚢

This small island is of great religious importance to Hindus as well as to Buddhists. Located near the jetty, the Naga Pooshani Ambal Kovil is a Hindu temple dedicated to the goddess Ambal, who blesses newborn babies. The original temple was destroyed by the Portuguese. The structure that you see today dates from 1788.

Nearby is the Buddhist Nagadipa Vihara, featuring a silver *dagoba* that marks the spot of the Buddha's second visit to Sri Lanka, when he is said to have restored peace to the area. Across the road by the bo tree is a seven-headed cobra fountain, where pilgrims often pose for photographs.

Did You Know?

The remotest of the islands, Kachchativu, is just 22 km (14 miles) from India.

popular stretch of sand. To the northwest is Kayts town, from where there are ferries to Karaitivu. The town also affords excellent views of the offshore Hammenhiel Fort, which dates from the 17th century, and is now the site of an upmarket hotel, run by the Sri Lankan navy.

← Nainativu's striking Naga Pooshani Ambal Kovil, and *(inset)* its brightly coloured interior

⑤
Karaitivu
🏠 33 km (21 miles) NW of Jaffna

Known as Amsterdam under the Dutch, Karaitivu is the most northerly of the islands. Karaitivu has churches, temples and shrines, but the highlight here is undoubtedly Casuarina Beach, which lies on the northern end of the island. Popular with locals and foreign tourists, this beach is safe for swimming. Basic facilities such as changing rooms and toilets are available on the beach.

③
Punkudutivu
🏠 24 km (15 miles) SW of Jaffna

The main reason to visit Punkudutivu is to catch a ferry to either Nainativu or Delft from the jetty in the west of the island. On the way, you'll see fishermen at work.

④
Kayts
🏠 6 km (4 miles) SW of Jaffna

The largest of these islands, Kayts is the nearest to Jaffna. It was christened Leiden by the Dutch and is called Velanai locally. South of the island is the Chatty (Velanai) Beach, a

EXPERIENCE MORE

3

Vavuniya

🅰D2 🚗63 km (39 miles)
N of Anuradhapura 🚉🚌

Two hours' drive north of
Anuradhapura, the bustling
provincial town of Vavuniya
marks the cultural border
between the Sinhalese south
and the Tamil north. As such,
the town found itself on the
front line of fighting for much
of the Civil War, and (during
the ceasefire) it became the
border point for entry into
the quasi-independent areas
controlled by the LTTE.

Vavuniya does not offer
many compelling reasons to
stop, but there are some
interesting *kovils* (temples) as
well as the golden-domed
Grand Jummah Mosque, an
architectural gem.

North of here stretches
the Vanni, one of the emptiest
regions of Sri Lanka, still
dotted with the patches of
impenetrable jungle which
once provided the LTTE with
their most secure hideouts.
Historically one of the least
populated areas of Sri Lanka,
the entire region remains
strangely, almost eerily,
deserted compared to other
parts of the island.

Running across the Vanni
from Vavuniya to Jaffna,
the A9 Highway was another
key war location, dubbed
the "highway of death" on
account of the lives lost along
it. Now immaculately restored
and enlarged, it offers few
reminders of its bloody past,
although passing drivers can
still be seen stopping at
roadside temples to offer
prayers for a safe journey.

Grand Jummah Mosque

🏠Horowapatana Road
🕐7am–7pm Sat–Thu, 7am–
noon & 2–7pm Fri

4

Kilinochchi

🅰D1 🚗N of Vavuniya 🚌

The major town of the Vanni,
bustling Kilinochchi offers a
vivid symbol of the island's
rebirth following two decades
of Civil War. Back in the war
years, the town served as the
capital of what was in effect
an independent Tamil state,
ruled by the LTTE. It was
an HQ for the movement's
leaders and administration.
Retaking
Kilinochchi
thus became

a key goal for the Sri Lankan
army following the resump-
tion of fighting in 2008. A
devastating two-month battle
for the town ensued, before
the LTTE were finally driven
out, leaving Kilinochchi
reduced to an enormous
pile of rubble.

The scale of reconstruction
since has been impressively
thorough, with few reminders
of the fighting now visible
beyond the occasional bullet-
scarred house. Two monu-
ments commemorate the
battle. The first, an unusual
war memorial, shows a shell
piercing a solid stone cube,
with a lotus blooming from
the top. More poignant,
however, is the second: a

The splendid golden-
domed Grand Jummah
Mosque in Vavuniya ↓

↑ The remains of an old Portuguese sea fort in Mannar Town, Mannar Island

TOP 5 MANNAR ISLAND BIRDS

Greater flamingos
Mannar's most eye-catching visitor is found on the wetlands.

Painted storks
Instantly recognizable thanks to their huge yellow beaks and slender pink legs.

Long-tailed shrike
This colourful little bird is one of Mannar's many Indian visitors.

Oystercatcher
Rare outside Mannar, this is one of the island's many waders.

Eurasian Curlew
Another species seldom seen in Sri Lanka outside Mannar.

huge, collapsed water tower, lying shattered on its side; it was blown up by the LTTE and now provides a vivid reminder of the devastation caused by the conflict.

---

5 Mannar Island

🅐 C2 🏠 63 km (39 miles) NW of Vavuniya 🚌🚆

Poking out of the northeast coast like a crooked finger towards India, Mannar Island is one of Sri Lanka's most remote but intriguing destinations. Badly hit during the Civil War, the island is now seeing tourists again for the first time in decades, including adventurous kitesurfers, attracted by the unspoiled beaches and excellent wind conditions. It is also a major bird-watching hotspot, with many migrant species making their first landfall in Sri Lanka here after crossing from India.

Scruffy Mannar Town is the island's major settlement, home to the interesting remains of an old Portuguese seafront fort. Just outside the town stands a short but immensely fat baobab tree, almost 20 m (66 ft) in circumference. The tree is said to have been planted in around 1480 by Arab traders, who are also believed to have

introduced the island's wild donkeys, which can still be seen roaming the town.

From here a single road runs across the island, through a beautiful landscape of sand dunes, salt flats and slender palmyra palms, to reach Talaimannar, just 30 km (18 miles) from India. The rusty remains of the old jetty from which ferries used to make the crossing survives, while out to sea a chain of islets and sandbanks known as Adam's Bridge outline the land bridge that once connected the two countries.

---

6 Elephant Pass

🅐 D1 🏠 90 km (56 miles) N of Vavuniya

A narrow causeway separating Jaffna Peninsula from the mainland, Elephant Pass was one of the island's most fiercely contested locations during the Civil War, and the site of two major battles between the Sri Lankan Army and LTTE. A large war memorial stands at the southern edge of the causeway, showing hands lifting a lotus-studded map of the island.

Further south, the burned-out remains of an armoured bulldozer offer a more moving and realistic reminder of the horrors of war. Used as a makeshift tank by the LTTE, the bulldozer was stopped only when a young Sri Lankan Army soldier, Gamini Kularatne, leapt in, detonating a grenade, and killing himself and everyone inside.

← The striking Elephant Pass War Memorial

NEED TO KNOW

The hullabaloo of Pettah, Colombo

BEFORE
YOU GO

Forward planning is essential to any successful trip. Be prepared for all eventualities by considering the following points before you travel.

AT A GLANCE

CURRENCY

Sri Lankan rupee (LKR), denoted by $ in this guide

AVERAGE DAILY SPEND

SAVE	SPEND	SPLURGE
6,000 LKR	**16,000 LKR**	**40,000 LKR**

BOTTLED WATER	COFFEE	BEER	DINNER FOR TWO
100 LKR	**400 LKR**	**500 LKR**	**5,000 LKR**

ESSENTIAL PHRASES

Hello	Ayubowan or kohomadah
Goodbye	Ayubowan or kohomadah
Please	Karuna karalah
Thank you	Sthuthi
Do you speak English	Obah ingireesi kata karanavaada?
I don't understand	Mata thereney nayhay

ELECTRICITY SUPPLY

Power sockets are type D, M and G. Standard voltage is 230–240 V and the frequency is 50 Hz.

Passports and Visas

Citizens of virtually all countries require a visa to enter Sri Lanka. These can be bought on arrival, although it's easier and cheaper to purchase an Electronic Travel Authorization (ETA) online in advance. Standard tourist visas are valid for 30 days, but can be extended for up to six months at the Immigration Service Centre in Colombo.
Electronic Travel Authorization
w eta.gov.lk

Travel Safety Information

Visitors can get up-to-date travel safety information from the **US State Department**, **UK Foreign and Commonwealth Office** and the **Australian Department of Foreign Affairs and Trade**.
Australia
w smartraveller.gov.au
UK
w gov.uk/foreign-travel-advice
US
w travel.state.gov

Customs Information

An individual is permitted to carry the following into Sri Lanka for personal use:
Tobacco products Not permitted.
Alcohol 1.5 l of spirits and two bottles of wine.
Cash You are not permitted to enter Sri Lanka with over 20,000 LKR in cash. If you plan to carry over 15,000 LKR (or the equivalent in other currencies), you must declare it upon arrival.
Medicines If bringing a large quantity of personal medicines with you it's wise to carry your prescriptions in case of enquiries.

Insurance

It's essential to take out an insurance policy including theft, loss of belongings, medical problems, cancellations and delays. Check, too, that your policy will cover you if you're planning on doing activities such as surfing, kitesurfing, diving and whitewater rafting.

Vaccinations

No inoculations are required to enter Sri Lanka, apart from yellow fever if you are arriving from an affected area. A Hepatitis A vaccination is often recommended by healthcare professionals.

Money

The official currency is the Sri Lankan rupee (LKR), denoted throughout this guide by the $ symbol. Some hotels require you to pay in US dollars. There are ATMs in all towns and most accept Visa and/or Mastercards, although you'll pay the local bank a transaction fee in addition to any other charges. Credit cards are sometimes accepted, although Sri Lanka remains an essentially cash-based country. You should always carry plenty of notes, especially outside Colombo.

Booking Accommodation

Sri Lanka offers a huge variety of accommodation, from five-star multinational chain hotels to tiny family-run guesthouses. Guesthouses are an island speciality, whether in hillside tea-planter bungalows or stylish boutique retreats along the coast. There are also plenty of informal kite-surfing camps and tented safari lodges, often in spectacularly remote locations. Local companies, such as **Red Dot Tours**, **Villas in Sri Lanka** and **Sri Lanka in Style**, can arrange tours and have access to the pick of the island's places to stay.

Red Dot Tours
W reddottours.com
Sri Lanka in Style
W www.srilankainstyle.com
Villas in Sri Lanka
W villasinsrilanka.com

Travellers with Specific Needs

Unfortunately, Sri Lanka presents a challenge for travellers with specific needs. Pavements (where they exist) are often jammed with parked cars, public transport is tricky or impossible to board and there are few specially adapted hotel rooms. The best advice is to contact a reputable tour operator and arrange private transport with a driver who understands and is sympathetic to your needs.

Language

Sinhala is the language of the Sinhalese, while Tamil is mother tongue of the island's Tamil population. English is widely spoken, often to a high standard, and even in remote areas there's usually someone who understands at least a few words. Most signs are trilingual in Sinhala, Tamil and English, although some buses are signed only in Sinhala or, in the north, Tamil.

Closures

Saturday and Sunday Sri Lanka operates a standard Monday to Friday working week, meaning that banks and offices are closed on weekends, although some post offices open on Saturday. Museums and other tourist attractions are generally open daily. A few might close for one or two days weekly, although not necessarily over the weekend. Most shops open daily, although a few close on Sundays.

Public holidays Banks, post offices and government offices close, although many smaller, independently owned businesses remain open.

PUBLIC HOLIDAYS	
January	Duruthu Poya
14 or 15 Jan	Thai Pongal
February	Navam Poya
4 February	Independence Day
Feb/March	Maha Sivarathri
March	Medin Poya
March/April	Good Friday
April	Bak Poya
13 & 14 April	Sinhalese and Tamil New Year
1 May	Labour Day
May (2 days)	Vesak Poya
May/June	Eid ul-Fitr
June	Poson Poya
July	Esala Poya
August	Nikini Poya
September	Binara Poya
October	Vap Poya
October	Milad un-Nabi
Oct/Nov	Deepavali
November	Il Poya
December	Unduvap Poya
25 Dec	Christmas Day

GETTING AROUND

Whether you're visiting for a short beach break or travelling around the island, discover how best to reach your destination and travel like a pro.

Arriving by Air

The country's only functioning international airport is the **Bandaranaike International Airport**, which is 6 km (4 miles) away from the city of Negombo. The airport has regular connections to numerous European, Asian and Middle Eastern cities. The Mattala Rajapaksa International Airport, near Hambantota, is not currently receiving commercial passenger flights, although it may in the future. For journey times between the airport and the major cities, see the table opposite.
Bandaranaike International Airport
🅦 airport.lk

Domestic Air Travel

The speediest way to travel across the island is undoubtedly by air. **Cinnamon Air** offers regular scheduled flights from Colombo to various other cities. Air travel is a great alternative to laborious travel by road. The seven-hour journey to Trincomalee from the capital, for example, takes a mere 50 minutes in the air. The main advantage, however, is the chance to see the island from above. The most stunning aerial views are enjoyed when flying to or across the verdant undulations of the Hill Country.

Some routes require the use of a seaplane, where you'll take off and land on various lagoons, including the remote Castlereagh Reservoir, which is set amid some of the Hill Country's highest and wildest peaks, and the palm-fringed south coast lagoons at Koggala and Dickwella. Seaplane destinations currently include Kandy, Castlereagh (for Adam's Peak), Koggala, Dickwella, Hambantota, Sigiriya, Trincomalee and Batticaloa. Fares range from around 27,000–45,000 LKR for a one-way journey. Chartered flights are also available to Nuwara Eliya, Anuradhapura and Jaffna. **Sri Lankan Airlines**' Air Taxi service operates seaplanes and chartered flights.
Cinnamon Air
🅦 cinnamonair.com
Sri Lankan Airlines
🅦 srilankan.com

GETTING TO AND FROM BANDARANAIKE AIRPORT

Destination	Journey time	Taxi fare
Colombo	1hr	3,000 LKR
Negombo	20min	800 LKR
Galle	2hr	8,000 LKR
Kandy	3hr	10,000 LKR

JOURNEY PLANNER

This map offers a handy reference for journey times by car or express bus between Sri Lanka's main towns and cities. The opening (planned for 2020) of the Kandy and Hambantota motorway extensions will significantly reduce some travel times.

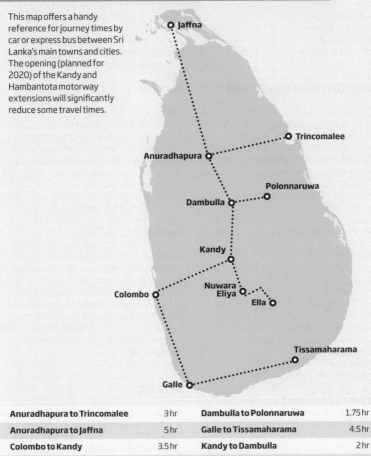

Anuradhapura to Trincomalee	3 hr		**Dambulla to Polonnaruwa**	1.75 hr
Anuradhapura to Jaffna	5 hr		**Galle to Tissamaharama**	4.5 hr
Colombo to Kandy	3.5 hr		**Kandy to Dambulla**	2 hr
Colombo to Galle	1.5 hr		**Kandy to Nuwara Eliya**	2.5 hr
Dambulla to Anuradhapura	1.5 hr		**Nuwara Eliya to Ella**	2.5 hr

Train Travel

Riding Sri Lanka's colonial-era railways (*p48*) is one of the best ways to get around the island, with 1,508 km (937 miles) of track. Recent upgrades to lines and rolling stock have also significantly reduced some journey times, although fares remain extremely cheap.

There are three classes. First class (only available on some routes) comprises modern air-conditioned carriages. Second and third class are similar, although second has slightly more comfortable seats. Unreserved tickets (second and third class only) can be bought on the day at stations, although you may end up standing. Reserved seats (available in all three classes) sell out fast and it's best to book in advance either through a tour operator or online at **Visit Sri Lanka Tours** or **12Go**. The **Sri Lankan Railways** website has full timetable and fare information.

12Go
🌐 12go.asia
Sri Lankan Railways
🌐 railway.gov.lk
Visit Sri Lanka Tours
🌐 visitsrilankatours.co.uk

Long-Distance Bus Travel

Buses remain the best way of getting to remote areas of the island, reaching even the smallest of towns. Services are run by a mix of private companies and the Sri Lanka Transport Board (SLTB), which operates the red buses. There are also private "luxury" services on major routes in smaller, minibus-style vehicles with curtained windows, although these can be rather cramped. Departures on major routes are frequent, running every 30 minutes or so, and fares are extremely cheap – averaging at around 100 LKR per hour's travel (except on toll motorway services). On the downside, Sri Lanka's buses aren't particularly comfortable, and can get packed to the rafters with standing passengers, while driving standards can be borderline hair-raising. An outline of major services can be found on the **Routemaster** website. A few services can be booked in advance or online, although in practice it's easiest to just turn up and buy a ticket on board.

Routemaster
🌐 routemaster.lk

Urban Transport

Tuk-tuks and taxis are the principal means of making short journeys in Sri Lanka. Colombo is the only place where it might be worth braving the local public buses, but even in the capital it is difficult to find the right stop. Tuk-tuks and taxis are far more reliable.

Tuk-tuks

Tuk-tuks (the motorized rickshaws, also known locally as "three-wheelers" or sometimes just as "taxis") are ubiquitous in Sri Lanka, and a standard means of getting from A to B for tourists and locals alike. Except in Colombo, there are no meters or set fares. Simply tell the driver where you want to go and they will name a price, which you're then free to accept or negotiate. Bargaining is universal, and some drivers will double their fares at the approach of a foreigner. It helps to ask what a reasonable fare should be at the reception desk at your accommodation before setting out, although bear in mind that you'll generally be charged more than a local. It's essential to agree a fare before setting off so you avoid any unpleasantness or scams at the end of the journey.

Metered tuk-tuks are widespread in Colombo, although many drivers will claim they're "broken" and there are also regular reports of meters being fixed to inflate prices. To ensure a fair fare, book a tuk-tuk through the **PickMe** app, which arranges a reputable metered rickshaw within minutes.

PickMe
🌐 pickme.lk

Taxis

You can hire a taxi in all large Sri Lankan towns, but be aware that these are often minibuses rather than cars, and aren't metered. As with tuk-tuks, you'll have to negotiate a fare before setting off. Larger towns often have designated taxi parking areas (opposite the entrance to the Temple of the Tooth in Kandy, for example), where you'll find a dozen or more vehicles waiting for custom. These ranks decrease the chances of drivers inflating their fares.

It's a lot easier to avoid being ripped off in Colombo, where you can book a taxi (car, not minivan) using the PickMe app. Taxi fares are often cheaper on the app than what you would pay if you hailed a tuk-tuk on the street. The app's service can be patchy outside the capital. The city also has several dedicated taxi firms, such as the reputable **Kangeroo Cabs**, operating modern radio-controlled metered taxis.

Kangeroo Cabs
🌐 kangeroocabs.com

Driving

Driving in Sri Lanka is not for the faint-hearted, and very few visitors get behind the wheel. Road conditions are challenging, with narrow, congested highways and a wide range of hazards including stray dogs, erratic cyclists, wandering pedestrians, kamikaze bus drivers and so on. If you do want to drive you'll need an international driving permit from your home country, which must then be authorized on your arrival at the **Automobile Association of Ceylon** (AAC) in Colombo. Reliable places to hire a self-drive car include **Malkey** and **Casons Rent-a-Car**.

Automobile Association of Ceylon
🅦 aaceylon.lk
Casons Rent-a-Car
🅦 casons.lk
Malkey
🅦 malkey.lk

Renting a Car and Driver

Given the stresses of driving yourself, the vast majority of visitors hire a car and driver, either for the duration of their stay or for individual journeys from place to place. All of the island's major tour operators can provide a vehicle, and there are innumerable smaller outfits, as well as freelance drivers offering their services. Reputable operators include **Sri Lanka Driver Tours** and **Destination Sri Lanka Tours**.

Destination Sri Lanka Tours
🅦 dsltours.com
Sri Lanka Driver Tours
🅦 srilankadrivertours.com

Rules of the Road

Sri Lankan traffic follows a generally accepted, and somewhat anarchic, set of unwritten conventions. Traffic drives on the left, and various speed limits apply. Who has right of way is a tenuous concept, although a definite pecking order applies. Larger and faster vehicles (buses especially) will expect smaller vehicles to slow and pull over to allow them to pass. Overtaking itself is often a hair-raising manoeuvre. An oncoming car facing an overtaking bus, for example, will be expected to slow down (or even leave the road) irrespective of the fact that the bus is technically on "their" side of the road. Horns are used freely, especially by bus and lorry drivers when indicating their desire to overtake a slower vehicle, and also to say thank you when a slower vehicle allows yours to pass. Right-side indicators are used to indicate to a vehicle behind that it is safe to overtake. Absent-minded pedestrians and erratic cyclists add further excitement, as do the island's innumerable dogs, a surprising number of whom have lost legs during their encounters with passing traffic.

Cycling

Cycling is one of the most pleasant ways of getting around the island, assuming you can deal with the heat and the traffic. Bicycling around Polonnaruwa and Anuradhapura is a great way to explore the sights, while a longer route through the Hill Country is also recommended. Tours are organized by a number of operators including **Chameera Cycling**, **Enviro Bicycle Tours** and **Beyond Escapes**.

Beyond Escapes
🅦 beyondescapes.com
Chameera Cycling
🅦 chameeracycling.com
Enviro Bicycle Tours
🅦 envirobicycletours.com

Bicycle Hire

Bike hire in Sri Lanka is usually a fairly ad hoc affair, with few places formally renting out cycles. Try asking at your guesthouse to see if they have a spare bike or if they know anyone who does. Your next best bet is to ask around local tour operators, who sometimes rent out motorbikes and bicycles. Don't expect to find quality rides either – most Sri Lankan bikes are antiquated affairs with clunky frames and dodgy brakes, although a couple of places in Negombo, such as **Pick & Go**, have relatively new mountain bikes for hire.

Pick & Go
🅦 pickandgotravels.com

Bicycle Safety

When it comes to cycling, Sri Lanka is definitely not Amsterdam or Copenhagen. Right of way is determined by size and power, and as a cyclist you are effectively at the bottom of the food chain, meaning that you'll be expected to get out of the way. Bus and lorry drivers can be particularly aggressive. Exercise caution at all times, expect the unexpected and wear a helmet (bring your own if you plan on doing a lot of cycling, since they're not often available for hire). Road surfaces are often in poor condition too: watch out for potholes and other hazards.

Ferries

There are currently no scheduled ferries to Sri Lanka, although increasing numbers of cruise ships visit the island. The ferry that formerly ran between Mannar and Rameswaram in India ceased operating in 1983 at the outset of the Civil War. Services were very briefly resumed between Colombo and Tuticorin in India in 2011, but soon floundered. Rumours that the Indian ferry will be revived continue to circulate, although it now seems unlikely ever to come to fruition.

The only regular ferry routes in Sri Lanka are those between the various islands surrounding the Jaffna peninsula. It's only a short hop over shallow water from Kayts to Karaitivu, and Punkudutivu to Nainativu, while it's a much longer, and potentially rougher, crossing between the mainland and Delft.

PRACTICAL
INFORMATION

A little local know-how goes a long way in Sri Lanka. Here you will find all the essential advice and information you will need during your stay.

AT A GLANCE

EMERGENCY NUMBERS

GENERAL EMERGENCY

118/9

AMBULANCE

110

FIRE SERVICE

110

POLICE

118/9

TIME ZONE
IST
There is no daylight saving time.

TAP WATER
Avoid drinking tap water as it may provoke a stomach upset.

TIPPING
Tipping isn't generally expected in restaurants and hotels although, of course, it's always nice to show your appreciation for good service.

Personal Security

Sri Lanka is generally a very safe country, and attacks against tourists are extremely rare, although it makes sense to avoid empty beaches and dark backstreets after nightfall. Sexual harassment of female tourists is, sadly, more common. If you are worried about it, dress conservatively and, if bothered in a public place, call out your abuser in a loud voice to make others aware of his behaviour.

After the 2019 Easter bombings, many hotels have tightened their security and you may have to pass through scanners.

Health

It's important to seek medical advice before travelling, especially if you will be spending a long time in the country. All visitors should take out comprehensive travel insurance before travelling. If you are sick, consult a doctor at a local clinic; for minor problems, see a pharmacist. Malaria has now been eradicated from Sri Lanka and the most common complaint remains stomach upsets from contaminated food or water. Heat-related problems are also a risk, including sunburn, prickly heat and sunstroke. Keep properly hydrated and adequately covered at all times.

Smoking, Alcohol and Drugs

Possession of all common recreational drugs, both soft and hard, is illegal, and possession is a finable or even imprisonable offence.

Smoking is banned in most enclosed public spaces, including onboard trains and buses, at stations and in offices. Needless to say, you should refrain from smoking in (or even near) any temples. Most indoor restaurants are also non-smoking, although you can still smoke in most bars and pubs.

The drink driving limit is 0.06 BAC (blood alcohol content) – less than most countries. Given the hairy driving conditions, it would be best to stay completely sober if getting behind the wheel.

Local Customs

The traditional Sri Lankan greeting is *Ayubowan* (may you have long life), which is accompanied by hands placed together in a prayer-like gesture. Westernized Sri Lankan men are more likely to offer you a handshake, but do not shake hands with a Sri Lankan woman unless she offers her hand first.

Away from the beach, dressing conservatively (especially for women) will avoid causing offence or inviting unwelcome attention. Similarly, avoid kissing or similar public displays of affection.

Buddhist iconography is a delicate subject, and tattoos showing images of the Buddha should be covered at all times.

If eating without cutlery, use your right hand.

LGBT+ Safety

Homosexuality is illegal in Sri Lanka and public displays of affection should be absolutely avoided. Despite this, same-sex couples are unlikely to encounter problems. Useful resources include **Equal Ground** and **Utopia Asia**.

Equal Ground
w equal-ground.org
Utopia Asia
w utopia-asia.com.

Visiting Temples

Always remove your shoes before entering a Buddhist or Hindu temple. Dress conservatively with your shoulders and knees covered. Be careful to behave respectfully, especially close to Buddha images. Do not pose for photos (or take selfies) in front of statues with your back facing the Buddha. If sitting, try to avoid pointing your feet at a Buddha.

Mobile Phones and Wi-Fi

Wi-fi is almost universally available in guesthouses and hotels, as well as many restaurants, although connections can be patchy.

Most international mobile phones work in Sri Lanka apart from some US phones. If you're going to be making many calls (and your handset is unlocked), it's well worth picking up a local SIM card. Special tourist packages are sold at the airport for around 1,800 LKR, and you can also buy SIMs and top-up cards at shops all over the island. Just remember that you need your passport to buy them. Two of the largest and most reliable networks are **Dialog** and **Mobitel**.

Dialog
w dialog.lk
Mobitel
w mobitel.lk

Post

Sri Lanka Post offices are generally open 7am–9pm Mon–Fri, and some open on Saturday mornings. When sending packages overseas, take the contents to the counter first for customs clearance, before parcelling them up (larger post offices have dedicated wrapping counters). Air mail takes around four days to reach Europe and North America.

Sri Lanka Post
w slpost.gov.lk

Taxes

A confusing variety of government taxes apply to some hotel rooms and restaurant prices, including VAT (15 per cent), Nation-Building Tax (2 per cent) and Tourist Development Tax (1 per cent). Prices are often quoted inclusive of all taxes (the so-called "nett" rate), but not always. In addition, some hotels and restaurants also levy a 10 per cent service charge. It's worth checking which taxes are, and are not, included with individual establishments to avoid unpleasant surprises when receiving the bill.

WEBSITES AND APPS

Sri Lanka Tourism
The official website of the government tourist board, srilanka.travel offers a useful range of visitor information.

Colombo Telegraph
The website of this online "newspaper", colombotelegraph.com is Sri Lanka's leading source for independent news reporting and investigative journalism.

Sinhala by Nemo
A useful app if you fancy diving into the basics of Sinhala, with native speaker recordings, plus written scripts.

INDEX

Page numbers in **bold** refer to main entries.

PHRASE BOOK

Sinhala, also known as Sinhalese, is the native language of the Sinhalese people, the largest ethnic group in Sri Lanka. Tamil, a Dravidian language, is predominantly spoken by the Tamil people of northeastern Sri Lanka. Of the various dialects used by Sri Lankan Tamils, the two major ones are Indian Tamil and Jaffna Tamil, with the latter spoken in the Jaffna Peninsula. The two dialects differ in styles of speech and accent, although both are mutually comprehensible. Other regionally distinct dialects are Negombo Tamil and Batticaloa Tamil, which are spoken in the coastal regions, and Hill Country Tamil, used by the tea plantation workers.

GUIDELINES FOR PRONUNCIATION

The Sinhala alphabet is referred to as an "abugida" or "alphasyllabary", meaning that consonants are written with letters while vowels are indicated with *pilla* (diacritics) on those consonants. The complete alphabet consists of 54 letters: 18 vowels and 36 consonants.

The current Tamil script consists of 12 vowels, 18 consonants and one special character, the *āytam*. The vowels and consonants combine to form 216 compound characters, giving a total of 247 characters. All consonants have an inherent vowel "a", as with other

Indic scripts. This inherency is removed by adding a title called a *pulli*, to the consonantal sign.

When reading the phonetics, pronounce syllables as if they form English words. Note that double consonants highlight the need to stress the sound, such as a "pp" instead of a single "p" or "dhdh" rather than a single "dh".

VOWELS

u	as in **u**p (short)
aa	as in f**a**r (long)
a	as in **a**pple
e	as in **e**ver (short)
ay	as in pl**ay** (long)
i	as in p**i**n (short)
ee	as in fl**ee** (long)
o	as in **o**ver (short)
oa	as in **o**ver (but longer)
oo	as in p**u**ll (short)
oo	as in c**oo**l (long)
ai	as in fl**y**
er	as in b**ur**n (don't pronounce the "r")
ei	as in w**ai**t
ouw	as in h**ow**
ull	as in g**ull**

CONSONANTS

dh	as in wea**th**er
d	as in **d**ay
th	as in **th**irty
ng	as in si**ng**
gn	as in Ke**ny**a
g	as in **g**un
j	as in **j**ug

ENGLISH	SINHALA	SINHALA PHONETIC	TAMIL	TAMIL PHONETIC
IN AN EMERGENCY				
Help!	**Udhaw karanne!**	*Udh-ouw ker-run-ner!*	**Udhavungal!**	*oo-dher-voo-ng-ull!*
Fire!	**Gindhara!**	*gin-dhe-rer!*	**Neruppu!**	*ne-roop-poo!*
Where is the nearest hospital?	**Langama ispirithaalaya kohedhe?**	*Lung-er-mer is-pi-ri-thaa-ler-yer ko-hay-dhe?*	**Arughil ulla aaspaththiri engay?**	*a-roo-hil ul-ler aas-pu-th-thi-ri eng-gay?*
Call an ambulance!	**Ambulance ekakata kathaa karanne!**	*ambulance e-ker-ker-ter ka-thaa ker-run-ner!*	**Ambulansai koopudungal!**	*ambulans-ai koo-poo-doong-ull!*
Call the police!	**Polisiyata kathaa karanne!**	*Poli-si-yer-ter ka-thaa ker-run-ner!*	**Polissai koopudungal!**	*Po-lis-sai koo-poo-doong-ull!*
Call a doctor!	**Dhostere kenekuta kathaa karanne!**	*Dho-sther-er-ke-ne-koo-ter ka-thaa ker-run-ner!*	**Doctorai koopudungal!**	*doctor-ai koo-poo-doong-ull!*
COMMUNICATION ESSENTIALS				
Yes	**Ow**	*Ouw*	**Aamaam**	*aam-aam*
No	**Nay**	*Ney*	**Illai**	*ill-ai*
Hello	**Ayubowan**	*aa-you-bo-wu**nn***	**Vanakkam**	*va-nerk-kum*
Goodbye	**Mung yunnung (I am going)**	*mung yun-n-ung*	**Naan porane (I am going)**	*Naan poa-ray-n*
Please	**Karunakara**	*ku-roo-naaker-rer*	**Thayavu seithu**	*thu-yer-voo sei-dhoo*
Thank you	**sthuthi**	*s-thoo-thee*	**Nandri**	*nun-dree*
I don't understand	**Mata theruney nay**	*mu-ter they-roo-nay ney*	**Enakku puriyavillai**	*en-uk-koo poo-ri-yer-vill-ai*
I don't know	**Mama dhanney nay**	*Ma-mer dhun-nay ney*	**Enakku theriyaadhu**	*en-uk-koo they-ri-yaa-dhoo*
Sorry	**Kanagaatui**	*kun-er-gaa-too-yi*	**Mannikkavum**	*mun-nik-ker-voom*
Excuse me	**Mata Sama venna**	*Mu-ter-sa-maa ven-**ner***	**Vali vidungal (give way)**	*va-li vi-doong-gal*
			Manniyungal (Pardon me)	*mun-ni-yoong-gull*
USEFUL PHRASES				
How are you?	**Oya kohomadhe?**	*o-yaa ko-ho-mer-dher?*	**Eppudi irukureengal?**	*ep-poo-dee i-roo-koo-reeng-gull?*
Very well, thank you	**Mama hondhing, sthuthi**	*mu-mer hon-dheeng, s-thoo-thee*	**Naan nalla irukiren, nandri**	*naan nal-la i-roo-ki-ray-n, nun-dree*
Not very well	**Vadi hondhing nemey**	*va-dee hon-dheeng nay-may*	**Romba nalla illai**	*rom-ber nal-laa il-lai*
What is this?	**Mey mokadhdhe?**	*may mok-**adh**-**dh**er?*	**Idhu enna?**	*i-dhoo en-**ner**?*
How do I get to...?	**...ekata yanney kohomadhe?**	*...e-ker-ter yu**nn**-ay ko-ho-mer-dher?*	**...iku povadhu eppudi?**	*...ikoo po-ver-dhoo ep-**poo**-dee?*
Where is the restroom/toilet?	**...eka kohedhe? Viveka kaamaraya/ vesikilya?**	*...eka ko-hay-dher? vi-ve-ker kaa-mer-rer-yer/va-si-ki-li-yer?*	**...engulladhu? toilet?**	*...eng-**gul**-ler-dhoo? Toai-let?*
Do you speak English?	**Oya ingireesi kathaa karanavaadhe?**	*oh-yaa ing-**gi**-ree-si ku-thaa ker-er-ner-vaa-dher?*	**Neengal aangilam pesuveerghala?**	*neeng-gal aang-gil-am pay-soo-veer-hala?*
I can't speak Sinhala/ Tamil	**Mata singhala/dhamila kathaa karanne behey**	*mu-ter sing-her-ler/dhu-mi-ler ka-thaa ker-run-ner bey-hey*	**Enakku singhalam/ thamil pesa mudiyaadhu**	*e-nuk-**koo** sing-herl-lum/ tha-mil pay-ser moo-di-yaa-dhu*
USEFUL WORDS				
I	**Mama**	*mu-mer*	**Naan**	*Naa-n*
woman/women	**geheniya/gehenu**	*gey-hey-ni-yer/ gey-hey-noo*	**pen/penghal**	*pe**nn**/pe**nn**-ghull*
man/men	**pirimiya/pirimi**	*pi-ri-mi-yaa/pi-ri-mi*	**aan/aanghal**	*aan/aan-ghull*
child/children	**lamaya/lamai**	*lu-mer-yaa/lu-mai*	**pillai/pillaighal**	*pill-ai/pill-ai-hull*
family	**pawula**	*pu-woo-ler*	**kudumbam**	*koo-doom-bum*
good	**hondhai**	*hon-dhai*	**nallam**	*nul-lam*
bad	**narakai**	*nu-rer-kai*	**koodaadhu**	*koo-daa-dhoo*
open	**erilaa**	*a-ree-laa*	**thirandhulladhu**	*thi-run-dhul-ler-dhoo*
closed	**vahala**	*vu-hu-laa*	**moodiyulladhu**	*moo-di-yool-ler-dhoo*
left	**vama**	*vu-mer*	**idathu**	*i-der-dhoo*
right	**dhakuna**	*dhu-koo-ner*	**valathu**	*vu-ler-dhoo*
straight ahead	**keling issaraha**	*ke-ling is-ser-rer-haa*	**neraagha munnaal**	*nay-raa-her **moon**-**naal***
near	**langai**	*lung-gai*	**arughil**	*a-roo-ghil*
far	**dhurai**	*dhoo-rai*	**dhooram**	*dhoo-rum*
entrance	**dhoratuwa**	*dho-rer-too-ver*	**vaasal**	*vaa-su**ll***
exit	**pitavena dhora**	*pi-ter-ve-ner dho-rer*	**veliyerum vali**	*ve-li-yay-room vu-li*

English	Sinhala		Tamil	
area code	praadheshaya kethaya	praa-dhey-sher-yer kay-thay-yer	paghudi kuriyeedu	pa-hoo-dhee koo-ri-yee-doo ther-yer
toilet	vesikiliya	va-si-ki-li-yer	toilet	taai-let
post office	thepel kanthoruwa	tha-pal kun-tho-roo-ver	thabaal aluvalagham	thu-baal u-loo-vu-ler-herm
address	yomuwa	yo-moo-ver	mughavari	moo-her-vu-ree
street	veedhiya	vee-dhee-yer	theru	they-roo
town	nagharaya	nu-gher-rer-yer	nagharam	nu-gher-rerm
village	gama	guh-mer	graamam	graa-mum

MONEY

I want to change £100 into Sri Lankan currency.	Mata, Engalanthayey salli powum seeyak, Lankavey salli valata maaru karanne oney	mu-ter, eng-ger-lun-ther-yay sull-i pow-oom see-yuk, lung-kaa-vey sul-li ver-ler-ter maa-roo ker-run-ner oan-ay	Enakku, Ingalandhin kaasu nooru powunghalai, Ilangaiyin kaasaaha maatra vendum	ey-nok-koo, ing-er-lun-dhin kaa-soo noo-roo pow-oon-hul-ai, i-lung-gai-yin-kaa-saa-her maa-trer vayn-doom
exchange rate	vinimaya anupathikaya	vi-ni-mer-yer a-noo-paa-thi-ker-yer	maatru vighidham	maa-troo vee-hee-dham
bank	bankuwa	bank-oo-ver	vangi	vung-gee
money/cash	salli/mudhal	sull-ee/moo-dhul	kaasu/panam	kaa-soo/pu-num
credit card	naya kaadpatha	nu-yer kaad-pu-ther	kadan attai	ku-den ut-tai

MAKING A TELEPHONE CALL

I'd like to make a telephone call	Mata dhurakathana emathumak karanne oney	mu-ter dhoo-rer ku-ther-ner amer-thoo-muk ker-run-ner alaipai etpaduththa oan-ay	Enakku oru tholaipesi see a-lai-pai ayt-pa-doo-vendum	e-nuk-koo o-roo tho-lai-pay-ther vayn-doom
I'd like to make an international phone call	Mata anthar jaathika dhurakathana emathumak karanne oney	mu-ter un-thur jaa-thee-ker dhoo-rer ku-ther-ner ema-thoo-muck ker-run-ner oan-ay	Enakku oru sarvadhesa tholaipesi etpaduththa vendum	e-nuk-koo o-roo surr-ver dhey-ser tho-lai-pay-see a-lai-pai ate-pa-du-ther vayn-doom
mobile phone	Jangama dhurakathanaya	jung-ger-mer dhoo-rer ka-ther-ner-yer	Kai pesi	kai pay-see

SHOPPING

Where can I buy...?	...ganne puluwang kohendhe?	...gun-ner poo-loo-wung ko-hen-dher?	...engey vaangalaam?	...eng-ay vaang-er-laam?
How much does this cost?	Meykhe keeyadhe?	May-ker kee-yer-dher?	Idhu evalavu?	I-dhoo ev-ver-ler-voo?
May I try this on?	Meykhe endhalaa balanne puluwangdhe?	May-ker an-dher-laa ba-lan-ner poo-loo-wung-dher?	Idhai uduthu paakalaama?	I-dhai oo-doo-thoo paa-ker-laa-maa?
I would like...	Mama kemathi...	Ma-mer ka-mer-thee...	Enakku viruppam...	E-ner-koo vi-roop-pam...
Do you have...?	...thiyanavaadhe?	thi-yer-ner-vaa-dher?	...irukiradha?	i-roo-ki-rer-dhaa?
Do you take credit cards?	Oba naya kaadpath gannavaadhe?	O-ber nu-yer kaad-pa-th gun-ner-vaa-dher?	Kadan attai eduppeerghala?	Ku-den at-tai e-doo-peer-ler-laa?
What time do you open/close?	Oba keeyatadhe arinney/ vahanney?	O-ber-Kee-yer-ter-dher u-rin-ney/va-ha-ney?	Ethanai manikku thirappeerghal/ saathuveerghal?	E-ther-nai mu-nik-koo thi-rer-peer-hal/ saa-thoo-veer-hul?
How much?	Keeyadhe?	Kee-yer-dher?	Evvalavu?	Ev-ver-ler-voo?
Expensive	Ganang vedi	Gu-nung va-dee	Kooda vilai	Koo-der vi-lai
cheap	Laabai	Laa-bai	Malivu	Mu-lee-voo
size	Pramaanaya	Prer-maa-ner-yer	Alavu	U-ler-voo
colour	Paata	Paa-ter	Niram	Ni-rum
department store	Departhamenthu Alevisala	De-paa-r-ther-may-n-thoo A-le-vi-sa-ler	Thurai kadai	Thoo-rai ka-dai
market	Velendha Pola	Ve-le-n-dher-Po-ler	Sandhai	Sundh-dhai
pharmacy	Farmasiya / Beheth saapuwa	Faa-mer-si-yer / Bay-heth saa-poo-wer	Marunthu kadai	Mu-roon-dhoo ku-dai
supermarket	Supiri velendha sala	Soo-pi-ri ve-len-dher sa-ler	Supermarket	Soo-per-maar-kayt
souvenir shop	Sihivatana alevi sala	Si-hi-vu-ter-ner u-lay-vee sa-ler	Ninaivu porulkadai	Ni-nai-voo po-rool-hull ka-dai

SIGHTSEEING

travel agent	Sanchaaraka niyojithaya	Sun-chaa-rer-ker ni-yo-ji-ther-yer	Prayana muhavar	Prer-yaa-ner moo-her-verr
tourist office	Sanchaaraka kaaryalaya	Sun-chaa-rer-ker kaarr-yaa-ler-yer	Suttrula aluvalaham	Soot-troo-laa a-loo-vu-ler-hum
beach	Vella / verala	Va-ler / ve-rer-ler	Kadatkarai	Ku-dut-ku-rai
bay	Bokka	Bok-ker	Virikuda	Vi-ree-koo-daa
festival	Utsavaya	Oot-ser-ver-yer	Thiruvila	Thi-roo-vi-laa
island	Dhupatha	Dhou-per-ther	Theevu	Thee-voo
mountain	Kandha	Kundh-dher	Malai	Mu-lai
temple	Pansala	Pun-ser-ler	Kovil	Koa-vil
museum	Kouwthukagaraya	Kouw-thoo-kaa-gaa-rer-yer	Arungkaatchiyagam	A-roong-kaat-chi-yer-herm

GETTING AROUND

When does the train for...leave?	...ter yana kochchiya, keeyatadhe pitath venney?	...ter yu-ner koa-ch-chi-yer, kee-yer-ter-dher pit-uth ven-ney?	...irku pohum rail vandi, ethanai manikku kilambum?	...ir-koo poa-hoom ra-yil vun-dee, eth-thun-ai mun-ik-koo ki-lum-boom?
A ticket to...please.	Karun karala...ter Eka tikattuwak...	Ka-roo-naa-ker-ler-laa... ter e-ker ti-kut-oo-wak...	Thayavu seydhu, ...ikku oru ticket tharavum.	Thu-yer-voo sei-dhoo, ...ik-koo o-roo ticket thu-rer-voom.
How long does it take to get to...?	...ter yanna velaava kochcharak ganeedha?	...ter yun-ner ve-laa-ver koch-cher-ruk gun-ee-dher?	...irku poha evvalavu neyram sellum?	...ir-koo po-her ev-ver-ler-voo ney-rum sell-oom?
I'd like to reserve a seat, please.	Karuna karala, Mang venuven eka aasayanak wen karanne	Ka-roo-naa-ker-ler-laa Maung ve-noo-veng eka aa-ser-ner-yuk veng ker-run-ner.	Enakkaaha oru seatai odhukavum.	E-nerk-kaa-her o-roo seat-tai o-dhook-ker-voom.
Which platform for the...train?	.... Kochchiya koi platform ekey dhe?	... koa-ch-chi-ya koi platform e-kay dher?	... rail vandiku endhe platform?	...ra-yil vun-dik-koo en-dher platform?
train station	Dhumriya pala	Dhoom-ri-yer per-ler	Rail nilayam	Ra-yil ni-ler-yum
airport	Guwan thotupala	Goo-wun tho-tooper-ler	Vimaana nilayam	Vi-maa-ner ni-ler-yum
bus station	Bus nevathumpala	Bus na-ver-thoom-per-ler	Bus nilayam	Bus ni-ler-yerm
a one-way ticket	Thani gaman ticket ekak	Thu-nee gu-mun ti-kat-e-kuk	Oru vali ticket ondru	O-roo vu-li ti-ket on-droo
a return ticket	Prathyaagamana ticket ekak	Prer-thyaa-gu-mer-ner ti-kat-e-kuk	Irandu vali ticket ondru	I-rern-doo va-li ti-ket on-droo

235

taxi	Kulee rathayak	Koo-lee ru-ther-yuk	Taaksi	Taak-si
car	Car eka	Car e-ker	Car	Car
bus	Bus eka	Bus e-ker	Bus	Bus
train	Kochchiya	Koo-**ch-ch**i-yer	Rayil vandi	Ra-yil vun-di
plane	Plane eka	Plane e-ker	Vimaanam	Vi-maa-num
plane ticket	Plane ticket eka	Plane ti-kat e-ker	Vimaana ticket	Vi-maa-ner ti-ke**t**
motorbike	Motor cycleye	Moo-tar cy-kel-er-yer	Motaar cykil	Mo-toa**rr** cy-ki**ll**
bicycle	Bysikalaya	By-si-kerl-er-yer	Cykil	Cy-ki**ll**
ferry	Dhoney	Dhoa-nee	Padaghu	Pu-der-ghoo

ACCOMMODATION

Do you have a vacant room?	Hiss kaamarayak thiyanavaadhe?	Hi**ss** kaa-mer-rer-yuk thi-yer-ner-vaa-dher?	Kaaliyaana arai ondru irukkiradhaa?	Kaa-li-yaa-ner a-rai on-droo i-roo**k-k**i-rer-dhaa?
Double/twin room	Dvithva kaamaraya	Dhvi-**th**-ver kaa-mer-rer-yer	Irattai arai	I-rut-**t**ai u-rai
Single room	Thani kaamaraya	Tho-ni kaa-mer-rer-yer	Ottrai arai	Ott-rai u-rai
I have a reservation.	Mang venuveng, veng kara etha	Mung ve-noo-veng, veng ker-er a-ther	Enakkaaha odhukka pattulladhu	En-uk-**k**aa-her o-dhoo-ker put-tool-ler-dhoo
hotel	Hotelaya	Ho-tel-er-yer	Hotel	Hoa-taal
guesthouse	Guesthouse eka	Guesthouse e-ker	Virundhinar vidudhi	Vi-roon-dhi-na**rr** vi-doo-dhee
room (single, double)	Kamaraya (thani, dvithva)	Kaa-mer-rer-yer (tha-ni, dhvi-**th**-ver)	Arai (ottrai, irattai)	A-rai (ott-rai, i-rut-**t**ai)
air conditioning	AC ethi	AC e-thi	AC ulla	AC oo**ll**-er
bathroom	Naana kamaraya	Naa-ner kaa-mer-rer-yer	Kuliyal arai	Koo-li-yull a-rai

EATING OUT

A table for two please.	Dhennekuta meysayak	Dhen-nay-koo-ter may-ser-yu**k**	Irandu peyarukku oru meysai	I-rem-doo pay-er-roo-koo o-roo may-sai
May I see the menu?	Mata Menu eka balanne puluwangdhe?	Mu-ter me-noo e-ker ba-lun-ner poo-loo-wung-dher?	Menuvai paarka mudiyuma?	Me-noo-vai paar-ker moo-di-yoo-maa?
I am a vegetarian.	Mama elavalu vitharai kanney	Mu-mer e-ler-ver-loo vi-ther-ai ku**n**-nay	Naan saivam mattum thaan saapiduven	Naan sai-vum mu**t**-toom thaan saa-pi-doo-ven
Can I have the bill, please?	Karuna kara bila dhennewadha?	Ku-roo-naa ker-er bi-ler dhe-ner-wu-dher?	Billai tharavum	Bill-ai thu-rer-voom
spicy (hot)	Dhevillai / serai	Dha-vi**ll**-ai / sa-rai	Urappu	Oo-re**rp**-poo

MENU DECODER

apple	Appel	A-perl	Aappil	Aa**p**-pill
banana	Kesel	Ke-sel	Valaipalam	Vaa-lai-pa-lum
bamboo shoots	Una dhalu	Oo-ner dhu-loo	Moongil kuruthu	Moon-gill koo-rooth-thoo
beef	Harak mas	Hu-ru**k** muss	Maatterachchi	Maat-**t**e-ru**ch-ch**i
bread	Paang	Paa-ng	Paan	Paan
chicken	Kukul mas	Koo-kool mu**ss**	Koli erachchi	Koa-li er-ru**ch-ch**i
chilli	Miris	Mi-ri**ss**	Kochchikai	Koch-**ch**i-kai
coconut	Pol	Poll	Thengai	Thayng-gaai
crab	Kakuluvo	Ku-koo-loo-vo	Nandu	Nun-doo
dessert	Athurupasa	a-thoor-oo-pu-ser	Palavaghai unavu	Pu-ler-vu-hai oo-ner-voo
duck	Thara	Thaa-raa	Vaaththu	Vaa**th**-thoo
egg	Biththara	Bi**th-th**er-er	Muttai	Moot-**t**ai
fish	Maalu	Maa-loo	Meen	Meen
fruit	Palathuru	Pu-ler-thoo-roo	Palam	Pu-lum
garlic	Sudhu loonu	Soo-dhoo lou-noo	Vellai poodu	Vell-ai pou-doo
ginger	Inguru	Ing-goo-roo	Inji	In-jee
lamb	Batalu mas	Bo-ter-loo muss	Aatterachchi	Aat-**t**e-rer**ch-ch**i
lemongrass	Sera	Say-rer	Sera	Say-rer
lobster	Pokirissa	Po-ki-ri-**ss**-aa	Periya iraal	Pe-ri-yer i-rool
milk	Kiri	Ki-ri	Paal	Paa-l
mushrooms	Hathu	Ha-thoo	Kaalaan	Kaa-laan
meat	Mas	Muss	Eraichchi	E-rai**ch-ch**i
onion	Lunu	Lou-nou	Vengayam	Veng-aa-yum
papaya	Gaslabu	Guss-lu-boo	Pappali	Pu**p-p**aa-li
pepper	Gummiris	Gum-**m**i-ri**ss**	Milaghu	Mi-ler-hoo
pork	Urumas	Ou-rou-mu**ss**	Pandri erachchi	Pun-dri er-ai**ch-ch**i
potato (sweet potato)	Ala (bathala)	A-ler (buth-er-ler)	Kilangu (vattraalai kilangu)	Ki-lung-goo (vu**tt**-raa-lai ki-lung-goo)
prawn	Isso	Iss-o	Iraal	I-rool
rice	Bath	Buth	Soaru	Soa-roo
salad	Saladhu	Sa-laa-dhoo	Salad	Sa-lud
salt	Lunu	Loo-noo	Uppu	Oo**p**-pou
sugar	Seeni	See-ni	Seeni	See-ni
vegetables	Elavalu	E-ler-ver-loo	Marakari	Mo-ruer-kur-ri
drinks	Beema	Bee-mer	Paanangal	Paa-nung-al
tea	They	Thay	Theyneer	Thay-neer
coffee	Kopi	Koa-pee	Kopi	Koa-pee
water	Vathura	Vu-thoo-rer	Thannir	Thun-neer
mineral water	Bothal kala vathura	Boa-thul ker-ler vu-thoo-rer	Pottilil adaikkapatta neer	Poa-till-il a-dai-ker-put-ter neer
milk	Kiri	Ki-ri	Paal	Paa-l
soft drinks	Sisil beema	Si-si-l bee-mer	Menpaanam	Men-paa-num
beer	Beer	Beer	Beer	Beer
wine	Vine	Vine	Vine	Vine
glass	Vidhuruwa	Vee-dhoo-roo-wer	Tumbler	Tumbler
bottle	Bothalaya	Boa-ther-ler-yer	Pottil	Poa-till

HEALTH

I do not feel well.	**Magey engata hari ney**	*Mu-gay ang-er-ter hu-ri ney*	**Ennudaya udambukku sari illai**	*En-noo-der-yer oo-dum-boo-koo sa-ri ill-ai*
I have a fever.	**Mata una vagey**	*Mu-ter oo-ner vu-gay*	**Enakku kaichchal adikiradhu**	*En-uk-koo kaich-ch-ul u-di-ki-rer-dhoo*
I'm allergic to	**Mata … ekata asaath-mikathvayak thiyanava**	*Mu-ter … e-ker-ter a-saath-mi-kuth-ver-yuk thi-yer-ner-vaa*	**Enakku … ikku ovvamai ondru ulladhu**	*En-ak-koo…ik-koo ov-vaa-mai on-droo ull-er-dhoo*
accident (traffic)	**Hadhisi anathurak (thadabadaya)**	*Hu-dhi-si u-ner-thoo-ruk (thu-der-bu-der-yer)*	**Vibaththu (pokkuvarathu)**	*Vi-buth-thoo (poo-koo-vu-ruth-thoo)*
ambulance	**Gilan rathaya (ambulansaya)**	*Gi-lun ruth-er-yer (ambulan-ser-yer)*	**Noyaali vandi**	*Noa-yaa-li vun-di*
antibiotics	**Prathijeevaka**	*Prer-thi-jee-ver-ker*	**Nunnuyir ethirpi**	*Noon-noo-yire-dhir-pi (aanti-biotic)*
blood pressure (high/low)	**Rudhirapeedanaya (adhiha/adu)**	*Roo-dhi-rer-pee-der-ner-yer (a-dhi/a-doo)*	**(adhiha / kuraindha) Iraththa aluththam**	*(a-dhi-her / koo-rain-dher) I-ruth-ther a-looth-thum*
diabetes	**Dhiyavediyaava**	*Dhi-yer-va-di-yaa-ver*	**Neerilivu noi**	*Nee-ri-li-voo noa-yi*
diarrhoea	**Bada burul veema**	*Bu-der boo-rool vee-mer*	**Bedhi**	*Bay-dhee*
doctor	**Dhostara**	*Dhos-ther-er*	**Maruthuvar**	*Mu-roo-thoo-ver*
flu	**Una**	*Oo-ner*	**Salikaichchal**	*Sa-lee-kaaich-chul*
food poisoning	**Ahara vishaveema**	*Aa-haa-rer vi-sher-vee-mer*	**Unavu nanjaaghudhal**	*Oo-ner-voo nunj-aa-hoo-dhul*
hospital	**Rohala**	*Roa-hu-ler*	**Aspathri**	*Aas-puth-thi-ree*
illness	**Asaneepaya**	*U-ser-nee-per-yer*	**Noi**	*Noa-yi*
injection	**Injection**	*Injection*	**Injection / oosi**	*Injection / ou-see*
malaria	**Maleriyaava**	*Ma-lay-ri-yaa-ver*	**Maleria**	*Mul-ay-riya*
medicine	**Beheth**	*Bay-hay-th*	**Marundhu**	*Mu-roon-dhoo*
prescription	**Beheth thunduwa**	*Bay-hay-th thoon-doo-ver*	**Marundhu cheettu**	*Mu-roon-dhoo cheet-too*

TIME AND SEASON

minute	**Vinaadiya**	*Vi-naa-di-yer*	**Nimidum**	*Ni-mi-dum*
hour	**Peya**	*Pa-yer*	**Manithiyaalam**	*Mu-ni-thi-yaa-lum*
day	**Davasa**	*Dhu-ver-ser*	**Naal**	*Naa-ll*
week	**Sumanaya**	*Soo-maa-ner-yer*	**Vaaram**	*Vaa-rum*
month	**Maasaya**	*Maa-ser-yer*	**Maatham**	*Maa-dhum*
year	**Avurudhdha**	*Uv-oo-roodh-dher*	**Varusham**	*Vu-roo-shum*
Monday	**Sandhudha**	*Sun-dhoo-dhaa*	**Thingal**	*Thi-ng-gull*
Tuesday	**Angaharuwaadha**	*Ung-er-hu-roo-waa-dhaa*	**Sevvai**	*Sev-vaai*
Wednesday	**Badhadha**	*Bu-dhaa-dhaa*	**Pudhan**	*Poo-dhun*
Thursday	**Brahaspathindha**	*Bru-haas-pa-thin-dhaa*	**Viyaalan**	*Vi-yaa-lun*
Friday	**Sikuradha**	*Si-koo-raa-dhaa*	**Vellikilamai**	*Vel-li-ki-ler-mai*
Saturday	**Senasuraadha**	*Se-ner-soo-raa-dhaa*	**Sanikilamai**	*Su-ni-ki-ler-mai*
Sunday	**Iridha**	*I-ri-dhaa*	**Gnaayiru**	*Nyaa-yi-roo*
spring	**Vasanthakaalaya**	*Vu-sun-ther-kaa-ler-yer*	**Vasandhakaalam**	*Vu-sun-dher-kaa-lum*
summer	**Gimhaanakaalaya**	*Gim-haa-ner-kaa-ler-yer*	**Kodaikaalam**	*Koa-dai-kaa-lum*
autumn	**Sarathkaalaya**	*Su-ruth-kaa-ler-yer*	**ilaiyudhirkaalam**	*I-lai-oo-dhir-kaa-lum*
winter	**Seethakaalaya**	*Shee-ther-kaa-ler-yer*	**Kulirkaalam**	*Koo-leer-kaa-lum*
rain (it is raining)	**Vahinava**	*Vu-hi-ner-vaa*	**Malai peyghiradhu**	*Mu-lai payi-hi-rer-dhoo*
wind	**Hulanga**	*Hoo-lung-ger*	**Kaattru**	*Kaat-troo*
sunny	**Awwa**	*Ouw-er*	**Veyil**	*Ve-yill*
weather	**Kaalagunaya**	*Kaa-ler-goo-ner-yer*	**Kaalanilai**	*Kaa-ler-ni-lai*
What time is it?	**Velaava keeyadhe?**	*Ve-laa-ver kee-yer-dher?*	**Mani enna?**	*Mu-nee en-ner?*
12:00:00 noon	**Dhaval dholaha**	*Dhu-vul dho-ler-haa*	**Nanpahal**	*Nun-pu-hul*
midnight	**Jaamaya**	*Jaa-mer-yer*	**Nalliravu**	*Null-i-rer-voo*
morning	**Udhay**	*Oo-dhay*	**Kaalai**	*Kaa-lai*
midday	**Dhaval**	*Dhu-vul*	**Paghal**	*Pug-hal*
afternoon	**Pasvaruwa**	*Pus-vu-roo-ver*	**Madhiyaanam**	*Mudh-dhi-yaa-num*
evening	**Havasa**	*Hu-ver-ser*	**Maalai**	*Maa-lai*
night	**Reh**	*Rey*	**Iravu**	*I-rer-voo*

NUMBERS

1	**Ekai**	*E-kai*	**Ondru**	*On-droo*
2	**Dhekai**	*Dhe-kai*	**Irandu**	*I-rern-doo*
3	**Thunai**	*Thoo-nai*	**Moondru**	*Moon-droo*
4	**Hatharai**	*Hu-ther-ai*	**Naalu**	*Naa-loo*
5	**Pahai**	*Pu-hai*	**Aindhu**	*A-yin-dhoo*
6	**Hayai**	*Hu-yai*	**Aaru**	*Aa-roo*
7	**Hathai**	*Hu-thai*	**Elu**	*Ay-loo*
8	**Atai**	*U-tai*	**Ettu**	*Et-too*
9	**Namayai**	*Nu-mer-yai*	**Onbadhu**	*On-ber-dho*
10	**Dhahayai**	*Dhu-haa-yai*	**Paththu**	*Puth-thoo*
15	**Pahalavai**	*Pu-haa-ler-vai*	**Padhinaindhu**	*Pa-dhi-nain-dhoo*
20	**Vissai**	*Viss-ai*	**Iruvadhu**	*I-roo-ver-dhoo*
30	**Thihai**	*Thi-hai*	**Muppadhu**	*Moop-per-dhoo*
40	**Hathalihai**	*Huth-ther-li-hai*	**Naapadhu**	*Naa-per-dhoo*
50	**Panahai**	*Pun-er-hai*	**Aimbadhu**	*Aim-ber-dhoo*
60	**Hettai**	*Ho-tai*	**Aruvadhu**	*A-roo-ver-dhoo*
70	**Hethewai**	*Ho-th-they-wai*	**Eluvadhu**	*E-loo-ver-dhoo*
80	**Asuwai**	*A-soo-wai*	**Embadhu**	*Em-ber-dhoo*
90	**Anuwai**	*A-noo-wai*	**Thonnooru**	*Thon-noo-roo*
100	**Seeyai**	*See-yai*	**Nooru**	*Nou-roo*
200	**Dheyseeyai**	*Dhay-see-yai*	**Iranooru**	*i-rer-nou-roo*
1000	**Dhaahai**	*Dhaa-hai*	**Aayiram**	*Aa-yi-rum*
10,000	**Dhaha dhaahai**	*Dha-haa dhaa-hai*	**Pathaayiram**	*Puth-thaa-yi-rum*
100,000	**Lakshayai**	*Luk-sher-yai*	**Latcham**	*Lut-chum*

The publisher would like to thank the following for their kind permission to reproduce their photographs:

Key: a-above; b-below/bottom; c-centre; f-far; l-left; r-right; t-top

123RF.com: Ievgenii Fesenko 106t; Angela Grant 99bl; Sergiy Lukutin 50cl; lzflzf 6-7; Yakov Oskanov 136-7t; Matyas Rehak 196-7b; Thomas Wyness 118tl.

4Corners: Guido Cozzi 8cl, 218-9; Jeremy Flint 18tr, 18bl, 132-3, 158-9; Tuul & Bruno Morandi 8clb, 92-3t; Ben Pipe 19bl, 82-3b, 206-7; Reinhard Schmid 59cr; Richard Taylor 59bl; Luigi Vaccarella 8cla.

Alamy Stock Photo: Mohammed Abidally 114-5b; AGE Fotostock / Christian Goupi 13br, 33br, 200-1b; Mark Andrews 67tl; Cedric Angeles 45tr; Arcaid Images / Richard Bryant 81b; Arco Images GmbH / TUNS 131cr; ArkReligion.com / Helene Rogers 140bl; Art Directors & TRIP / ArkReligion. com / Helene Rogers 187cla; Avalon / Photoshot License / Andy Rouse 36-7b; Peter Barritt 196clb; BE&W agencja fotograficzna Sp. z o.o. / BE&WON99 72cra; Georg Berg 46-7t; Sabena Jane Blackbird 90br; Jon Bower - Sri Lanka 115tr; Michele Burgess 54cr; Wojtkowski Cezary 171tr; Jui-Chi Chan 178-9t; China Span / Keren Su 53bl; Stuart C. Clarke 181tl; Justin Cliffe 148tl; Peter Cook 40-1t; David Crausby 96tl; Cultura Creative (RF) / John Philip Harper 144-5b, / Benedicte Vanderreydt 32tl; Mark Daffey 165tl; dbimages / Marcia Chambers 164-5b; Marius Dobilas 128t; Alison Eckett 36tl; eFesenko 20, 30-1b, 68t, 181cr; EyeEm / Francisco Rama 131cra; Daniele Falletta 174bl; Philip Game 31br, 199cb; Paul Gapper 199tr; Thomas Haensgen 30tl; hemis.fr / Christophe Boisvieux 59cl, / Franck Chaput 181bc, / Jean-Pierre Degas 60-1, / Gil Giuglio 212-3b, / Franck Guiziou 109br, 129b, 201tl, / Camille Moirenc 22tl, / Bertrand Rieger 185br, / Alain Schroeder 11cr, 119b; Image Professionals GmbH 39cb; imageBROKER / Stefan Auth 67bc, / Peter Giovannini 56bc, / Harry Laub 172clb; INTERFOTO / Travel 79bl; Ivoha 176cla, 202b; Olga Khoroshunova 129crb; Joana Kruse 26clb; Abhishek Kumar 82cb; Adrian-Catalin Lazar 44tl; Lebrecht Music & Arts / Lebrecht Authors 128bc; Llewellyn 187cl; Lookinglost 10clb; Terry Mathews 24bl, 163; mauritius images GmbH / Cash 33cla, / Harald Schön 13t; MehmetO 72crb; Tuul and Bruno Morandi 12t, 47b, 114cra, 122tr, 123b, 153cl, 198bl, 203cl; Nature Picture Library / Edwin Giesbers 17br, 102-3; Anne-Marie Palmer 31tr, 84clb, 113clb;

Photopat 41cla; The Picture Art Collection 53tl; Rob Pinney 26crb; Paul Quayle 35cl; Simon Reddy 11br, 31cl; Frederic Reglain 50cr; Robertharding / Christian Kober 43cr, / James Strachan 152tl, / Matthew Williams-Ellis 120b; Pep Roig 58cl; Marco van Rooijen 37tr; Shalom Rufeisen 121t; Vipula Samarakoon 125t; Peter Schickert 124bl; Nick Servian 113br; David South 93br; Paul Springett C 10ca; Kumar Sriskandan 39cl; Dave Stamboulis 73; Jochen Tack 33t; Travel Pictures / picturescolourlibrary.com 168tl; Travelib Asia 46br; Matthew Wakem 32br; wanderluster 95br; Finnbarr Webster 194-5t; Hilda Weges 182b; Westend61 GmbH / Christian Vorhofer 143cr; Jan Wlodarczyk 20bl, 28cr, 42crb, 141ca, 186bl, 187clb (Dhyana Mudra); Xinhua / Ajith Perera 51tr, / Gayan Sameera 72bl; Ariadne Van Zandbergen 51clb, 52bc, 101br, 170cl, 175bl, 183tr, 210t; ZUMA Press; Inc. / © Andrey Nekrasov 97b.

AWL Images: Peter Adams 168-9b; Katja Kreder 17tl, 86-7, 174-5t, 187clb; Ludovic Maisant 8-9b, 213tr; Nigel Pavitt 76b, 156tl; Bertrand Rieger 48-9t; Jane Sweeney 2-3, 10-1b; Ian Trower 16c, 62-3, 74-5b.

Bridgeman Images: Leemage / ©The British Library Board 52t, 54tl; © British Library Board. All Rights Reserved 54-5t, © Giancarlo Costa 54br; Pictures from History 54cla; The Stapleton Collection 55clb.

Dorling Kindersley: Idris Ahmed 67cra, 109tc.

Dreamstime.com: Jaromír Chalabala 127tr; Tomas Ciernik 90-1t; Dinozzaver 121cr; Mikhail Dudarev 147br; Anna Dudko 189tr; Feathercollector 37br, 156tr; Evgeniy Fesenko 4, 20cr, 23tl, 23tr, 41br, 85tr, 187t, 200tl; Filipp Filipovich 98b; Kevin Gillot 164cra; Mykola Ivashchenko 54clb; Izanbar 121crb; Olga Khoroshunova 166bl, 170-1b; Sergii Kolesnyk 45br; Krivinis 150-1t; Kyslynskyy 22tr; Len4foto 94b; Dmitry Malov 28t; Msanca 12clb; Njarvis5 177br; Oskanov 165cra; Kuganathan Priyatharsan 53crb; Saiko3p 24t, 24clb, 24crb, 34br, 66-7b, 126-7b, 197tr, 217tl; Saletomic 39tr; Scaliger 126tl; Vadym Soloviov 22-3ca; Takepicsforfun 176-7t; Thilankaperera 131crb; Toxawww 77tr; Travelvr 143bl; Trofoto 42clb; Pavel Trubnikov 108cl; Hilda Weges 34-5t, 142; Thomas Wyness 26t, 38tl, 38-9b, 43crb, 116bl, 139cl, 139b.

Geoffrey Bawa Trust/ Lunuganga Trust: 80crb, 81cra; Luca Tettoni 80t.

Main Contributors Gavin Thomas,
Rachael Heston
Senior Editor Ankita Awasthi Tröger
Senior Designers Sarah Snelling, Ben Hinks
Project Editor Rebecca Flynn
Project Art Editor Van Le
Designers Stuti Tiwari Bhatia,
Hansa Babra, Simran Lakhiani
Factchecker Emma Boyle
Editor Ruth Reisenberger
Proofreader Kathryn Glendenning
Indexer Helen Peters
Senior Picture Researcher Ellen Root
Picture Research Sophie Basilevitch,
Åsa Westerlund, Sumita Khatwani,
Rituraj Singh, Vagisha Pushp
Illustrators Chingtham Chinglemba,
Sanjeev Kumar, Arun Pottirayil
Cartographic Editor James Macdonald
Cartography Ashutosh Ranjan Bharati,
Rajesh Chhibber, Simonetta Giori
Jacket Designers Sarah Snelling, Bess Daly
Jacket Picture Research Susie Watters
Senior DTP Designer Jason Little
DTP Coordinator George Nimmo
DTP Designer Rohit Rojal
Technical Prepress Manager Tom Morse
Image Retouching Steve Crozier
Producer Rebecca Parton
Managing Editor Hollie Teague
Managing Art Editor Bess Daly
Art Director Maxine Pedliham
Publishing Director Georgina Dee

First edition 2014

Published in Great Britain by Dorling Kindersley Limited,
80 Strand, London, WC2R 0RL

Published in the United States by DK Publishing,
1450 Broadway, Suite 801, New York, NY 10018

Copyright © 2014, 2020 Dorling Kindersley Limited
A Penguin Random House Company
20 21 22 23 10 9 8 7 6 5 4 3 2 1

A CIP catalog record for this book
is available from the British Library.

A catalog record for this book is available
from the Library of Congress.

ISSN: 1542 1554
ISBN: 978 0 2414 1133 9

Printed and bound in Malaysia.

www.dk.com

MIX
Paper from
responsible sources
FSC
www.fsc.org   FSC™ C018179

**The information in this
DK Eyewitness Travel Guide is checked regularly.**
Every effort has been made to ensure that this book
is as up-to-date as possible at the time of going to
press. Some details, however, such as telephone
numbers, opening hours, prices, gallery hanging
arrangements and travel information, are liable to
change. The publishers cannot accept responsibility
for any consequences arising from the use of this
book, nor for any material on third party websites,
and cannot guarantee that any website address
in this book will be a suitable source of travel
information. We value the views and suggestions
of our readers very highly. Please write to: Publisher,
DK Eyewitness Travel Guides, Dorling Kindersley,
80 Strand, London, WC2R 0RL, UK, or email:
travelguides@dk.com